Woodrow Wilson

Woodrow

A Biography

Wilson

by Silas Bent McKinley

FREDERICK A. PRAEGER   *Publishers*   *New York*

ACKNOWLEDGMENT is made for permission to quote the following herein:
P. 21, line 32, to p. 22, line 5; p. 61, lines 6-11—From *Woodrow Wilson: The Man, His Times and His Tasks*, by William Allen White. Copyright 1924 by William Allen White, 1952 by W. L. White. Published by Houghton Mifflin Company.
P. 29, line 34, to p. 30, line 4; p. 50, lines 19-25; p. 139, lines 29-35—From *The Life and Letters of Woodrow Wilson*, by Ray Stannard Baker. Copyright 1927 by Doubleday & Company, Inc. From *Woodrow Wilson: Life and Letters*, by Ray Stannard Baker. Published 1928 by William Heinemann Ltd., London.
P. 132, lines 2-6—From *The Intimate Papers of Colonel House*, ed. Charles Seymour., Vol. I. Copyright 1926 by Houghton Mifflin Company.

First published in the United States of America in 1957
by Frederick A. Praeger, Inc., 150 East 52 Street, New York 22

Copyright © 1957 in the United States of America
by Frederick A. Praeger, Inc.

Library of Congress Catalog Card Number 57-5962
Printed in the United States of America

For

NANCY WALLACE McKINLEY

FOREWORD

This is a biography which is fundamentally sympathetic to Wilson, yet seeks to be critical and judicious. It emphasizes the effect of his unusual boyhood and youth upon his development as a man. It discusses his writings as a whole; and it shows how egotism and a stubborn spirit grew in a man whose intense desire was to be the champion of the whole human race. His failures are recorded, but so are his spectacular achievements in behalf of democracy, of liberal reform and finally of lasting peace. He emerges from these pages a complex character as well as a great hero.

CONTENTS

FOREWORD		*vii*
I	The Presbyterian Preacher's Son	*1*
II	The Growth of a Divided Mind	*14*
III	"A Most Persuasive Talker"	*24*
IV	Romance and Happy Marriage	*35*
V	Scholar and Popular Professor	*49*
VI	Princeton's Progress under Wilson	*63*
VII	Conflict and Defeat at Princeton	*79*
VIII	The Dynamic Development of Wilson's Mind	*93*
IX	Destroying a Political Machine	*111*
X	A Professor's Presidential Campaign	*124*
XI	Putting an End to Dollar Diplomacy	*138*
XII	Tariff and the Federal Reserve System	*152*
XIII	Meddling in Mexico	*165*
XIV	Trust Busting and Proposed Reforms	*179*
XV	Failure to Prepare for War	*189*
XVI	Capable War President	*205*
XVII	The "Fourteen Points" and Germany's Collapse	*215*
XVIII	The Dizzy Pinnacle of Human Fame	*227*
XIX	The League of Nations Is Born	*238*
XX	Fighting for Democratic Principles	*248*
XXI	Disaster at the Senate's Hands	*258*
XXII	Only the Unbending Will Remains	*268*
A BRIEF BIBLIOGRAPHY		*279*
INDEX		*281*

Wilson and Poincare, Paris, Dec. 14, 1918.

CHAPTER I

THE PRESBYTERIAN
PREACHER'S SON

Thomas Woodrow Wilson was born three days after Christmas 1856 at Staunton in the slave state of Virginia. It was just after Buchanan had been elected President as a compromise candidate, in the hope that the desperate issues of slavery and disunion might somehow be settled without war.

The baby's father, Joseph Ruggles Wilson, of Scotch-Irish ancestry, had graduated from the Princeton Theological Seminary, while his mother, Jessie Woodrow, the daughter of a Scotch Presbyterian divine, had been born in northern England and brought to America across a stormy sea at the age of nine. Since they already had two little girls aged six and four the parents must have welcomed the arrival of a son, one who might carry on the tradition of serving in the Presbyterian ministry which was so strong in both their families.

Staunton, the county seat of Augusta County, was then a city of four thousand, located 136 miles northwest of Richmond on a tributary of the Shenandoah River. It had several female seminaries, iron foundries, a brick yard and a dozen churches. It was even then no new frontier town recently carved out of the wilderness, but a community regarded by its members as settled and likely to endure without much change. In a conservative and carefully stratified society of planters, artisans and Negro slaves the popular Presbyterian pastor was readily conceded a high and honored place.

The Wilsons lived in a frame house with a wide veranda on one of the main streets of the town. The two small sisters probably were delighted at the arrival of a baby to play with and spoil with loving care. He was named after his maternal grandfather and he soon grew so fat and bouncing that his father described him as looking dignified enough to be moderator of the General Assembly, the periodic gathering of leaders of the church.

But in spite of the tender attentions of his mother and sisters, Tommy began to lose his chubbiness as he grew out of babyhood and developed into a thin and spindly boy, with yellow hair and luminous eyes, as well as a somewhat delicate digestion. His mother seems to have recognized that she had a high strung little boy on her hands for she was in the habit of describing him to her friends as "a mischievous bundle of nerves." Even before he went to school he had to wear spectacles, and although he had plenty of nervous energy he was lacking in general physical vigor.

It was not long before Tommy began to be conscious of the Presbyterian atmosphere of prayer and hymns and catechism with which he was surrounded. While he knew his mother took good care of him, his real enthusiasm was reserved for his father whom he regarded as undoubtedly the greatest man in the world. It was natural that the companionship and intimacy of his father was the most pervasive influence in his childhood and young boyhood, for they were together almost constantly during the first nine years of little Tommy's life.

This companionship was well suited to give health and vigor to the boy's mind and character, for his father loved the world of books as well as the sonorous fullness of a well-turned phrase. Yet the pastor was always full of fun, with a joke or pun and a friendly word for everyone. Even the casual friendship of such a man would have been an inspiration to any youngster.

Before Tommy was two years old his father was called to the First Presbyterian Church in Augusta, Georgia, which was an active city of about twelve thousand with iron foundries and cotton warehouses along the reddish waters of the Savannah River. Since

Augusta was at the head of navigation, its growth was to be expected. It became the seat of a Federal arsenal which the Confederates seized during the Civil War, and from which the citizens turned out a great deal of ammunition for the Confederate armies.

The church was one of the most distinguished in the South. It had a congregation which was founded in 1804 and a missionary society which had been active and wise enough to advance Alexander Stephens, later Vice-President of the Confederacy, the money for his education. In its new pastor it found a man with a gift for preaching. He always read his sermons, which probably made them more finished literary productions than they would otherwise have been; and no member of the congregation was more stirred by them than little Tommy who sat gazing up in awed admiration of his father.

At home Joseph Wilson used to sit on the floor, lean his back against the bottom of an overturned chair and read aloud to his family books of travel, poetry or the novels of Dickens or Scott, while his young son often lay flat on his back on the floor. The father's deep bass voice would give feeling to each pictured emotion, then suddenly his ringing laughter would burst out over a hilarious passage in *Pickwick Papers* or some other favorite. Or on a summer evening the family might have a discussion in the garden, with the good minister always the leader of the little group. No day was allowed to pass without family prayers, when the entire family knelt together. The Bible was read each day; and on Sunday evenings they sang their favorite hymns without an accompaniment.

Although Tommy did not go to school until he was nine years old, his father had taken great pains to teach him at home. On weekdays the handsome minister would take him to see a corn mill or cotton gin in action; and during the Civil War they visited the ammunition factories and iron foundries. Tommy always had to discuss afterward what he had seen or what he had read, for the pastor believed that the clear expression of ideas was essential to a clear understanding. He was accustomed to say: "My son, the mind is not a prolix gut to be stuffed; it is a digestive organ, it is an assimilating organ and what it does not assimilate it rejects and gets no profit from."

The father also told him: "When you frame a sentence don't do it as if you were loading a shotgun, but as if you were loading a rifle; shoot with a single bullet and hit that one thing alone."

Later they would take an excerpt from some author whom the parson admired, say Charles Lamb, and the two of them would work on it together, taking it to pieces and seeing if its ideas could be expressed better and more concisely in some other fashion. The difficulties of such a process are obvious on the face of it, so that when they applied the same method to Daniel Webster's orations, it is not surprising that the boy's verdict was: "We never got far with Daniel." It is hard to see how a youngster could have found better training in the proper use of words or in the importance of wisdom, culture and Christian character. Later in life he was inclined to judge the changes going on around him by comparing them to the simple disciplined life of his father's family and often found in them a growing lack of harmony with the Jeffersonian form of society which he had experienced.

After the war a young Confederate officer named Derry opened a private boys' school beside the river near the Episcopal Church. Here were great warehouses filled with cotton, where the boys could play among the bales. When Tommy Wilson began going there, although he showed ability in lines that he enjoyed, the teachers reported that his general work was below the average, "not because he was not bright enough, but because he was not interested." They found him a sensitive child who was concerned with things of the spirit and with what he chose for himself rather than the school curriculum. A young woman who sometimes substituted for the organist at Sunday services said that although she thought the minister's boy was shy and reserved he was peculiarly affected by music. She even sometimes saw him crying during a doleful hymn, like "'Twas on That Dark and Dreadful Day," which was often sung during the Communion service.

Tommy was sensitive to other things beside church music, for in later years he quoted *The Golden Age* by Kenneth Grahame as saying of children: "They live in a world of delightful imagination; they pursue persons and objects that never existed; they make an Argosy laden with gold out of a floating butterfly," while grown-up people, "stupid Olympians try to translate these things into uninteresting facts."

But the impressionable youngster also had elements of strength. It was while sitting in church that his friend Will Fleming noticed the sharpness of his nose and chin as well as the great size and broadness of his head. Will was so impressed with these characteristics that when he went home he hunted them up in a phrenology book, which stated that they indicated force and ambition. Will said that ever after that he watched with interest for great achievements from his friend. At the same time older men remarked that Tommy had a high and impetuous temper.

It is difficult to know how much effect the Civil War had on the mind and spirit of the little boy, but it must have been considerable. Although he was only four years old when the war began and only eight when it ended, and had no relatives in the army, the atmosphere of war was all around him. Two thousand men enlisted from his town of twelve thousand. His father was an enthusiastic Southern sympathizer and his church was turned into a hospital. Tommy later told how he recalled a man passing in the street who cried in great excitement that Lincoln was elected and that there would be war. Recognizing the deep feeling in the man's voice, he ran in to ask his father what it meant. So it happened that his very earliest memory was concerned with politics and war.

Later he sat on a gatepost in front of his house as a ragged company of men going to join the Confederate Army marched past. He jeered at them in the slang of the day: "Oh, Joe—where's your mule!" Then later still he peered through the drawn blinds of the manse to see Jefferson Davis and Alexander Stephens driven by in a carriage when they were prisoners of the Union Army on their way to a Federal jail.

The boy also remembered one Sunday morning when his father

5

climbed the pulpit and said with dramatic intensity: "A great battle is raging today in Virginia, and the forces of the Confederacy are suffering from a lack of ammunition. This congregation must do its duty and immediately at the close of these services the ladies will repair to the munitions factory and help with the cartridges. You will now rise and sing the Doxology and be dismissed." Tommy sat there lost in admiration for his father, but he must also have been aware of the seriousness of a war which could even disrupt a Presbyterian Sabbath.

On quiet Sundays the family frequently drove out in the country to the house of their friends the Flemings, whose son remembered all the Wilsons crowding out of the carriage after church, as well as the deplorable fact that he and Tommy had to keep their shoes on all day. Tommy also often visited with his cousin Jessie Bones out at her parents' place in the district called "Sand Hill," one of those sandy stretches around Augusta with plenty of space for a gallop over the fields or into the pine woods. Reading *The Deerslayer* and *The Last of the Mohicans* gave these two such ideas of Indian exploits that they would decorate themselves with feathers and pokeberry warpaint with the idea of luring little pickaninnies into an ambush among the pine trees. If no other children appeared, Jessie was the victim to be burned at the stake.

At other times the little boy would have only himself to play with in the woods behind the manse, where he could sail toy boats in the rushing gullies filled with water after a rain, dreaming of glorious exploits on land and sea. This vivid dream world which was recorded in the imaginary logs of ships which he was sailing held adventures enough to serve as compensation for his delicate physique. If he had been more robust he would probably have been so busy playing with the other boys that he would have had little time to concentrate on dreams.

Perhaps it was a sign of his lack of physical vigor that he was always called by the name of Tommy rather than Tom or some other sturdier nickname. The weakness of his body was one reason why he did not go to school until he was nine. He was further

6

handicapped by his spectacles, and by his two older sisters' efforts to keep him in the ways of cleanliness and sedate behavior. He was sensitive and delicate; there are no stories of his fights with other boys nor even of his being subjected to teasing or razzing by his gang, for they were well-bred boys and perhaps had some special respect for the preacher's son. This failure to get out in the rough and tumble of the boy-world and find his own place by his courage and his fists was a serious weakness in his education. He was not used to opposition from his playmates, to taking their jokes and submitting to the punishments of fights with the tougher boys around the town. When the manse gate crushed one of his fingers so that it became stiff for life, this became another handicap to prevent his fighting and wrestling with his companions. He was inclined to be too sedentary, too much wrapped in dreams, with little Tommy always as the central figure.

Yet before he left Augusta at the age of fourteen he was able to take command of his friends in surprising fashion. He organized a gang of boys, "The Lightfoots," who were in the habit of holding meetings in his father's barn. They faithfully followed the rules of parliamentary procedure under his direction. He succeeded in drilling them until each of the boys knew perfectly well what the "previous question" was and that only two amendments could be offered. Even on a rainy day it must have been surprising to see a group of small boys engaged in such debates rather than in the hunting, wrestling and fighting natural to youngsters of that age.

But when the Lightfoots played baseball against other gangs, Tommy always took an enthusiastic part, for he liked the game and was a good player. Although he avoided fights and physical conflict he had excellent co-ordination and was never awkward or clumsy. He enjoyed organized sports, but he was almost too ready to stand up for his rights. The old folks said that if he felt he had suffered an injustice in some decision he would throw down his bat and go home. In all these activities it appears that he was showing himself a natural leader, although not so much on the athletic field as in things of the mind. For things intellectual were already the realms where his greatest interest lay, and it was this interest, combined with the intensity of his nature, which made it possible for him to keep the boys in his father's barn engaged in discussions conducted in accordance with parliamentary procedure and operating under a constitution of their own making.

Tommy had a cultural inheritance from Presbyterian forebears on both sides of his family, although his father's ancestors included fewer pastors than his mother's. His paternal grandfather, James Wilson, was not a preacher of the gospel, but an active businessman; yet his business was the editing and ownership of newspapers in which he delighted to write columns dealing with politics and economics as well as personal matters. He was quick to use his editorial powers for his own advancement and that of the community in which he lived, and he possessed many qualities of leadership which might be expected to reappear in different forms somewhere among his grandchildren. He was one of those men of primarily Scotch descent whose ancestors had lived in the north of Ireland for generations. When he first migrated to America from County Down in 1808 he became an apprentice to William Duane, who owned and edited a famous liberal newspaper in Philadelphia. This periodical, printed in the former home of Benjamin Franklin and called the *Aurora*, was the first muckraking sheet to appear in America. Philadelphia was then the capital of the country so it was a good location for Duane's paper, which was influential in bringing about the election of President Jefferson.

Later James Wilson went west by way of Pittsburgh to Steubenville in the new state of Ohio. There he became owner of the town's leading newspaper, the *Western Herald,* and took part in bringing the first railroad to the city. He was elected to the Ohio legislature; later in life he even became an associate judge of the Court of Common Pleas without ever having been a lawyer. He was "a man of great size . . . gay, candid and friendly"; but he could be bitter and quick in his attacks on those he disliked. One of these was Samuel Medary, once governor of the state, whom he referred to as "Samedary," and made the frequent butt of jokes and ridicule. Once when "Jimmie" Wilson's birth as a foreigner was contrasted with that of Medary, "born in Ohio," Editor Wilson commented in his paper: "So was my dog, Towser."

James had married Anne Adams on November 1, 1808, soon after they landed from the same ship in Philadelphia. She was four years younger than he, full of health, with big features, a mouth and chin so firm that they denoted will power verging on stubbornness. She too must have come from County Down or Antrim, for she always liked to tell how they could see the white linen flying on a line in Scotland across the Irish Sea from her childhood home. The Scottish faith and stubbornness came with her too. Once when one of her three daughters disobeyed her she declared that she would never see her again, nor did she relent even on her deathbed. She brought up all her ten children in the strict doctrine and discipline of the Presbyterian Church, and whenever her husband was away in the legislature or busy with a newspaper he started in Pittsburgh, she and her boys were able to bring out the Steubenville *Herald* by themselves.

The youngest son of this strong-willed and aggressive couple was Joseph, the father of Tommy Wilson. The older sons had been put straight into business, but Joseph showed such an interest in learning that it was decided he should have a college education. Even as a youngster Joseph had printed his own little paper, and later he carried his part of the financial burden of the family by working at the printer's trade while he was still going to school. After joining the Presbyterian Church by profession of faith on May 3, 1840, he entered Jefferson College at Cannonsville, Pennsylvania. When he had completed the course he was chosen valedictorian of his class, indicating high scholarship and perhaps some skill in oratory.

Joseph was a tall young man, generally merry but with sudden angers. He had a handsome face and figure, attractions of which he was probably well aware. After teaching for a year at Mercer, Pennsylvania, he prepared himself for the pulpit by going to the Western Theological Seminary at Alleghany and to Princeton. When he came

9

back to Steubenville with a license to preach, he taught in the Male Academy there for two years while waiting for a church of his own.

One autumn day in Steubenville as Joseph was raking leaves in the family's yard he noticed a girl with gray eyes and yellow curls walking down the street. The young lady, Jessie Woodrow, returned his glance and saw through a picket fence a stalwart youth so careful of his hands that he was raking in gloves. Whatever her original impression, however, Jessie soon became so fond of the young instructor that she became Mrs. Joseph Wilson three years later. The pair were married by Jessie's father in his manse at Chillicothe, Ohio.

If the Wilsons were Scotch-Irish, the Woodrows were pure Scotch. The line of Presbyterian scholars and preachers is easy to follow; it has been traced back to Professor James Wodrow of Glasgow University, born in 1637, a teacher who prepared more than six hundred young men to be ministers of the Gospel. This distinguished divine, a scholar in Greek, Latin and Hebrew, was said to have had the principal part in formulating "the polity and discipline of the Church of Scotland, and in securing their adoption as fundamental principles of that domination" in the seventeenth century.

Thomas Wodrow, the grandfather after whom the new baby in Staunton, Virginia, was named, was also versed in the classics and in Scotch Presbyterianism. He left Scotland in 1820 with his bride, Marion Williamson, to take a church in Carlisle, England where he changed his name to Woodrow, because the English pronounced it that way. While living in Carlisle for fifteen years they had eight children of whom a girl named Jessie was the fifth. They took this whole brood, all of whom were under sixteen, with them when they sailed for America from Liverpool in November 1835. On this voyage the weather was so stormy that after almost reaching Newfoundland the ship was carried back within sight of Ireland. There is a family legend that during this gale little Jessie, then aged nine, was on deck one day clinging to a rope when a big wave breaking across the bow carried her over the side, but that she kept clutching the rope until she was swept safely back on the deck again.

10

The winter tempests and wild seas were such a strain and worry for the poor mother with so many small children on her hands that she died four days after landing, while her husband was off preaching at Poughkeepsie. Her sister, Isabella Williamson, took over the care of the children. After a year as missionary at Brookville on the St. Lawrence River, the father moved his family to Chillicothe. In this pioneer village he sought to uphold the light of learning contained within the precious volumes of his own personal library of ancient and modern authors. In 1850 he was called to the Hogg Presbyterian Church, located in the state capital at Columbus, where he remained until his death in 1877. He is said to have been "especially powerful in prayer . . . conservative in his views and thoroughly Presbyterian in his belief."

These were the Woodrows, Scottish and Covenanter to the core, serious and scholarly, sure that they were in the right and intolerant of opposition. From them Tommy would naturally learn doctrines of stern devotion to duty and to the truth as he saw it. The Irish Wilsons, far less serious and fond of songs and laughter, also had a strict Presbyterian background. The Wilsons sought success and they achieved it in ways more worldly than the Woodrows, but the members of both families were fired by Calvinistic zeal.

A month after he was married in June 1849, and after being ordained a Presbyterian minister, Joseph Wilson began to look around for a way to improve his condition. He was always seeking to rise to something better by using his greatest asset, a remarkable gift of expression. His first practical use of it was to win the position of professor of rhetoric at Jefferson College, where he had been a student. After a year there, he made his move to the south in 1851 when he became a teacher of chemistry and the natural sciences at Hampton Sidney College in Virginia. He remained there four years and was able to add to his teaching income by preaching. He was so ambitious and successful that by each move he obtained a post superior to the last one, gaining always more prestige and greater opportunity.

It was in 1856 that he became pastor of the Presbyterian Church in Staunton. He made a fine figure, with his bass voice, his brown eyes, a shock of straight hair, neck whiskers and sideburns. He relished a hearty dinner to make the quiet of the Sabbath more enjoyable, nor was he loath to accept a drop of Scotch whisky on a weekday. The courtesy and courtliness of this dashing parson did not prevent him from using his Irish wit to make remarks that often left a sting, for he took a delight in joking and teasing. In spite of this, people liked to have him around, for it was almost true, as his son later observed: "If I had my father's face and figure it wouldn't make any difference what I said."

Although the minister enjoyed playing chess and billiards, he shared the Presbyterian aversion to cards. That he was a happy companion for his children is evidenced by the tradition of a boisterous game of tag between him and little Tommy, with the boy running from the study into the garden and dodging behind trees until he finally was caught trying to climb over the fence. "I've caught him, the young rascal," called the father as the rest of the family ran out to see the fun.

On the other hand his wife, Jessie, was much more remote and reserved, with even her soft and gentle voice indicating aloofness. She had such a strong religious feeling that as a girl she copied out under the heading "Best Wishes" a poem which began: "Thine be the love, refined from sense, That seeks its object in the skies." Although she was a well-trained musician, she seldom played except for the family. She had a pride which made her dislike receiving the gifts of such things as fruits and preserves so often sent to a minister's household. With no flair for sociability or friendliness, she could hate anyone who she thought was injuring her family. She was the strong character who spent her time in the home, concentrating on the training of her children to place them on the paths she wanted them to follow.

Tommy Wilson obviously had a powerful heritage. Although no single individual of real genius can be found among them, most of his ancestors had exceptional force of personality. To all this Presbyterian strength and severe Calvinistic training was added a spark of Gaelic gaiety through his father's line; while Tommy himself displayed a curious talent of which no example had appeared among his forefathers. This was an ability to organize individuals into groups and to sway their behavior. Somewhat handicapped in his physical development, he early gave proof of superior intellectual powers. He seemed to be a boy, not too lovable perhaps, but well worth watching.

CHAPTER II

THE GROWTH OF
A DIVIDED MIND

The departure of the Wilson family from Augusta in 1870 came when Tommy was almost fourteen, his boyhood behind him, his adolescent period ahead. He had become a lanky youth with spectacles and freckles beneath a thatch of straw-colored hair. Although too tall and thin he was never really awkward. He must have had a charm about him with his active mind, his tenor voice and some new signs of interest in the companionship of girls.

The town to which the Wilsons moved was Columbia, the capital of South Carolina, whose business district, a mile long and three blocks wide, had been burned by the Yankees and not yet restored. This evidence of the ruthlessness and waste of war burst upon the boy not only at an impressionable age but also with a sudden violence for which he had received no adequate preparation. Augusta had been out of the direct track of all Federal armies. In Columbia he saw not only desolation but social and political disintegration.

The change to a different city broke Tommy's ties with his "gang" of friends. And this was probably hard on him, even worse than it would have been for most boys of fourteen for never again during his boyhood did he become an integral member of any group outside his family.

On the other hand the change to Columbia was an advancement for his father. It was an honor to be selected to teach pastoral theology in the well-known Presbyterian Seminary, and, before long,

Dr. Wilson was also called to be minister of the First Presbyterian Church at $1,500 a year. When his wife inherited a substantial sum from her brother the Wilsons began to build a solid roomy mansion of their own, about a block from the seminary. Although it was not comparable to one of the old Colonial residences, since it was built in the rococo style of the period, it was comfortable and even pretentious for that time and place. The position held by the mother in the family's affairs is indicated by the fact that its building was planned and supervised by her.

Tommy's life in Columbia was quiet and serene in spite of the devastations of war, because he was thrown mostly with the families of those who were teaching in the college. These men were so devoted to the Presbyterian faith and immersed in the intellectual life that they could rise above the desolation and poverty around them. Tommy continued his education at a private school for boys, but he also needed some extra tutoring to get him ready for college. He was not an outstanding student and he did not take much interest in science or most of his other subjects. His Uncle James Woodrow, a Doctor of Science from Heidelberg, teaching in the college, is reported to have once exclaimed: "Tommy, you can learn if you will. Then for Heaven's sake, boy, get some of this. At least if you have no ambition to be scholar, you might wish to be a gentleman."

As was only natural for this time of life, Tommy's interest for the moment seemed to be centered in girls rather than in his studies. As a boy he had not only played Indians with his cousin Jessie Bones, but he had also occasionally been seen rough-housing some small girl in Augusta, with perhaps a little feeling of love entering into the horse play. After he moved to Columbia he became more serious about it and even wrote letters to the girls. The few surviving specimens available, although couched in the restrained and stilted fashion of the day, contain occasional would-be poetic flashes of emotion.

Family gossip relates that when his mother sent him one evening to bring his older sisters from the MacMasters' house, since young ladies in the South could not be out alone after dark, he just stood

15

on the porch and rattled the blinds, too embarrassed to enter. His mother worried so much about this incident that she asked Mrs. MacMasters what she could do to give the young man more poise. Yet it was only a few weeks later that Mrs. MacMasters reported seeing Tommy and her daughter Ellen walking together, hand in hand, with lagging steps. Then Tommy's mother ceased to be concerned about his bashfulness.

But a great new fountain of emotion, which he felt to be far more engrossing than his interest in girls, suddenly burst upon him in the winter of 1872-73. Religion and the Bible were the sources of that stream, which he suddenly began to believe would bring him strength and refreshment all his life long. However true this may have been, there can be little doubt that his vivid religious experience at this time suggested rather an adolescent emotional upheaval, with the psychological strains showing themselves in religion rather than in sex.

It was in the winter when he was just sixteen that Tommy started to attend religious meetings which an older student named Francis J. Brooke began to hold in his room. Although Brooke had received very little prior education he was so full of zeal for the faith that it was not long before the gatherings had to be moved to a little one-story brick stable which served as a chapel for the seminary. This had a low rostrum facing rows of wooden benches with pictures of leaders of the church on its walls. Tommy said later that he never heard greater speeches than those uttered from that rostrum, talks which stirred him so much that the little chapel became for him "holy ground." Religious enthusiasm was fanned to even greater heights in the following months until finally the call to join the church became so strong that he applied for membership on July 3, 1873. The minutes tell of the application of "three young men out of the Sunday School and well known to all. . . . After a free confession during which they severally exhibited evidence of a work of grace begun in their hearts, [they] were unanimously admitted to the membership of this church."

Even though all this may have been due more to the emotions

of youth than to any calm reasoning of the mind, his ardor seems to have been altogether sincere. It became his habit not only to read the Bible every day but also to kneel down daily to his prayers. It is clear that this habit of prayer remained with him, for many years later he wrote: "I do not see how anyone can sustain himself in any enterprise in life without prayer. It is the only spring at which he can renew his spirit and purify his motive." Religion became so much a part of the core of his being that he later said: "So far as religion is concerned, argument is adjourned."

He followed the good Protestant doctrine concerning the Bible, for later he said: "It reveals every man to himself as a distinct moral agent, responsible not to men, not even to those men whom he has put over him in authority, but responsible through his own conscience to his Lord and Maker. Whenever a man sees this vision he stands up a free man, whatever may be the government under which he lives, if he sees beyond the circumstances of his own life." And as a corollary of this sense of personal responsibility he became convinced that in order that a man could have his own faith and serve his God in his own way, the state must grant religious freedom. He felt that this freedom could be used wisely only if the citizens were given education. Consequently it was not long before young Wilson's interest began turning toward the three fields of religion, government and education.

These new convictions, which appealed to his mind as well as his emotions, had enabled him in the spring of 1873 to begin to "command his own development," as he expressed it later. There was a definite turning away from passive drifting to a stern determination to work toward a set purpose. He subsequently discussed the development of a man's purpose in life in an essay called "When A Man Comes to Himself," in which he spoke of the time when a man begins to understand "the secret of social and individual well-being, for the two are not separable." This was the period when the realization of this secret seems to have first come to him, and his change from vague dreams to a dawning sense of purpose was soon recognized by those about him, as is shown in a letter written by his Uncle James to his son in the early spring of 1873, which says: "Tommy Wilson still attends Mr. Barnwell's school, opposite their house, and is said to be studying well. He seems to have improved." The change was also marked by the appearance, at this time, of Gladstone's portrait above Tommy's desk; and he informed his young cousins that it was a picture of a great statesman and that he "intended to be a statesman too."

The next fall a small legacy received by his mother made it possible for him to enter Davidson College, twenty miles north of Charlotte, North Carolina, a strict Presbyterian school, which had expressed disappointment when his father declined an invitation to be its president. The classrooms and dormitories were all in one big building, embellished by a façade of dignified stone columns and set in rolling hills of reddish soil on which the natives raised corn and cotton, sheep and wheat. The few stores in town catered mostly to the students, who had been purposely located out in the country away from temptation and diversions. The only railroad was so slow that a story tells how an indignant conductor shot a man on a mule who was going faster than the train.

His fellow students regarded the sandy-haired youth with spectacles as "witty, genial, superior but languid." He does not seem to have become especially intimate with any of them, perhaps because he had so much studying to do, for he entered with "conditions" in Cicero and ancient geography as well as on probation in two other subjects. His poor health made his work all the harder so that he almost had a complete breakdown before the end of the year. This was due principally to troubles with his digestion, which led to a general debility that required rest and recuperation.

This same lack of physical energy made trouble for him in other ways. The boys had to carry their own water and firewood as well as undertaking numerous other chores, which were a drain upon his strength. When he played center field in the baseball games the captain of the team once burst out: "Tommy Wilson would be a good player if he weren't so damned lazy." Doubtless the other boys agreed with him. But actually the trouble with Tommy was not laziness, he just did not have the strength to work harder at baseball after attending to his studies and his chores.

His greatest interest was in the Eumenean Debating Society, whose constitution he copied out in full almost as soon as he became a member. It debated such subjects as the benefits of slavery, and whether John Wilkes Booth acted as a patriot in the shooting of Lincoln. On December first he made his earliest recorded appearance in public when he upheld the negative of the question: "Resolved: That republicanism is a better form of government than limited monarchy." On January 17 he delivered an original oration, a month later he argued in favor of compulsory education. In May he was excused from several meetings because of illness and his family decided that he had better stay at home the next year to regain his strength.

That fall when Tommy was almost eighteen his father became minister of a church in Wilmington, North Carolina. This new location suited his father better than any place in which he had ever lived, but except for his interest in the ships and docks, Tommy seems to have found few vital contacts in the town. Calling upon some young ladies led to a stilted exchange of letters with one of them, as well as occasional excursions and picnics, but he found little in the way of intellectual companionship or community of ideas with most of the young people. Because the fathers and older brothers of most of the boys had been killed in the war and they were needed to help support their families, very few of them went to college. John Bellamy became his particular friend, next to his own father, and an old family servant has reported that "if he wasn't reading a book with one, he was talking about a book with the other."

He spent his time studying Greek, reading, thinking and dreaming. He and Bellamy used to roam through the woods and swim in the Cape Fear River. When they read romances of Walter Scott together Tommy liked to talk about the characters, discussing their peculiarities and which one he liked best. In *The Pirate* he enjoyed the fun of Yellowley calling out Latin quotations from the back of a Shetland pony, and when they got through laughing over this episode they could discuss the qualities and comparative charms of the two girl heroines, Minna and Brenda.

Tommy looked like his father, with the same luminous eyes, the same big teeth set in a heavy jaw, and a prominent nose and cheek-bones. But his face was longer, perhaps something of a horse face with its straight profile and large protuberant teeth. Although he was not as handsome as his father, his jaw was more finely molded and his eyes flashed with a keener intelligence. They could leap with laughter too, while the straight firm line of his mouth seemed to indicate exceptional fixity of purpose.

In spirit he was more like his mother , who never turned a beggar from the door but was so standoffish that people thought her cold and distant. It is quite possible that in reality Jessie was kind, but she had a strange sort of pride which prevented her from making friends. There is a story of her refusing to let her family eat on the deck of an excursion boat as everyone else was doing one summer day on a picnic, not even relenting to let them join the Bellamys in some cake which was offered. Then on a winter night when she was ill of typhoid Miss Ellen Bellamy came over to sit up with her, but the presence of an unmarried woman for the night must have hurt the mother's sensitive pride, for Ellen was never invited to the house again.

The leisure and the opportunity to dream which the young man had while he was in Wilmington were influences that stayed with him all his life. They seem to have added to his nature something of softness and repose, which would occasionally give a touch of light-ness to his determined spirit. He wandered among the docks and wharves and talked to sailors ashore from all the ports of East and West. He was a constant comrade of his friend John in the stately old pillared home of the Bellamys, with its high-ceilinged rooms and rich Victorian furnishings. John loved his friend and felt that the

20

only trouble with Tommy was that he was "a confirmed and con-founded Calvinist."

Although his father and John kept Tommy busy with books, those discussed in the minister's study being serious volumes of philosophy, history and religion, there is still evidence that Tommy became involved in some sort of mild and very tentative romance with one of the maidens of the neighborhood. He paid her bashful visits and they may even have held hands a little. He sent her an occasional rose and sometimes a note which the recipient preserved and held dear. It was no great romance, but he had begun to show some genuine interest in girls.

One of the peculiarities of Tommy Wilson's temperament was that although he was neither unselfish nor self-sacrificing for other people, not even for his family, he was willing and eager to devote himself wholeheartedly to a cause. This was true almost from his boyhood to his death.

The central focus of his thoughts in those days was placed upon his faith in an all-powerful and all-seeing God: "God, whose I am and whom I serve," as he was accustomed to say. This strongly entrenched faith might in the future become a too intoxicating wine if he began to feel that he had the wisdom and the strength to carry out God's will. For he was a preacher's son, the offspring of the Lord's anointed, a product of the aristocratic South and not of the rough and tumble democracy of the Middle West. He was not used to having other boys stand up and steadfastly maintain ideas opposed to his. Such confidence on the part of a serious youth could lead to great achievements, but it did not encourage any idea of compromise or conciliation.

Suddenly, this confidence was increased by a new thought that came to him concerning his abilities. His father, jocund and delighted, spoke of it to Dr. William Bellamy, as he caught up with him in the street one day and said: "See here, Will—I've something to tell you. Says Tommy to me at breakfast this morning, after he had been reading until way after midnight last night: 'Father, Eureka,' and I say, 'Eureka, Tommy, and why?' 'Eureka,' he repeats, all fine and gay, 'Eureka, I have found it!' says he. 'Found what?' says I. 'A mind, sir. I've found I have an intellect and a first class mind,' says he. He had been reading an abstruse book and the ease which he mastered it convinced him that he had a mind!'"

The father was pretending to make it a joke, but it was obvious to Dr. Bellamy that he was very pleased and proud. Although this was an unusual statement for a boy to make, many a clever youth may well have had the same sudden thought about himself. Was it egotism to put this into words? It does not seem so; it seems to have been the simple statement of what appeared to the boy to be a fact, a statement made the more readily because he and his father were such friends. Even if this has been interpreted by some as a declaration that he meant some day to run the world, there is no real reason to believe that it was any such thing. It seems rather the mere utterance of a youth who for the first time was recognizing something of his powers and who took pleasure in announcing the discovery to his best friend, his father.

Yet there was peril in this too. It was possible that Tommy might come to think he had one of the great minds of the world, and so begin to disdain the third- and fourth-rate minds of others, grow to ignore them and be scornful of them, not recognizing that his own might not be so very superior. It was an excellent tool, that brain of his, but it was not one of the great intellects of all time; and he might grow to think it better than it was. Perhaps he would come to rely upon its power until he would start to think he could ignore the feelings and ideas of others and even trample ruthlessly upon them if he wished. From this could develop an intellectual pride, which with his great faith in God might lead him to believe that with his first-class mind he could become the chosen instrument of God's will—a source of strength, but dangerous to quaff too deeply.

All this gives evidence of the not uncommon phenomenon of a divided mind or personality. On the one hand was an almost pathological introversion with his attention focused on his own thoughts,

22

passions and intellectual achievements, including in his late teens an emotional upheaval which he regarded as a religious awakening. On the other side was a gay and affectionate youth, interested in his family, the girls and his friend John Bellamy. These general interests even were extended to include the fictional characters of Scott and other writers. Two sides appear, both fundamentally parts of the same Tommy, as he struggled with the strains of adolescence. Both serious introvert and lively extrovert were there, both made the man.

CHAPTER III

"A MOST PERSUASIVE
TALKER"

One of the real turning points of Tommy's career came when his family decided to send him to college at Princeton. It was the first time he had left the South, with its primarily rural economy dependent largely upon cotton and its undertone of bitterness and frustration consequent upon war and reconstruction. Now he came to the North with its more advanced industrialization and its greater variety of activities. And at the same time he became part of a community where investigation and study were matters of general concern. Here for the first time he found an atmosphere entirely congenial to his own tastes.

When he entered Princeton in the autumn of 1875 he was a good-looking youth of eighteen with a thick shock of blond hair. He was not a distinguished athlete and his digestion always gave him trouble, but he had built up his strength at Wilmington. He was almost six feet tall and of good sound build, weighing 165 pounds. Behind his spectacles his eager and intelligent eyes often lighted up with a lively twinkle. The training in the exact use of language and in the development of broad intellectual interests which his father had given him had both tempered and sharpened an already powerful mind inherited from his Scotch-Irish ancestors. He was now prepared to turn this excellent instrument to his own special purposes.

24

In many ways he was a promising member of the class of 1879 and it semed very possible that in this new world of college he would win the admiration and affection of his fellows. Even in Augusta he had managed to assert a definite supremacy over the other boys of the Lightfoot gang when he gathered them together in his father's barn for a parliament of debate and discussion. But the authority which he exerted over them there had a tendency to fall to pieces on the baseball diamond or the rough and tumble field of sports. Now things of the intellect were beginning to interest all his companions, so that Tommy's exceptionally alert mind gave him a more and more commanding position among them as his college life progressed. He gave indications that he might achieve one intellectual success after another. Debating was his favorite pastime, but oratory and writing were also great fun for him. One of his classmates reported that "what he called 'the play of the mind' was as exhilarating to him as play of the body to the athlete"; in itself it gave him a keen delight, quite aside from fame or profit.

Tommy came up from the South carrying a dignified old black bag his father had used, as well as a letter to President James McCosh, which his shyness forbade him to deliver. He lived in a boarding house with sixteen other students, largely freshmen like himself. Not many of his classmates were Southerners, for that region was still suffering for the poverty and bitterness engendered by the war. He had something of this feeling himself for, although he sat up all one night discussing without apparent resentment the causes of the Civil War, yet on another occasion after an argument concerning the vengeful intemperance of Reconstruction his face turned white and he slammed out of the room crying: "You know nothing whatever about it."

His long lean jaw may have contributed to the impression of self-control and determination in his face, quite different from the lordliness, conceit and polite self-confidence shown in his father's fleshier countenance. And with this determination went an air of distinction. His classmate Robert Bridges said: "No one ever could put pomp in a college parade like Tommy Wilson. He had a gift for it." He was fresh from the South but it was not long before he began to make himself felt in the college and acquire lifelong friends.

This was a time of revival of interest in universities and educational problems all over the country. Dr. McCosh had come to Princeton a few years before, and Eliot to Harvard; Cornell and John Hopkins were just being organized, Yale and Columbia had outstanding leaders in Woolsey and Barnard. The theory of evolution was arousing interest everywhere and Dr. McCosh took the position that "our first inquiry is not whether it is consistent with religion, but whether it is true. If it is found to be true on the principle of the induction of Bacon, it will be found that it is consistent with religion on the principle of the unity of truth."

Since Joseph Wilson was a graduate of Princeton, Dr. McCosh had visited the family in Columbia while Tommy was home on vacation from Davidson College and looking the lad over with an appraising eye had observed to his father: "The boy'll be coming to Princeton no doubt"—a remark which Tommy long remembered, together with the personality of Dr. McCosh himself and the Scotch burr of his speech, which Tommy learned to imitate to perfection.

Tommy had a great fund of general reading, and in many ways he was more mature and mentally alert than the other boys, but he was poorly prepared in mathematics and not sufficiently familiar with Greek roots for one who was supposed to read Demosthenes and Herodotus in the original. Nor was he fluent in translating from Latin the poems of Horace and the histories of Livy. These required subjects interested him so little that all through his college courses his purpose with regard to them seems to have been merely to comply with the minimum demands of the faculty. But in other fields his enthusiasm was so intense that the humorous historian of the class said of him: "Tommy Wilson, upon entering college, rushed to the library and grabbed Kant's *Critique of Pure Reason*."

Actually Tommy soon discovered that he wanted to study, not Greek or Latin authors nor philosophy nor pure literature as such, but political essays and discussions of government by authors like Burke and Bagehot. Henry W. Lucy, who later wrote for *Punch*

26

under the name of "Toby, M.P.," was then painting vivid pictures of leading figures of the British Parliament for the *Gentleman's Magazine* as well as contributing articles on "The Orator" and "The Democratic Party in the United States." These essays showed Wilson the field of endeavor which appealed to him by giving him some understanding of the English methods of democratic government and political arrangement. These well-tried methods aroused his admiration and in the field of government he felt that he might one day win a great place, for he could debate, he could orate and he might learn to lead.

He first found the numbers of the *Gentleman's Magazine* which contained Lucy's articles when he stopped at the head of the south stairs of the college library early in his first term and saw the volumes there on the shelf beside him. When reading these essays he could comprehend the workings of the British form of Parliamentary government. He could see Gladstone with his swift flow of words, able to bewilder his audience before he began to enlighten and convince; he saw Disraeli with his awkward gestures and John Bright with his polished witticisms. He saw the lesser luminaries; he apprehended that their debate was free and open so that all the world might understand just where each of them stood.

He realized that the British system led to drama and to direct responsibility of all the actors to those who had elected them. He soon came to the conclusion that this arrangement was far superior to the American method, where so many of the decisions were made by various committees of Congress who could kill a bill merely by never bringing it before the House or Senate. He kept thinking about this until he began to feel a definite urge to speak his mind by writing upon what he considered the evils of our system.

While he did not follow any routine college method of instruction, even sometimes ridiculing the requirements, he was very busy pursuing as far as possible the bent of his own mind. He soon definitely determined to seek a public career, and with this in view he spent all his energies on the study of government, including

27

the history and theory of government and the careers of political leaders. Literature interested him only if it dealt with the lives of statesmen. He even refused to try for a literary prize which his facility in writing might have enabled him to win because he found the work would have entailed a study of Ben Jonson and two Shakespearean plays. His classmate Robert Bridges speaks of the "confident selection" of his work and his "easy indifference" to all subjects not in accord with his purpose.

One of Wilson's greatest enjoyments was participating in the activities of a literary society know as Whig Hall, whose constitution had been written by James Madison. This organization, which specialized in debating, brought its activities to a climax each year with a debate against the rival society known as Clio. He liked this sort of thing so much that he organized another group called the Liberal Debating Club whose meetings were patterned after those of the British Parliament, so that certain members represented the government party which was obliged to go out of office if it lost the confidence of the chamber.

He did not win many college prizes, although an oration on Cobden and an essay on the Earl of Chatham are said to have gained much applause. The works of Burke received his especial attention, with those of Pitt, Disraeli, and Bagehot not far behind. He developed his voice by reading aloud and by declaiming from a volume of Burke either in the woods at Princeton or in his father's church at Wilmington.

But after all this training, when it came to the big prize of his senior year, the Lynde Debate against Clio, Wilson did not participate. The members of Whig Hall now recognized him as probably their best orator but when the preliminary debate took place to choose their champion he put his hand into the hat and drew a slip which required him to argue in favor of a protective tariff. He tore it up in anger and refused to go on, for he was such a strong adherent of the principle of free trade that he declared nothing would induce him to present arguments against his heart's conviction.

28

On the surface this may seem a childish attitude for him to have taken, as William Allen White has suggested, and certainly it was a disappointment to his comrades who were largely depending upon his talents to win the great debate. But Robert Bridges said the society had not made him its debater and staked its game upon him, nor had he been chosen for the final team, as White implies later in his discussion. On the contrary, Bridges stated: "We were all sorry that he withdrew, but he had not been chosen and had not accepted any trust. Any one of us could have dropped out in the same way."

Under these circumstances the issue became simply a question of how much the doctrine of free trade meant to Wilson at that time. Doubtless to the average undergraduate it would have been of little consequence which side he upheld, but to Wilson, with his passionate interest in human institutions combined with his sense of the importance of good government, the doctrine of free trade was of so much concern that even in an undergraduate debate he could not bring himself to deliver an attack upon it in public. That was the stand he took, that was his nature; he would not speak against this principle because he believed in it so firmly and because its adoption seemed so vital to him.

At the same time he found all the life and activities of college thoroughly congenial. He was not a sufficiently good player to get on the baseball team but he became its manager, and also was secretary of the board of the football association. He belonged to an eating club called "The Alligators" in which he found companionship that thoroughly suited him. His bedroom was number seven in the new Witherspoon Hall, on the second floor with a view of the main street of Princeton in the distance. Here and in number nine a group called the "Witherspoon Gang" frequently gathered in the evening after prayer meeting and held long discussions on any topic that came up, whether it dealt with philosophy, politics, religion or some subject more directly related to their daily lives.

Robert Bridges, who was one of his best friends, said of him: "He took great pleasure in the writers who used language with precision and with imagination. He would trail a word or a phrase

29

with that eagerness that R.L.S. so exalted. They would pop out in his conversation at the club table as part of a jest or noisy dispute. There was a twinkle in his eye, but he knew and you knew that he had scored."

His classmates also have told us more about his college career. Bridges went on to say: "This comradeship of his which began on this campus had a strong hold on him always. It included all kinds of men on the campus and diverse interests. He never lost the joy of it and I know it often lightened his burdens." Again Bridges reported that Tommy had a jesting phrase in college which went: "When I meet you in the Senate, I'll argue that out with you." With his friend Charles Talcott, Wilson made a solemn covenant "That we would drill ourselves in all the arts of persuasion, but especially in oratory, that we might have facility in leading others into our ways of thinking and enlisting them in our purposes."

But it was evident that Tommy could turn from these high endeavors to things less serious, for he frequently went serenading in a quartet with his clear tenor voice under the windows of the Princeton maidens. The spirit of romance mixed with jollity on those carefree evenings must have appealed to his never-failing love of fun and attractive women.

Besides graduating 28th in a class of 106, he was for two years a member of the editorial board of *The Princetonian* and its managing editor in his senior year. We know that he kept copies of his serious writings, since some of his essays, orations and debates were later collected and published under the title *Mere Literature*.

One of his greatest triumphs came at the very end of his college course when the editor of the *International Review* accepted an article of his on "Cabinet Government in the United States." Published in the number for August 1879, this essay attacked the American Congress as "a legislature which is practically irresponsible" and argued that this could be corrected by giving Cabinet ministers a seat in Congress as well as a voice in its debates. He believed that this procedure would do much to develop both a strong Cabinet and a strong Congress because it would focus the attention of the whole nation on Congressional arguments since they might lead at any time to the fall of one Cabinet and the creation of a new one. He also felt that the work of Congress should be done not in secret committees but "as if in the presence of the whole country, in open and free debate." All this was the logically reasoned consequence of his reading and thinking about the differences between the British system of government and our own. And added to his intellectual achievements was his gift for speaking. One of his classmates, later Dean H. B. Fine of Princeton, said that "publicly and privately he was one of the most persuasive talkers I ever heard," and his teachers recognized that "He had an earnestness that was really intense."

The fall after graduation Tommy entered the University of Virginia Law School. But before this, on July 7, 1879, he wrote a letter to his Princeton classmate Charles Talcott in which he mentioned how hard it had been to part from his friends and went on to declare how their mutual promises to prepare themselves for work on behalf of a cause made it easier for him to persevere in his daily efforts at composition and the preparation of his voice for public speaking. His cause was good government. His law school career was primarily intended to serve the purpose of fitting himself for public service, perhaps for Congress; and with this in mind he frequently stayed up working late into the night. At Charlottesville he almost immediately joined the Jefferson debating society as well as the Phi Kappa Psi fraternity. He used to sing in both the chapel choir and the glee club which, like the group at Princeton, was accustomed to warble such ditties of the day as "Marguerite," "Speed Away," "Golden Slippers" and "Forsaken," as serenades beneath the windows of their favorite girls. It was a life of simple gaiety combined with hard work that he had in the Law School at Charlottesville, just as it had been at Princeton.

Although he was no athlete he was selected to present the medals on December 20 at the close of the University Field Day. His speech on this occasion was greeted with much laughter and loud cheers. He began with a medley of absurdities which were followed by pretended gallantry and ended with a little earnest eloquence. The mixture included these original verses concerning a young lady whose whereabouts were unknown:

> "But where in thunder is she now, I wonder?
>   Oh, my soul be quiet, and my sad heart hush!
> Under the umbrella of another fellow
>   Ah! I think I see her, paddling through the slush!"

In more serious moments he was busy developing his ability in speech-making by tramping off along toward Jefferson's home at Monticello to pour forth the orations of Demosthenes or addresses by one of his heroes in the British Parliament. Once a student met him taking a long walk with a volume of Shelley's poems in his pocket. There can be little doubt that his persistence in hard work was due to a feeling that he was training himself for what one day might develop into greatness.

Evidence that he felt the urge of some unusual power within himself and yet feared it might be mere empty pride is shown in a letter he wrote to Charles Talcott on May 20, 1880, in which he says: "Those indistinct plans of which we used to talk grow on me daily, until a sort of calm confidence of great things to be accomplished has come over me, which I am puzzled to analyze the nature of. I can't tell whether it is a mere figment of my own inordinate vanity, or a deep-rooted determination which it will be in my power to act up to."

When the young law student was scheduled to deliver an oration on John Bright, some of the ladies of the college community were so eager to come that for the first time in history they were allowed in the halls of the "Old Jeff" debating society. There in the heart of postwar Virginia, Tommy Wilson had the courage to try to justify John Bright's opposition to the Confederacy, saying: "I yield to no one present in love for the South. But *because* I love the South I rejoice in the failure of the Confederacy. . . . The Northern union would have continued stronger than we, and always ready to use her strength to compass our destruction."

32

Just as he had succeeded in teaching rules of order to the Lightfoots in Augusta, so now when he agitated for a new constitution for the Jefferson Society he aroused such interest in the project that for several months most of the club meetings were occupied with discussions of the new document's provisions, although the minutes show the members also took time to argue about some of Wilson's favorite topics such as the tariff and the British system of ministerial responsibility.

At the same time Tommy took part in the many-sided activities of the university. When the whole student body gathered together after a fight between some of the students and the roustabouts of a circus, belligerent youths were arguing that everybody go to the circus grounds to "wipe them up" until Tommy mounted a chair, lifted his hand for silence and said: "I have listened with much attention to the plan you have outlined to whip the circus. I want to make a few remarks on how not to do it." After his speech, the students all went quietly home to bed.

His university activities still left him time for a mild love affair with his cousin Harriet Woodrow, who was a student in the Augusta Female Seminary at Staunton over the mountains. He could get over there and back easily on a weekend. Once his other cousins thought him too boisterous in his applause at a concert when Harriet performed. After spending the Christmas holidays of 1879 in Staunton he kept up an active correspondence with Harriet until the summer of 1881 when he visited her family in Chillicothe, made his proposal and was promptly rejected.

All this time he was becoming tougher of mind, gradually developing into manhood. While he sang and played baseball, gave orations on John Bright and continued his study of the British Parliamentary system, his sense of purpose and his determination to become a leader in the world were constantly before him. An indication of this came at the end of his stay at Charlottesville, when he started calling himself Woodrow Wilson. He did this deliberately, for he probably realized that his first appeal to a large public must be based on his books and essays. He wrote Robert

Bridges saying, "I find I need a trademark in advertising my literary wares. . . . Woodrow Wilson sticks in my mind."

He had now grown into an earnest young man determined to make a place in the world, but something of his boyishness always remained a part of him. All his life he loved to sing and often had a most un-Calvinistic impulse to dance, while boyish moods of anger and of exultation were to burst forth from him occasionally until he died.

In this persistent youthfulness he retained a human quality which did not detract from his determination to achieve noble ends, but which makes it easy to understand how those who knew him well could both admire and love him. College life had proved to be the kind of existence that suited him; it was as a student at Princeton and Charlottesville that his keen mind first found a sympathetic climate outside of his own home, so that he there began to develop a definite intellectual leadership that gave promise of greater things to come. He had sung in glee clubs, put pomp in college parades, and been a genial companion; while at the same time he had devoted most of his waking hours to his chosen work, the study of government, perhaps spurred on in this by the anticipation that it might one day lead him to a seat in Congress or the Senate. The emotions of adolescence had developed into the tenacity of young manhood.

CHAPTER IV

ROMANCE AND HAPPY MARRIAGE

In December 1880 Wilson left the University of Virginia on account of his health but he occupied himself with the study of the law in his father's manse at Wilmington. He went back home because the family doctor found his "digestive organs seriously out of gear" and thought that systematic medical treatment under careful supervision would improve the condition. He did seem to get better, and even found some time to visit with the girls of the city, but reported that he was somewhat restrained from "bestowing too much attention upon any one of these interesting creatures" by his young brother, James Ruggles, Jr., born 1866, who was "constantly and slyly in wait" for an opportunity to tell the family at home all about it.

His interest in British politics continued. He reported reading with delight Trevelyan's *Early History of Charles James Fox* and later could not help rejoicing over the death of Disraeli. He renewed his work in Latin while teaching his brother and reported that he found the exercise of teaching an excellent training for himself. He attended church picnics without enthusiasm, but took pleasure in singing in various "musicals."

By the spring of 1882 he was twenty-five years old and felt himself sufficiently improved in health and prepared in the study of law to embark upon the practice of that profession. The intricacies and majesty of the law, however, had no real appeal for him.

35

The whole family discussed together the question of where he had best set up in practice and decided upon Atlanta, because it seemed to be the only town in the South which had recovered from the war sufficiently to show signs of becoming a center of commerce and industry. The only trouble with this selection was that many other young lawyers and their families were coming to the same conclusion at the same time, so that the city directory for 1883 showed that there was more than one lawyer for every four hundred of the population including children and Negroes.

Nevertheless, to Atlanta Wilson set forth. As soon as he arrived, with his license in his pocket, he looked up an acquaintance from the University of Virginia named Edward Ireland Renick; the young men found their minds to be completely in accord with one another and immediately established the law firm of Renick and Wilson in an office on the second floor at 48 Marietta Street. They also roomed together at the house of a widow at 344 Peach Tree Street, where Wilson made friends with his landlady's niece, Katie Mayraw. The two often read aloud together and he tried to teach her stenography. Wilson and Renick also had long talks and walks when they read *The Aeneid* together. They used to discuss the best ways to build up the South, fight the Northern high-tariff men, and make Congress responsible to the will of the people.

The young lawyers had plenty of time on their hands since their profession was so greatly overcrowded, and they had no local connections to bring in clients. Wilson's family was providing the money for his keep, consequently it was easy for him to go back to his college reunion at Princeton that June, as well as to help his father as clerk of the General Assembly of the Southern Presbyterian Church. Then one day in September a young man from the New York *World*, Walter Hines Page, came into the office. He was accompanying the Tariff Commission which Wilson and Renick had known was traveling about the country presumably taking evidence but actually seeking to give a hearing to all those who wanted a high protective tariff upon one item or another. Page had recently come from John Hopkins University and he was busy overthrowing the superficial dignity of the commissioners by his ridicule. Wilson thought this a good opportunity to make a plea for free trade which would as a matter of course be published in the record of the proceedings. He appeared before the Commission in the breakfast room of the Kimball House and put forward an argument on behalf of a tariff for revenue only, which showed a grasp of the subject and skill in presentation that won him the admiration of the local congressman and the few other young men who were present. That same evening he gathered in his office a group of men interested in public questions and four months later organized a branch of the Free Trade Club of New York, which met every two weeks during the winter to discuss all manner of problems, with almost all talking done by Wilson.

He also sat in the gallery of the Georgia Senate where he was badly disillusioned about the character of the members of that august body, which he had envisioned as something like the British Parliament, with wit and wisdom marking its debates. In Atlanta he found instead a group of country merchants, lawyers and farmers, ignorant and with no training in the art of government, assembled to write the laws for the great State of Georgia. On one of the first occasions that he visited the legislature he found its members considering a resolution requesting the state's Senators and Representatives in Washington "to do all in their power to secure a grant from the federal treasury in aid of education." This idea, which has since become more widespread, was contrary to his whole theory of government, for he believed that all men should stand on their own feet and depend upon their own efforts to take care of their own problems. The resolution carried with only one speech opposing it and Wilson expressed his indignation in a letter to Robert Bridges written several years later.

So far as is known Wilson never had a case of his own to try in court although he was once assigned by the judge to represent a Negro who had no other attorney. His mother became almost his only client when she gave him control of her small property. The Bellamy family cherishes a story that the Reverend Joseph Wilson asked Tommy's old friend John Bellamy how much he was making at the law in Wilmington and on receiving the answer, "About eighteen hundred dollars," the old Doctor muttered: "Well, so you are, are you? The boy down in Atlanta isn't making his salt."

Probably Wilson did as he pleased, allowing his afternoons for writing and for reading the *American Statesmen* and *English Citizens Series,* both altogether to his taste. He forwarded to the *Nation* several articles which he wrote on American congressional government, but received them back with "Mr. Garrison's extremely unfavorable opinion." Meanwhile he became steadily more restless all through the spring of 1883 because he came to feel that the practice of the law "for the purposes of gain is antagonistic to the best interests of the intellectual life." He noticed with sympathy that some of his heroes like Burke, Bagehot and Sir Henry Maine were "trained as lawyers, but found the legal profession unsatisfying." He felt that he could not practice law properly when he was studying history and politics at the same time. He was becoming convinced that the profession of teaching would give him more time to study and write upon the subjects that really interested him.

Then in April 1883 he made a short visit to Rome, Georgia, to talk over his mother's business affairs, which she had now entrusted to him, with her brother-in-law James Bones. Bones had been handling her affairs in the past, so Wilson took with him a typewriter and his mother's power of attorney. Rome was a beautiful old town with a broad central street, great trees, and fine old houses where his family were ready to receive him.

Jessie Bones, with whom he had played in Augusta had just married and become Mrs. A. T. H. Brower. Not far from the Browers lived Agnes Tedcastle, a friend and contemporary of Jessie's, who knew about the young man's arrival. Another friend of Miss Tedcastle's was Ellen Axson, daughter of the Presbyterian minister, a girl whom a cousin has described by saying: "She always had a flower-like appearance; her hair was a bronze gold, her eyes ever a deep brown and her face was all aglow with the marvelous color that she never lost."

38

Ellen was twenty-three and, when her mother had died two years previously leaving her the eldest of four children, she had taken a vow never to marry. Nevertheless when she saw a tall well-dressed young man with silky mustache and short blond side-whiskers pass by the Tedcastles' porch she immediately asked: "Who is that fine-looking young man?" Her friend answered: "I don't know whether to tell you or not, you man-hater; that is Tommy Wilson."

He went on walking past and did not see her until the next day when he observed her in church wearing a heavy crepe veil and thought: "What a bright pretty face, what splendid mischievous laughing eyes! I'll lay a wager that this demure little lady has lots of fun and life in her!" When she spoke to Mrs. Bones after the service, young Wilson took another good look at her and determined to learn her name and seek an introduction. He discovered she was "Miss Ellie Lou Axson" and remembered that their fathers were friends; there is even a story that he had once insisted on holding her in his arms when he was about six years old and she about two.

An intense desire to meet this attractive young person seems to have taken immediate hold on him, for he went almost at once to call upon her father, who asked him to sit down and undertook to entertain him. Wilson asked rather pointedly about his daughter's health. The good minister seemed somewhat surprised but summoned her to the parlor where the older man kept them busily engaged in conversation on the question, "Why have night congregations grown so small?"

Ellen was serene and sweet as well as lovely and vivacious. She walked for miles in conversation with Tommy; he "could not keep away from her" and "had to call every afternoon." Numerous little notes went back and forth; her first two were on black-bordered cards addressed to "Mr. Wilson," and the third somewhat more intimately to "Mr. Woodrow."

She knew things that Wilson did not know; her intellectual interests were broader than his if not so intense. She had been brought up in "a house of books and religion," she talked to him about

39

Browning and Sidney Lanier, Wordsworth and Laurence Sterne; and she had a real talent for painting which later led her to study at an art school in New York.

One story goes that on the very first evening after taking her home from a family gathering he stood on a bridge over the little river and swore to himself that one day he would marry Ellen Axson. Another records a picnic when Woodrow and Ellen sat on the straw with their feet dangling out of the rear of Colonel Brower's wagon and never appeared for lunch. It took him a little time to persuade her to be his wife; at first she refused to consider it even though she also felt the attraction.

Although quite a correspondence began when he left Rome after seeing her less than a dozen times, nothing seemed to be developing from it. Then apparently quite by chance, when he was going north to Baltimore and Johns Hopkins to study in September and had to change trains at Asheville, North Carolina, he saw her sitting on the veranda of the hotel, while he was walking up the principal street. When he recognized her hat with a peculiar braid upon it he rushed up the steps. She had been called home by the sudden illness of her father and she also was waiting between trains. As they walked up and down the porch he quoted Bagehot's remark that a bachelor is "an amateur in life," and before they had to separate they were engaged.

She told her brother about it with shining eyes when she reached home, asuring him that Woodrow was "the greatest man in the world and the best." This love was a deep and new experience for Wilson. He wrote a few months later that until he met her he could not become "fully himself," that he had at last discovered how to use his "unguided strength." It gave him a "new realization" beyond anything that he could have imagined.

He wrote her a month after their engagement that he used to think as he supposed other young men do, that he should "never pay any but entirely voluntary homage to a woman," had thought a wife would be a mere "leisure-moment companion, dispensing with intellectual sympathy." But he now felt quite differently and when he heard her expound the significance of the plot of *Middlemarch* as they returned from "a certain walk up a hill" he realized that she was the kind of wife he needed. He did not want a wife such as John Stuart Mill married who would furnish him with opinions, but he was delighted to have found one who would come into his studies as "a close companion."

Even after her swift agreement to marry him, Ellen Axson had some misgivings. She told a cousin a little later that "if I had not promised him just then it would never have happened." It was indeed lucky for them both that he proposed and was accepted exactly when he did.

Her indecision stemmed from the fact that she was the oldest child in the family, coupled with the realization that with her mother dead she had become the feminine head of the household two years before. Now she arrived home after her adventure with Wilson at Asheville to find her father seriously ill from a nervous disorder which led to his death shortly afterward. She was overcome by her responsibilities arising from two younger brothers and a baby sister, hence it was then that she expressed doubts whether she should not forego marriage altogether.

Wilson was sunk into violent misery by her indecision, for even two years after their first meeting he wrote to her on April 15, 1885: "It's a matter of life and death with me." But at the same time he told her about his shortcomings, accusing himself of a "sensitive, restless, overwrought disposition" and of "restless, unappeasable ambition."

They also discussed at length her prospective career as an artist, since she had a real talent for painting, nor could Wilson deny "a woman's right to live her own life." However he felt that they really needed one another for he wrote, "It is not peculiar to women, my darling, to fail to find contentment in living for themselves. Men are quite as unable to satisfy themselves with self-service."

There were practical difficulties, too, because he had only "about $500 in all to get married on" in addition to the prospect of a position in Bryn Mawr College at $1,500 a year. Certainly this was not much, but it evidently seemed sufficient to the young people for they were married in the manse of the Independent Presbyterian Church of Savannah on June 24, 1885. Ellen had been living there with her grandfather, the Reverend I. S. K. Axson, since the death of her father and had taken charge of the dignified old house nestled among the trees behind the church.

The old-fashioned parlor had Victorian furniture, a fireplace and a high Southern-style ceiling. The young couple stood in a corner of the room, he tall, keen-eyed and happy, with his long silky mustache, and she a beautiful blond girl full of pride in her husband. His father and her grandfather had tears in their eyes as they went through the simple ceremony uniting their offspring. All the Wilson and Axson relatives were there, as well as some of the Woodrows, and while they were waiting for the bride to come downstairs Wilson and her brother Stockton Axson sat talking about the books in the old minister's library.

Everything was properly connubial, with the scent of orange blossoms in the air and all the relatives assembled, when two small boys, the bridegroom's nephew Wilson Howe and the bride's younger brother Edward "mixed it up in a joyous fight over some difference in boyish opinions." Stockton Axson related later that the bride was much shocked but he "caught a twinkle in the bridegroom's eye which seemed to say, 'Let's separate them, but don't let's be in too desperate haste about it.'" Here was an incident which showed up the characters of the bride and groom; Ellen was inclined to regard even small affairs in a serious light, while Wilson had the Irish gift of loving life and seeing fun in everything. He could even thoroughly enjoy a good fight between two little in-laws on his wedding day.

Yet Ellen understood people probably better than her husband did; she gave him wise advice, sympathy and counsel. She felt that she wanted to take care of him and make his life comfortable and lovely, but when she became ill having her first babies the attention which he gave her and the solicitude he felt took him out of himself and made him happy. She knew far more about poetry, philosophy and literature in general than he did and she built up his interest in these things. Her love of music as well as her genuine ability in painting were completely congenial to his tastes.

While he took his Presbyterian faith as being something he would never question, Ellen had her religious difficulties. In trying to solve them she found that Carlyle helped her with his doctrine of work and that Kant and Hegel were quite comprehensible, as well as interesting reading.

The threads of her life became woven into his until they were quite inextricable. Her appearance had a dainty sweetness which covered up a will of iron and a somewhat gloomy spirit, traits not unlike those of Wilson's mother. She possessed the external gentleness and laughter of a Southern woman and an appearance of vivacity in her youth, but with no sense of fun underneath. The joyous lightheartedness of her beloved husband never aroused her to merriment. But she did her best for him; if she could not join in his gaiety she kept young people around him who could, her brother and various cousins, as well as his father, who never grew old in spirit. Besides doing all this for his happiness she gave him the support of her powerful will and wise intellect, invaluable helps to his career.

The honeymooners went to a little one-story cottage surrounded by trees at Arden in the hills of North Carolina. Vines clung around the windows and the porch had a broad roof. Ellen reported that "We are out of doors most of the time, walking together and reading, unless I can coerce him into singing, for he has a beautiful voice."

Hers was a nature no less intense than his when it came to marital devotion but she could look upon others and upon the outside world with somewhat more of calm and less excited feelings. From the beginning she entered into all his thoughts and plans; she protected, guided and influenced his life. Although she had the youthful vivacity of a healthy, happy, high-spirited girl, she was the only one with whom he could relax and she understood him from the first. She insisted that he should not cut short his work at John Hopkins to marry her. If he had taken this step it would probably have completely frustrated his future progress. She gave him wise advice at every point of his career.

He wrote her a year later that his thoughts, impulses and affections had no outlet save through her and again in a few months he gave her an assurance which was undoubtedly the simple truth that she was the only person in the world to whom he could "tell all that his heart contains."

His affection and his need for her grew greater with the years long after their marriage. He wrote her every day that he was away from her, not just telling her of the trials and successes of the moment, but real love letters, with continual little reminders of how she refreshed his spirit and how lonely he was away from her. Then as soon as he got back he would immediately sit down and recount everything. It has been asserted that neither ever tried to conceal from the other any slightest happening or even passing thought. The stream of letters was to continue for thirty years and they were always full of tender love and of devotion to the family but above all to each other.

His engagement to marry this brown-eyed, vivacious girl with all her capacity for love and her interests in religion, philosophy, literature and art was one of the most fortunate events of his entire career. She did her best to turn him from an egotistical self-centered boy and youth into a man willing and eager to devote his life to the service of mankind.

Yet his nature had already showed itself. We have almost no early instance of self-sacrifice on his part on behalf of another. So through all his life his great sacrifices were for principles, not for individuals. Already he had often abandoned boyish games for dreams of greatness, left the ball field if he felt some wrong was threatened, refused to debate on behalf of a high tariff, told a Virginia audience that the South was better off back in the Union, and left the law to study government. He had the Presbyterian awareness of the awful respon-

44

sibility of the individual soul answerable to its God. Tender, loving sympathy and fellow-feeling for another individual he does not seem to have possessed. There was little free outpouring of his spirit to any other person, except perhaps to Ellen. But when it came to working and fighting for the right as he saw it, he seldom spared himself. And with Ellen Axson's help, this desire to serve the cause of humanity became established in him through the years. In it lay the great source of his strength. Ellen broadened his curiosity to add new aspects of life and human achievement to those problems of politics and government which had absorbed his attention up to the time of their marriage. She gave him the affection which he needed, the absolute devotion to his ideas and problems which increased his strength through all the years of her life.

Wilson seemed absolutely to require the love and interest of women. In addition to Ellen Wilson he soon had three admiring and adoring daughters who formed an exceptionally united and devoted family. And yet even to them he added other cousins and distant relatives, largely from the South. His cousin Jessie Bones remained an intimate of the family. Others stayed with them while they were students and Wilson was a young professor. He had admiring females around him all his life. They caused his soul to blossom and gave strength to his spirit.

Much as he loved Ellen he recognized in himself this need for feminine companionship. Early in 1907 when she sent him to Bermuda for a rest during a strenuous conflict at Princeton he remained aloof at first from the attractive and unattached women in his great hotel. But soon he became friendly with a Mrs. Mary Hulbert Peck. When he returned to Bermuda in 1908 he walked along the sands with her, he quoted poetry, he told her his problems and asked her advice. Later she loaned him and Ellen her cottage on the island for use during a vacation.

During the next seven years Wilson frequently wrote Mrs. Peck once or twice a week telling what was on his mind and when she received these letters she read them or showed them to anyone who was interested. She visited the Wilsons and they visited her; his letters were light and cordial but they showed no rise or fall of sentimental emotion. It seems most unlikely that any tense or passionate letters should have been inserted into the sequence. Wilson was straightening out his thoughts by putting them into words. It is hard to believe that the friendship was anything but innocent, at least during the time Ellen was alive.

Spiritual friendships with women of outstanding character and charm were always characteristic of Wilson. He seemed to need that feminine touch of personal interest and appreciation, of understanding for his moods and thoughts, to bring out the very best in him. And he had much to offer them. He was an excellent companion, for his wit was combined with an almost boyish exuberance of spirit which was brought out by the society of women, while his never-failing delight in the play of the mind always kept them interested. He was accustomed to flatter them not by direct compliments but by his pleasure in matching wits and minds with them.

Mary Hulbert Peck was enchanting and sympathetic, with a gay voice and understanding eyes, with apparently no mean nor malicious thoughts, altogether a delightful companion and confidante for Wilson's ideas about the world and his own problems. He saw her three years in a row and she has told of a talk they had one bright day in 1909. It was "in a frame of roses, of oleander and gray-green cedar, a picture of shore and reef, never to be forgotten," that Wilson asked her if he should run for governor of New Jersey, with the hope of later becoming President of the United States. She encouraged him to try it, saying: "Why not? Statesmanship has always been your natural bent, your real ambition all your life."

Then after leaving the definite problem before him to talk in general about life and destiny he turned to her again and began quoting the last poem in the *Oxford Book of English Verse*, by an Irish poet dear to Wilson's heart, a poem that seemed to foreshadow his own destiny and at the same time indicated the nature of their fellowship. The poem began: "In the hour of death, after this life's whim," and ended:

For even the purest delight may pall
And power must fail and pride must fall,
And the love of the dearest friends grow small—
But the glory of the Lord is all in all.

When Mrs. Peck was divorced shortly before the Presidential election of 1912 she took again the name of her first husband, Hulbert, by whom she had had a son. Scandal surreptitiously connected her name with Wilson's implying if not asserting an improper intimacy between them, but it is probable that nothing of that sort existed at that time. There can be no doubt that Wilson found refreshment in Mary Hulbert's spirit and her intellect, but Theodore Roosevelt pretty well took the issue out of the campaign by saying that you might as well ascribe illicit relations to an "apothecary's clerk."

After Ellen Wilson's death in August 1914 stories were bandied about which intimated scandal again. It is not possible to be so certain of his innocence at this time, for the strong threads of his life were broken, threads which had tied him to Ellen so that they had almost seemed like one individual, and it was only natural that a change should come upon him. He was always uxorious. He had always loved women with a passion which was psychic rather than physical, and Mary Hulbert must have been really a more congenial companion mentally than his beloved Ellen. She could supply a gaiety of spirit which might help to support him temporarily in his grief over his loss.

When Ellen died, the European war had just broken out, so that he was faced with all sorts of unexpected and almost insoluble problems. This made the loneliness of his high office even more difficult to bear. His very nature demanded a wife. Before long, even less than a year after Ellen's death, he fell in love with Mrs. Edith Bolling Galt, another beautiful and intelligent woman. A few months later he married her. She had charm and good sense and was accustomed to the social whirl of Washington. She became his confidante and unquestionably his closest companion, devoting herself without stint to his well-being.

47

All his life Wilson felt the need for women. He relied upon their help, their love and their understanding. It was not women in the mass; it was always a few women who were his intimates and closely devoted to him. His spirit and ambition soared higher with their help. They helped him rise to the very best that was in him. The urge to turn to them, to pour his spirit out to them, to seek strength in their understanding and sympathy was part of his nature from the days he courted Ellen until he died.

CHAPTER V

SCHOLAR AND POPULAR PROFESSOR

His new and absorbing love for Ellen Axson after their meeting in 1883 made Wilson more eager than ever to find the career for which he was properly fitted. He was constantly becoming more convinced that he was making no progress in Atlanta. The law had captured his interest in the first place as a step toward political power and leadership, since he felt that most of those who sat in Congress and the law-making bodies of the nation were trained as lawyers. But he cared little for the study of legal problems as such, nor had the demand for his services been sufficient to kindle any sparks of enthusiasm for the law which might have lurked in his mind. Once persuaded that the law was not the career for him, he abandoned it after less than a year.

Nor did he find it hard to think of leaving Atlanta. He wrote his friend Dabney that: "Here the chief end of man is certainly to make money, and money cannot be made except by the most vulgar methods. The studious man is pronounced impractical and suspected as a visionary." His strictures were too severe for there he had discovered Renick and other "companions of the mind." Atlanta had also given him a contact with the rough and genuine world, from which he had been too long sheltered; and this experience was good for him. Nevertheless he felt he had no ties there that could not be easily broken.

Walter Hines Page, when he came to Atlanta traveling with the tariff commission, had told him about the new Johns Hopkins University which was gathering together a group of established thinkers and students to do graduate study in various fields. Although Wilson's family were still supporting him, he could not go to Germany, where his friend Dabney was, because he could not speak the language nor raise such extensive funds; and besides he was in love with a Georgia girl. Consequently he thought that the institution at Baltimore was his best opportunity for study in his favorite fields. He reached this determination at almost the same time that he first met Ellen, and when he arrived for the winter term on September 18, 1883, he had become engaged just two days before.

He wanted an intellectual life and he was also conscious of a "strong instinct of leadership," two urges which might be difficult to satisfy at the same time. But he believed that he could best prepare for this by study at John Hopkins, so he went there in the fall of 1883. He wrote Ellen Axson a few weeks after his arrival:

> What l have wished to emphasize is the *object* for which I came to the University: to get a special training in historical research and an insight into the most modern literary and political thoughts and methods, in order that my ambition to become an invigorating and enlightening power in the world of political thought and a master in some of the less serious branches of literary art may be the more easy of accomplishment.

He had no idea of joining a group of pseudo-intellectuals in New York or Paris. But he had met the rough and callous-minded world in Atlanta and had not enjoyed it nor been successful in it, so he very sensibly changed direction. He wrote of Atlanta without enthusiasm and perhaps with some disillusion or bitterness, but he probably failed to realize that he felt this way because it was the politicians and small storekeepers whom he had seen at their money-grubbing rather than the gay and gracious life which was more truly typical of the town. His inner spirit was not embittered nor had he changed his purpose, he still wanted to train himself to become a leader of men and their thoughts. Only he now realized that he could work toward his purpose better, for the moment, by writing about government than by pursuing the practice of the law, especially when there appeared to be so little practice to be had.

He wanted to study modern governments. Especially was he still eager to compare the British system, a prime minister and Parliament working together, with the American system of checks and balances, leaving Congress and the president largely independent of one another. When he first arrived in Baltimore he was worried because he felt that the professors wanted to require all students to spend their time on "institutional history by making them dig in the dusty records of old settlements and colonial cities," which was not the sort of "grand excursions amongst imperial policies" which he had planned for himself. This was his thought when he first gathered with the others, students and instructors alike, on Friday nights around the long red table of Dr. Herbert B. Adams' celebrated historical seminar. Among those who attended were many who later were to become distinguished as editors, economists and the like. But he was not to be held back for long before giving free expression to his own ideas and desires. Three weeks after his arrival he went to see Dr. Adams after tea, told him that he had a hobby he had been riding for some years from which he was loath to dismount. The professor was sympathetic, readily freed him from "institutional" work and told him to go on with his constitutional studies, saying the work proposed was just what he wanted to see done. Wilson naturally felt elated and encouraged at this verdict.

He was asked to discuss Adam Smith before the seminar and started in to read all the volumes written by his subject. Then Dr. Ely, who wanted to spread a thorough knowledge of economic ideas, suggested to Wilson and Davis R. Dewey that they write together a history of American economic thought. Wilson did a lot of reading on this also and wrote about a third of the book, but he came to despise the work and the manuscript was never published.

He then got busy on his favorite constitutional studies, finishing an article on "Committee or Cabinet Government" which was published by the *Overland Monthly* in January 1884. He also began working on "four or five essays on 'The Government of the Union,'" a project which grew into a book on Congressional government. He drove himself to keep on working, gathering and co-ordinating information even when he was thoroughly fatigued. He wrote Ellen: "If a man does not find duty agreeable he does not deserve gratification."

Then he tried to develop his literary style and his ability in speaking and holding an audience, realizing that these arts were essential if he was to win any sort of leadership over men. His success in this was recognized both by those who read his article and those participated with him in the seminar, in fact one of the other students even asked Wilson to help him put his thoughts in the proper literary form. Wilson observed that: "Oratory is not declamation but putting things so as to appeal irresistibly to an audience."

He labored so assiduously that he did not even go home for the Christmas vacation; but he worked with such concentration that he was able to find considerable time for activities outside his studies and he had a rollicking good time with his leisure. He loved to talk, taking special pleasure in "opening the eyes of Northerners" to the Southern attitude toward the Civil War and Reconstruction. He told tall tales in dialect, Irish, Scotch or Negro. He joined the glee club, agreeing to "warble with them every Monday evening;" nor was it long before he became its leading spirit. One of their best concerts was before an audience of factory workers, mostly girls, who enjoyed the classical pieces and milder college songs but found that "The Three Kittens" and a silly song called the "Hip-po-pot-a-mus" went straight to their hearts. The club came home from the Methodist Church in the suburbs where the concert was given with all its members packed into a four-horse bus "roaring and rattling thro' the quiet streets."

The glee club under Wilson's leadership got into a dispute with the president of the University. The club needed money to pay its expenses and Wilson wanted to raise this amount by an admission charge to those who attended its concerts. When the president offered to pay the expenses from funds at the disposal of the university because he thought it undignified for the university to allow admission to be charged on its premises, Wilson replied that the glee club had its pride to preserve as well as the University. Fighting for his principles, Wilson persuaded the other members to support him until at last he won his point. When he showed that he was ready to stand up for what he thought was the right way, the president gave in and permitted the glee club to collect its admission fees.

At times he went to candy parties where they "compounded the caramels in the dining room, boiled them in the kitchen and ate them in the parlor," while again he attended baseball games with groups arranged by his old college friend Hiram Woods, now a young doctor. Wilson was always a delightful dinner companion, and in those days was able to set the table in a roar; later his wit naturally became less boisterous.

Mrs. Edith Reid, who later developed into a lifelong friend, says that when she first saw him he was "a tall young man, with a formal oversensitive manner." This was when she had invited him to a reception attended principally by the wives of professors and older people. One of the group about her asked: "Now how does he manage that bedside manner and make his dress clothes look like a preacher's? He's terribly clever, but he's provincial." After taking a long look at the young man, who was naturally feeling an unaccustomed shyness among so many older people, Mrs. Reid replied: "If he's provincial he's making the provinces look bigger than the city. He has personality, he is distinctly the personage in this room." She felt he had a remarkable face, strong and heavily marked, naïvely young but full of power. After talking to him about his work and ambitions she led him on to make "a swift-running appraisement of our Presidents from Washington to Cleveland. She says: "There was a diffident graciousness in his manner and in the quality of his voice that marked him as coming from the South; but the moment the talk touched on the problems of the country all diffidence and youth were lost, and he led the conversation with vivid brilliance."

He felt that perfunctory teaching such as some of the professors inflicted upon the students was of little value, but he delighted in James Bryce who gave a series of lectures and in Josiah Royce whom he found "to have the faculty of bringing masses of detail into a single luminous picture." On the other hand he felt that although Henry Ward Beecher gave them splendid entertainment for an hour and forty minutes. "nobody carried away much instruction."

He wrote a new constitution and by-laws for the Hopkins Literary Society, presiding over the meeting at which they were adopted in December 1884. In writing to Ellen about this he added a paragraph which explained very well why he was always so much more self-giving and consequently successful in addressing large groups than in private talks with individuals.

> I have a sense of power in dealing with men collectively which I do not feel always in dealing with them singly. In the former case the pride of reserve does not stand so much in the way as it does in the latter. One feels no sacrifice of pride necessary in courting the favor of an assembly of men such as he would have to make in seeking to please one man.

He took care to prepare his talks even to the small group in the seminar so that they would in reality be finished speeches. They were received with enthusiasm and he told Ellen: "I enjoy it . . . it sets my mind—all my faculties—aglow. . . . There is absolute joy in facing and conquering a hostile audience . . . or in thawing out a cold one."

Along with this pleasure in using his power to convert and convince others came a conviction that government in the United States was rapidly degenerating from the high levels set a generation earlier by Webster, Clay, Calhoun, Lincoln and Douglas. Since then had come the two administrations of Grant and those of Hayes and Arthur, with all manner of spoils and corruption, with apparently an utter lack of broad vision or intellectual power among those in public life. Bright, Gladstone and Disraeli were dominating the

English political scene; why should not men of their caliber become the leaders of America? He was fired with a wish to discover what the trouble was and if possible to bring forward some sort of remedy.

His first thinking along these lines had germinated in college and flowered in his essay on "Cabinet Government in the United States." Then he had kept on developing the same subject in the article published in the *Overland Monthly* for January 1884 where he suggested specific improvements in the American system which he felt would make Congress and the President more quickly and effectively responsible to the people. Now he wanted to go on and work out these ideas with more completeness, incorporating the results into a book which would give them permanence and he hoped might lead to actual changes in some of our methods of government.

He got to work right away and wrote Ellen during the Christmas holidays: "I've opened the new year by a day of diligent work on my favorite constitutional studies. I've planned a set of four or five essays on 'The Government of the Union.'" Then he went on to say that his desire and ambition was to treat the American Constitution as Bagehot had treated the English Constitution, with a fresh and original method. He wanted to show how it grew and how it actually worked; he pointed out that many changes had come to pass which made the practice of government different from that envisaged in *The Federalist*. That day he spent in writing a historical sketch of the modifications which had been wrought in the federal system until they had resulted in establishing a peculiar position for Congress in the federal government. He intended to follow this up with essays upon Congress itself which would examine at length the legislative machinery and the relations of Congress to the Executive.

Later he went on to show how the system of referring bills immediately to specific committees which had to pass upon them first, and which could alter or suppress them, destroyed the sense of leadership in both the President and members of Congress. In April he sent the first few chapters to Houghton Mifflin and received an encouraging letter in reply. He worked at the book all summer and sent the completed manuscript under the title *Congressional Gov-*

ernment to the publishers as soon as he got back to Baltimore in September. It was the end of November before he finally heard that it had been accepted and that they would offer him as good terms as if he were already a well-known writer. He dedicated the book to his father and sent the first copy to Ellen.

The first edition was sold out within a few weeks and most of the reviews were favorable. Gamaliel Bradford, lawyer and writer on politics, wrote in the *Nation* that if there was any previous expositor of what the government established by the Constitution had actually become after a century of history it had escaped his search. "This want Mr. Wilson has come forward to supply." Bradford recognized that the book was modeled on Bagehot's *The English Constitution* and said it could, "although the praise is so high as to be almost extravagant, bear comparison with that inestimable work."

Its argument was presented clearly and the reforms suggested were calculated to improve the efficiency of our government as well as make it more sensitive to the will of the people. The conception may not have been entirely original, the method and style as well as some of the ideas undoubtedly came from Bagehot, and other theories which were included had already been published in the speeches and *Nation* articles of Gamaliel Bradford, as Professor Link suggests; but Wilson was the first to carry the argument through all its diverse ramifications. He presented it in a form that brought it before the public, so that it stood some chance of leading the people of the country to demand action and reform.

The book started a whole new line of thinking among political scientists; a school of anglophile writers and professors arose which soon began to win a large following. This enthusiasm for English institutions increased and persisted long after Wilson had turned to other fields of endeavor. The book influenced English writers too, for James Bryce read it and quoted from it in his work, *The American Commonwealth,* and he was only one of many who publicly recognized its importance.

Wilson praised the idea of having a Prime minister who must resign if he suffered an adverse vote in Parliament, largely because he realized that this meant the head of the state necessarily had the legislative body ready to support him. Yet he stated his doctrine with enough qualifications so that it turned out he was not seriously embarrassed by it in any activities of his later life.

This book along with the two magazine articles which preceded it and a restatement and amplification in *Constitutional Government,* years later, contain the main essence of Wilson's studies and meditations about the ideal form of government and how it should be conducted. They pointed out clearly the usages in the American system he thought should be corrected.

It has been a subject of regret that Wilson did not set forth his speculations on improving the American government in any other book for so many years. Instead he turned to other fields which combined both history and government. At the same time that he made a reputation with his first book he had assured himself of a teaching position; for the Universities of Michigan, Arkansas and Tulane as well as the new college of Bryn Mawr made tentative offers for his services.

All of the experience at John Hopkins had been good for him. The clash of minds and ideas with other intelligent, alert young men, many of whom were to go far in varied intellectual fields, could not fail to quicken his resolution and energize his spiritual fervor at the same time that he must have been a stimulation to his fellow students. The labor he put into his book together with his other hard work at the university helped to develop a strength of mind and purpose which gave him a power he needed badly in the struggles of his later life.

In the autumn of 1885 Wilson went to the new women's college just being established at Bryn Mawr. He had selected it after having an interview with its president as well as with Miss M. Carey Thomas who was its dean and real executive head. She was a brilliant, capable woman, a Doctor of Philosophy from Zurich and five days younger than Wilson. After his arrival he found her authority difficult to bear, but at least he had the department of history all to himself.

57

He did not care for Bryn Mawr, although he stayed there three years, which gave him his first experience as a teacher. He found the girls dull and uninteresting, as is shown by his remarking that they wrote down notes on his jokes just as they did any other part of his lectures. In one class he had only one student, and the whole student body numbered less than fifty girls. He found no inspiration in teaching such classes.

Two daughters were born to the Wilsons while they were in Bryn Mawr; and while they were very pleased at these additions to their family, their life was necessarily made harder by the care of the babies as well as by the uncomfortable quarters the family had to occupy. At first they had only the second story of a cottage called the Betweenery, because it was between two others called the Deanery and the Scenery. The roads were muddy in winter, the cottage had inadequate heating and kerosene lamps for light. When the children came the family moved into the parish house of a deserted church on a country road.

In March 1886 Robert Bridges arranged for Wilson to address a meeting of Princeton alumni in New York, but his speech on "The College and the Government" was too serious as well as too long, so that many men left before it was over. Two weeks later Renick tried to find a job for him in the State Department where he could see more of the "inside of the Government," but without success. Then on April 16 his first daughter Margaret was born, in Gainesville, Georgia, where Ellen had gone to be with one of her aunts.

He sent his book on *Congressional Government* to Johns Hopkins as the thesis for his degree of Doctor of Philosophy which he received in June 1886, and he undertook to write a book on comparative government for Heath and Company. This was planned to develop the origin and early history of government, going on to the governments of Greece, Rome and the Middle Ages, with especial emphasis on the American and English constitutions in the modern world.

In August 1887 a second daughter, Jessie Woodrow, was born to Ellen at Gainesville and Wilson was busy working in German tomes for this book, which was to be called *The State*, at the same time that he was preparing a series of lectures he was to give at Johns Hopkins. But he was beginning to find himself "hungry for a class of *men*" and was convinced that his salary at Bryn Mawr was totally inadequate for a family of four; so when he got a chance to go to Wesleyan University at Middletown, Connecticut, in the fall of 1888 at higher pay he accepted the opportunity with alacrity.

These years of teaching were his halcyon days when the gaiety of the Wilsons kept bubbling forth from him. He was an ideal professor, original and interesting in his lectures and companionable with the students. He had a chance to read extensively in government and economics, he worked hard and was able to turn out books and articles which not only won him greater prestige in his profession but also helped to supplement his small salary.

He had shaved off his silky mustache, showing a powerful sensuous mouth in his long face, flanked by big ears. His long legs were brisk and agile, and although his movements were not too rhythmical he was never awkward. He seemed full of fun and was generally a delight to those around him.

If he missed something of the movements going on through those years in the industrial development of the East, he was aware of the growing spirit of protest in the West, voicing itself in the Populist movement; and he was keenly interested in the political scene. He was not satisfied with either of the national political parties, and had dreams of starting a new party with fresh ideas. He thought perhaps this could be done by getting together a group of young men who could contribute articles with a new viewpoint to the leading periodicals, even though he found that the market for essays of this sort was somewhat limited.

Although he was successful and happy, he sometimes felt dissatisfied, a feeling that he once expressed by saying: "A man may be defeated by his secondary successes." He probably felt and

59

hoped that these were years of preparation for the part he hoped one day to play upon a greater stage.

When they moved to Middletown the Wilsons lived in a white frame Colonial house with elms and maples on a broad lawn. It was located across from the campus on High Street, which Charles Dickens had called "the most beautiful avenue in America." There Wilson had two happy years, with a wife and little children who adored him, simple but adequate living arrangements, a scholarly environment and interesting work to do.

He lectured with an earnestness and enthusiasm which communicated itself to the students until they were so interested they forgot to take notes. One of them said later: "I can see him now with his hands forward, the tips of his fingers just touching the table, his face earnest and animated, many times illuminating an otherwise dry and tedious subject by his beautiful language and his apt way of putting things." He wanted to be master of the class and said he wished to make sure they "get exactly what I have to give them."

He went after the moribund old debating society where members attended in order not to be fined for staying away and changed it into the "Wesleyan House of Commons." Here "governments" could be overturned by a vote after debate and men argued on the side in which they really believed; for Wilson said that "To argue any case on any side without the basis of a conviction of any sort, is mental suicide." Meetings became crowded, debates became hot and serious, one group after another would form the government and then be thrown out in its turn.

As a leader in coaching the football team he was equally successful. Although he had never possessed the physical stamina to play the game in college, he squelched the interference of the secret societies so that the best men should be chosen for the squad and developed one of the greatest teams that ever represented Wesleyan, one which administered defeats to Pennsylvania, Amherst, Williams, Rutgers and Trinity. After working out many trick football plays, Wilson told the boys from this college of slightly over two hundred that they should try to win even from the great universities, saying: "Go in to win; don't admit defeat before you start."

An example of his enthusiasm came on Thanksgiving 1889 when a severe storm made the field "a sea of mud." After two easy Lehigh touchdowns it looked like certain defeat for Wesleyan

> . . . when suddenly, from the Wesleyan bleachers a man walked out in front, clad in heavy rubber boots and a raincoat. He shouted to the Wesleyan contingent, reproaching them for not cheering for their team; and at once began to lead them in the Wesleyan yell, beating time for them with his umbrella. This he continued violently until . . . the tide of the game turned.

The cheer leader was professor Wilson and it was said that the spirits of his boys were so aroused that they came back and tied the score.

Wilson became so popular that the students marched to serenade him and he responded with witty speeches. "He made everything he touched interesting." The college annual, *Olla Podrida,* summed up the student view of him:

> Prof. W-i-n.
> A merrier man
> Within the limit of becoming mirth
> I never spent an hour's talk withal.

It is noteworthy that all of his personal relations seem to have been happy at Middletown; if he made enemies he forgot them. A new baby, Eleanor Randolph, was born to the Wilsons in October 1889. Stockton Axson, Ellen's brother, came to live with them and attend the university, while Mary Hoyt and other young relatives made occasional visits. The Congregational minister became one of his best friends; and when Wilson received proposals that tempted him to leave, the officers and faculty of the university made every effort within their power to induce him to remain.

But as early as January 1887 he had written Robert Bridges, "What I am waiting for is a chance to give all my time to political science." In July 1889 when Dr. Patton, the new president of Princeton, interviewed him and suggested a chair of "Public Law," Wilson was interested both because he loved Princeton and because he felt that Wesleyan was "not a sufficiently *stimulating place.*" After some further correspondence he accepted the appointment, and began his new duties in September 1890.

CHAPTER VI

PRINCETON'S PROGRESS UNDER WILSON

They were happy days for Wilson, those days at Wesleyan followed by the early years at Princeton. He had a most loving wife and children who adored him. His father, his brother-in-law and other relatives often stayed with them, keeping the household always cheerful and full of activity. When he walked the floor at night with a crying infant, he told his class about it the next morning and asked them to bear with him. He loved to joke and be friends with people. He was successful in his teaching and writing, as well as in winning a distinguished place among his associates. Four times the Princeton students voted him the most popular of their professors.

When he went there in the autumn of 1890 he was able to concentrate his teaching on the subjects in which he was most interested; public law, government and the science of politics. He had more time for writing and the urge within him led him to keep right on working on his books and essays in the afternoons as well as all through the summer vacations. He soon became known as a brilliant college lecturer, generally starting the hour by giving the students a few sentences to write down and then developing, explaining and embroidering his theme. Tradition has it that Booth Tarkington on first coming out of Wilson's class cried out: "Say, there's a man!" Wilson worked hard on his lectures, had a happy way with him, and spoke well-rounded sentences in a well-trained voice.

Stockton Axson, who had become a teacher of English literature at Princeton, tells of the cheerful home life of Wilson and his family, which he called a life ruled by love so firmly rooted that its foundations were never even slightly shaken. Wilson aroused his wife's interest in Burke and Bagehot, while she taught him to care for Wordsworth, Browning and water-color painting. If there was a disagreement upon any policy or any undertaking it was settled amicably because of their respect for one another's opinions. But if Ellen said, "Woodrow you know you don't think that!" he would often grin and say, "Madam, I was venturing to believe that I thought that until I was corrected."

Ellen was able to devote herself without stint to the task of bringing happiness to her husband and children. She filled his need for affection and love so that he wrote her that his feelings were best expressed in Wordsworth's poems: "She was a phantom of delight," except for the blondness of her hair. She read all that he wrote and provided wise criticism to help him improve it, she was careful and saving so that he should have few worries over money and she brought friends around to keep up his gaiety and good spirits. His writings and his lectures earned money enough for them to have an attractive half-timbered house near the campus with a study where he used to sit writing hour after hour. In their free evenings she would read Scott, Dickens or Wordsworth aloud to the family, or he would read while she occupied herself with painting.

At Princeton he lectured to classes of one hundred even at the very start and they kept on increasing in numbers until they filled halls seating four hundred as his career progressed. He felt that he was training future leaders for the nation not only in the classrooms but in other activities as well. There was a story that he helped work out plays for the football team, and watched daily practice for ten weeks in autumn. He was said to have set up a "House of Commons" modeled on the British form of government just as he had done at Wesleyan, and he fought successfully for the installation of the honor system among the students. President Patton opposed this innovation, but Wilson succeeded in convincing the faculty that he understood the idealism of young Americans far better than the president who had been brought up in England. Consequently it was the new professor's persuasiveness and enthusiasm that swept the faculty along into introducing this change, which made the students feel their responsibility not to cheat in examinations.

Professor Bliss Perry described Wilson as a "long-jawed, homely, fascinatingly alert man" in whom there was little that was youthful "except high spirits, energy and self-confidence." Some of his colleagues thought he was sometimes too contemptuous of slowness and dullness in older men, although at first it was said "he betrayed no arrogance of opinion." Self-confidence was one of his most attractive virtues says Bliss Perry, even if it was sometimes excessive; and Wilson himself enjoyed quoting the saying that "While a Yankee always thinks he is right a Scotch-Irishman knows that he is right." At times he was undoubtedly autocratic. At Wesleyan he could scarcely forgive undergraduates who overthrew a "ministry" in the "House of Commons" which stood upon a platform he approved, and some students at Princeton regarded it as impolitic to differ with Wilson's more fundamental opinions.

George Armour, a book collector who lived near the Wilsons, used to tell how one of their children asked his daughter, "What is a dilettante?" and she replied, "I don't know, do you?" The little Wilson said, "No, but that is what my father says your father is." Wilson was very much the opposite of a dilettante, keeping definite hours of work in his study, and his power of concentration was shown when he would sit with hand poised over his typewriter while waiting for the proper word to come. When he talked at teatime the subject was usually books or general principles of living and Bliss Perry says it was often more delightful just to listen to Wilson than to argue about his views.

Wilson's "Calendar of Great Americans" published in 1894 showed something of what those views were so far as his own country was concerned. He rejected from his list all Englishmen bred in America like Hamilton and Madison, those who were provincial like John Adams and Calhoun, and those whose thought was universal like Emerson and Asa Gray. He turned instead to those who "created or exemplified a distinctly American type of greatness." This left him such men as Franklin, Jackson, Clay and Lee, with Lincoln as the most perfect type of all. "The whole country is summed up in him: the rude Western strength . . . the Eastern conservatism. . . . He even understood the South." The influences of these different sections of the country were blended in Wilson himself, with his Middle-Western ancestry, his boyhood in the South, his schooling and later life spent in the East.

His first important address on educational problems came at the Chicago World's Fair in July 1893, when he asserted that a full four-year college course of liberal studies ought to be a prerequisite to professional studies in medicine, theology or law, saying: "Let leading universities and colleges that have or can get money enough to make them free to act without too much regard to outside criticism, first erect professional schools upon a new model of scholarship, and then close the doors of those schools to all who have not a first-rate college training." He repeated this thesis the next year in a speech to the American Bar Association, again demanding that students be required to have a general liberal education before being admitted to the specialized study of the law.

These were happy and successful years, but as they progressed a new restlessness began to stir in Wilson, a new desire for more activity, for a more strenuous part in the political life of the nation. Most afternoons during this period he spent an hour or so in pleasant talk in the library or garden with his father and Stockton Axson. But in the spring of 1896 Wilson barely escaped having a nervous breakdown and Ellen sent him off alone to England for the summer, since she could not leave the children. When he came back he began to seem impatient with his lot and to desire a larger part upon a greater stage. He no longer had much time for the long afternoon conversations in the library, and Dr. Wilson would say: "Something has come over Woodrow; he is restless. He can't sit down happily and talk as he used to."

Wilson evidently never put this feeling into words, but Robert

Bridges believed that political ambition was always in the back of Wilson's mind. His father sensed it and in his old age half jokingly told an old family retainer in Wilmington to cast his vote, the father's vote, some day for Woodrow Wilson as President of the United States.

About a month after his return from England Wilson had an opportunity to express his views on educational problems in a way that gave him great prestige in the academic world. When Princeton was making plans to celebrate the completion of its first 150 years of existence, he was chosen as the principal orator of the occasion and he took for his theme "Princeton in the Nation's Service." After pointing out that the school was founded in quiet Colonial times to give young men training for the pulpit and for citizenship, he went on to tell how it became "in some visible sort the academic center of the revolution," with so many of its graduates among the leaders of the movement. Then when more peaceful times returned again graduates reverted to "the elder type . . . of sound learning and stout character, without bold impulse added or any uneasy hope to change the world."

He proceeded with the idea of national service and active participation in world affairs which seemed to be always in his mind, pointing out that, "A God of truth is no mean prompter to the enlightened service of mankind." He then remarked upon the danger that America, in boasting of her newness and her achievements, would disregard the past; a danger which he felt was increased by the discoveries of scientists, who while carrying on their experiments, had been able to do their work with no knowledge of history or literature. He declared, "You do not know the world until you know the men who have possessed it and tried its ways before ever you were given your brief run upon it." He went on to say, "It is not learning but the spirit of service that will give a college place in the public annals of the nation. It is indispensable, it seems to me, if it is to do its right service, that the air of affairs should be admitted to all its classrooms."

He felt that colleges owed a responsibility to the nation to train a few scholars but many more students who would become good citizens and "the world's servants." It did not matter so much what these men learned as that they should possess a "vision of the true God" and be readily moved to action by things of the spirit. Science was valuable but it could not do this, it could not make them less greedy for wealth and power, it could not incline them to righteousness. For this they must go to a study of the past, they must go to history, philosophy and literature. These ideas might not have been entirely new, but he expressed them clearly and vividly. He ended his speech by describing the sort of university he would like to see established in the modern world and asking: "Who shall show us the way to this place?"

This speech was received with such enthusiasm that it put Wilson in line as the logical choice for next president of the University. In fact one of the aspirants for that office is reported to have said that day that he saw his hopes were gone; no one but Wilson would have a chance.

Wilson's attitude toward social and political problems did not undergo any great change during the decade of the 1890's. His economic life had been safe and secure; even during the bad times which led up to the panic of 1893 his fortunes had constantly improved and although not wealthy he had no fear of poverty nor worry about the future. He never came into close contact with the workers in the factories or on the farms during those quiet years as a professor and he continued to be a follower of the British Manchester school which advocated free trade and laissez-faire. At the same time he realized that the country was facing new economic problems and regretted "the fact that the 'East' has made no effort to understand the desire for the free coinage of silver in the 'West' and the South."

He did not approve of the growth of great monopolies and trusts since he feared that they gave "to a few men a control over the economic life of the country which they might abuse to the undoing of millions of men." He did not want to "leave the economic liberty of the individual or the freedom and self-respect of the workingman unprotected." But while putting some curbs on vast aggregations of capital he thought it important not to impede the growth of the nation if only at the same time the "equalitarian tradition of American democracy" could be preserved.

By the end of the century many thoughtful men were beginning to be concerned about just what stand the American government ought to take on the new problems of imperialism which were an aftermath of the war with Spain as well as on questions pertaining to the money power in politics at home. Consequently it was natural that a man of Wilson's ambition and desire to serve his country should have felt even by 1900 an urge to find his duties in a larger sphere than teaching and writing could afford. Already he had been offered the presidencies of six large universities but had refused them all to continue his career at Princeton.

He made no public remarks about the Spanish-American War, but believed that the most important result was "the greatly increased power and opportunity for constructive statesmanship given the President by the plunge into international politics and into the administration of distant dependencies." He also argued that an "impulse of expansion is the natural and wholesome impulse which comes with a consciousness of matured strength." Possibly his attitude toward the Filipinos and imperialism was a sort of sophisticated and semi-religious expression of the idea of the "whiteman's burden" as Profesor Link has suggested. At any rate he did not appear to be opposed to the new American imperialism which was spreading into the Caribbean and the Pacific.

At the Princeton commencement in June 1902 President Patton, probably knowing that the younger members of the faculty, headed by Wilson and others, were pushing scholastic reforms with which he was not in sympathy, suddenly handed his resignation to the Board of Trustees. In doing so he recommended Wilson as his successor, a suggestion which was immediately adopted, one of the trustees commenting that it was the only time he had ever known that group to be unanimous about anything. This quick election probably avoided a lot of ill feeling which might have grown up if different candidates had been allowed time enough to build up their own determined groups of supporters.

As soon as the selection had been made and the meeting of trustees adjourned, Wilson's three classmates on the board hurried off to tell him the good news, so that he was able to go with shining eyes from his home to a reception at his friends the Hibbens' and there report the great event to his most intimate friends. That evening the alumni and students took the new president to the steps of old Nassau Hall, gave him many a cheer and called on him to speak. The official announcement was made at a luncheon the next day, where he replied to the applause by saying: "How can a man who loves this place as I love it realize of a sudden that he now has the liberty to devote every power that is in him to its service?"

Since Wilson was one of the leaders of the liberal and reforming group, the faculty and trustees of Princeton probably foresaw that the new president would want to introduce far-reaching changes in the life of the university. His inaugural address repeated much that was said in his speech of 1896 with its emphasis upon the need to train men to serve their country "with the spirit of . . . the religion of Christ, and with the energy of a positive faith." However he went on to be more specific about certain university problems, stating his opposition to an "elective system" such as had been adopted at Harvard and giving voice to the hope that funds might be obtained for building a "college of residence" for graduate students "as nearly as may be at the heart, the geographical heart, of the university." He pointed out that "growth that is a manifestation of life . . . builds upon old tissue," a sentiment which, like the whole speech, could be interpreted as favoring progressive or conservative views as the hearer chose. The curious result was that Walter Hines Page, whose friendship dated back to those days in Atlanta when Wilson appeared before the tariff commission, began to feel that here would be an excellent leader for the liberals of the nation, while at the same time George Harvey, editor of the *North American Review,* thought the big business wing of the Democratic Party might be able to use such a man.

Meanwhile Wilson's work lay at Princeton, where plenty of problems awaited him. In fact he was faced with a great change in his career. For he was now a recognized leader, the chosen head of the university. When he had finished boyhood and entered the world of teaching and of books, the leadership which he had won with such difficulty from the Lightfoot gang of boys came much more easily to him, for he was now in a sphere where the activities were intellectual rather than physical. Popularity had come also, a far greater and more genuine popularity than he had ever won as a boy. But the leadership which he had gained as a professor had been merely one of pre-eminence in his profession rather than one in which he was the active leader of an organization. It had been possible to live a shy, retired and secluded life and yet fulfill that career to the uttermost. Now he was called to something quite different, to a life of conflict, a career of combat. This daily struggle was to follow him to the end of his days.

How well was he prepared to meet the new problems which lay before him? A great asset was his courage, a courage which, although it shrank from physical contact and rowdy methods, never wavered nor failed to drive him forward. Along with this came an inner gaiety, a restrained yet irrepressible liveliness, which he showed mostly to his family and intimate friends but which was nevertheless an essential part of him. Also he had wisdom and a quietness of spirit which failed him only when his egotism or temper got the better of him. He had a good mind and unusual abilities, as well as a firm and resolute character. But his greatest quality was faith, an unfaltering belief in the goodness of God and the inherent dignity of man. Because of this faith he was prepared to throw all his mental, moral, and physical power into the service of his God and of his fellow men; but he wanted all things to be done his way and himself to be the leader.

Gradually, as time went on, the new president discovered how to accomplish the purposes which he believed to be so just, and found ways in which to overcome opposition. He used persuasion when persuasion would get results, but he did not hesitate to have recourse to subtle contrivance, and perhaps even artifice and stratagem if necessary. He could also resort to mere force. He hated to compromise, especially on a matter of principle but he learned to do even that at times, although his occasional refusal to do this at critical moments later resulted in his failure to carry some of his greatest projects through to a successful conclusion.

In becoming president of Princeton he brought a new spirit into the university world of America, a spirit which caused Professor Slosson to write in 1910 in his book on *Great American Universities* "Princeton is the most interesting of American Universities to study just now. . . . [It] is going forward by leaps and bounds." This spirit had been voiced in Wilson's address of 1896 which had shown his preoccupation with liberal education; with education which would give the students joy and satisfaction and broader interests for the rest of their lives rather than merely preparing them to make more money as doctors or lawyers or teachers. And along with this change of direction, he explained, must come higher standards of scholarship and behavior, getting rid of those who drank too much or cheated in examinations and even those who did not want to bother to study. The new president said, "I'll not be president of a country club"; and he intended to lift the scholastic standards of Princeton until they equalled any in the land. His achievement of this goal was recognized by President Lowell of Harvard, who wrote: "He certainly did raise Princeton very much in grade among the institutions of higher learning in the country. He was also, so far as I am aware, the first head of a college who strove to raise the respect for scholarship among the undergraduate body."

Wilson's reputation was enhanced a few days after his inauguration when his five-volume *History of the American People* was published. The book received favorable notices from the critics and has remained ever since one of the most readable general works on American history. At the same time the trustees, on motion of ex-President Cleveland, gave him more power by authorizing him to "create such vacancies in the teaching force as he may deem for the best interests of the university." He immediately used this power to eliminate some of the less active members of the faculty, indicating sympathy with those who were removed but paying no heed to protests from them or their friends.

He turned next to student discipline. When some boys were suspended for intemperance at a beer party and Stockton Axson asked what had happened, Wilson replied: "It has happened that there is going to be some discipline in this college." When a mother came to plead, "I am to have an operation and I think I shall die if my boy is expelled," his answer was, "We cannot keep in college a boy reported by the student council as cheating; if we did we should have no standard of honor." But he came from the conversation so shaken that he could eat no lunch; and ten years later after a difficult conversation with Orlando of Italy in which he rejected some seemingly reasonable Italian demands, he still referred to this necessary refusal of a parent's entreaties as the most painful interview of his life.

Besides enforcing orderliness and decent behavior, Wilson undertook to raise the standard of scholarship, making the examinations more difficult, and demanding that those who failed should be forced to leave the university. The trustees gave him their support in this even though it led to an immediate decrease in the number of students. Wilson promised that the loss would be quickly recovered and this proved to be substantially true.

When the faculty had been weeded out and the students made to realize that they must come to learn and not to play, the next problem was that of planning a course of study. An elective system like Harvard's had led to "a multiplication of courses which have in large part remained unco-ordinated" said Wilson. This result was almost unavoidable when a free choice was made by freshmen. Soon the president, as chairman of a Committee on Course of Study, worked it out so that courses in the first two years were almost entirely prescribed and in the last two they must be chosen not "from a miscellany of studies, but . . . from a scheme of related subjects." Even Harvard soon followed this example and it was not long before similar assistance in the selection of subjects was offered to the students at Cambridge, with rules to prevent the spread of their interests over too wide a range of topics. These regulations for the grouping of courses have become a model for more and more colleges ever since, especially because this was one of Wilson's innovations which did not involve extra expense.

Development of a strong graduate school was another matter of concern to the new president. Few graduate students had come to Princeton and there was no building to house them, but in 1900 an enterprising and generous trustee was made chairman of the committee on the graduate school, while Andrew F. West was elected dean. Because under President Patton "nothing ever happened," West was given extensive powers. This action seemed sensible at the time but was later to be the source of a bitter battle between West and Wilson.

During the summer of 1903 Wilson and his wife went to England. They also visited the Continent, especially France and Italy, for the only time before his famous journey of 1919. His health still bothered him: "The Garfields have the art of getting up a dinner of delightful dishes not one of which I ought to eat," said he. He went to Muskoka Lake in the Canadian woods in 1904 and came "near being a progressive Republican," as Theodore Roosevelt ran against Parker that fall. A minor operation in February 1905 required five weeks of convalescence in Florida, but even in cases such as this he was always busy working out his plans for improving the university and developing new ideas to be taken up in due course.

Almost as soon as he had been elected, at a great dinner of alumni at the Waldorf Astoria in December 1902 Wilson had set forth his plan for a tutorial system "resembling Oxford, but better than Oxford." The local name for this became the preceptorial system; fifty young men were to be added to the faculty as tutors, or preceptors. These men were expected to keep in close touch with the students, living in dormitories with them and helping them with their work and problems at all hours. They were to stay at this sort of job not longer than five years so that they would not become restless or stale and he announced to the assembled guests: "All of that, gentlemen, costs money. Now I am coming to business. To start that particular thing fairly and properly would cost two millions and a quarter. [Whistles from the audience.] I hope you will get your whistling over, because you will have to get used to this, and you may thank your stars I did not say four millions and a quarter, because we are going to get it. [Applause.] I suspect there are gentlemen in this room who are going to give me two millions and a quarter to get rid of me. They will be able to get rid of me in no other way that I know of."

The alumni admired his courage and some of them agreed to make annual gifts large enough to give the scheme a fair trial even though the principal amount was not raised. Andrew Carnegie was approached by letter but he did not contribute to the preceptorial system. Later, when Wilson again applied to the generous steel magnate, he received the reply, "I have already given Princeton a lake," to which Wilson retorted not too graciously, "We needed bread and you gave us cake."

But Wilson's new plans and his enthusiasm carried many of the trustees and alumni along with him. When he invited his fifty bright young scholars to be tutors at Princeton forty-seven of them accepted. This did much to give Princeton the combined advantages of a small college with its close relationship between student and faculty and of a large university with its more famous teachers and professors.

Wilson believed that the preceptors "could transform this place from a place where youngsters are doing tasks to a place where there are men doing thinking, men who are conversing about the things of thought, men who are eager and interested in the things of thought." He wanted courses to consist of reading outside the classroom, with lectures to illuminate and supplement the reading. The plan soon began to work so well that men were reported beginning to talk about their studies at the clubs and the seniors sang: "Here's to those preceptor guys, fifty stiffs to make us wise."

When it came to getting the men he wanted for higher faculty positions Wilson's enthusiasm and zeal were a great help in persuading those whom he selected to accept his offer. When he asked Professor Frank Thilly to come, that distinguished psychologist said: "Woodrow Wilson's epistle was so gracious, so wholehearted, so human, that I accepted his invitation to visit him at Princeton without further consideration." Another professor reports that a colleague asked him, "What brought you to Princeton?" and they both agreed that it was Wilson, because both "were inspired by his ideals of a university, of education, of life."

Turning from teachers to buildings Wilson decided that all new buildings should be in the Tudor Gothic style of Oxford and Cambridge, believing that "by the suggestions of that architecture we shall find the past of this country married with the past of the world." He insisted upon this plan being carried out; when it meant an argument with some prospective donor who wished to give a building to be built in some other style the chance of losing the gift did not divert Wilson from his purpose.

Next the board of trustees came in for his attention because he believed that some of the members were worse than useless when there was work to be done and might well be a deterrent to those thinking of making gifts to Princeton. Wilson went right after the problem and personally presented the undesirable trustees with a request for their resignation. He then got the approval of the board to appoint a financial secretary for the university to take routine matters of business off his hands.

It is perhaps unfortunate that Wilson had only daughters instead of some sons who could have contested his supremacy and disputed his authority at home. Possibly the problem of dealing with sons would have made him less unyielding, so that in the long run he would have come to understand better the importance of considering other people's feelings and opinions.

Yet his home life in the presidential mansion called "Prospect," remained cheerful, carefree and happy. His daughter Eleanor told later how they had games of billiards and whist, celebrations at Christmas and New Year's, reading aloud in the evening, and how her father took part in charades, once dressing up as a pompous old lady in a velvet curtain, a feather boa and one of his wife's hats. He always liked to dance and sing, crack jokes and recite limericks. A favorite verse was: "My face, I don't mind it, I'm always behind it, It's people in front that I jar." He could impersonate an enthusiastic orator on the Fourth of July gesticulating not with his arms but with his legs. One of his wife's relatives who had lived in their house wrote that: "He loved gay nonsense. He could play the fool enchantingly."

He overflowed with excellent conversation both at tea and at dinner parties. The wife of a colleague, Professor H. D. Thompson, reports him as the most delightful of dinner companions. Most of the faculty in those days knew the townspeople and storekeepers, and Wilson had a friendly manner, but it did not indicate any real personal interest on his part. He was probably an intelligent introvert, who was clever enough to build up a façade of geniality; and if he became somewhat more inaccessible during those years when he was head of the university he endeavored to conceal it. But he gave up his games of billiards at the Faculty Club because he said he was so frequently approached by some player or spectator with a favor to ask or a problem to discuss that he found the game and the friendly spirit constantly interrupted by business.

He might well have been content to lose some of his privacy, for all his reforms of these first four years had gone through with no serious opposition and even met with unqualified approval from almost everyone. But in the spring of 1906 he suffered with arteriosclerosis from overwork and nervous strain, so he spent the summer with his family in the Lake District of England. There he rested and at the same time began to consider how to accomplish other educational reforms.

His days of easy leadership at Princeton were over. Already he had inaugurated great changes; including higher standards for students and faculty, a well-integrated course of study and the preceptorial system. He had largely succeeded in his announced purpose of transforming Princeton "from a place where youngsters are doing tasks to a place where there are men doing thinking." But the projects which he was now about to undertake met with far more concerted and serious resistance.

CHAPTER VII

CONFLICT AND DEFEAT
AT PRINCETON

His almost complete success in putting through his plans to improve the university and the ease with which the task had been accomplished to this point caused Wilson to underestimate the opposition his new principles would arouse. He thought that men needed only to have what seemed to him to be principles of justice and reason placed before them to make them embrace those principles with an ardor something like his own. He did not realize that many of them would disagree with him both as to what was best for the university and what was possible.

His next idea was to abolish the upper-class eating clubs, whose buildings, large and small, lined Prospect Avenue. These had sprung up gradually after Greek-letter fraternities had been abolished under Dr. McCosh. They took in two thirds to three quarters of the sophomore class, to replace those who were graduating. Those who were left out had their feelings badly lacerated, some of them even left college, and with some of the students the clubs had come to consume an unduly large proportion of their time and interest. Making a club was apt to mean more to many of them than achievements in Latin or mathematics, this occasioning Wilson's remark that "The side shows are swallowing up the circus."

He presented his proposals on this subject to the Board of Trustees on December 13, 1906, without first consulting the faculty. His notes for his report to the meeting indicate his thought:

> The Upper Class Clubs—decrease of democratic, increase of
> social feeling—Increase of luxury—the buildings, etc.
> *Remedy*—We must *reintegrate*—and create a *college* comrade-
> ship based on *letters*. We have tutor and pupil. Now we must have
> pupil and pupil in a comradeship of studies.

He proposed creating colleges out of the clubs and out of new
quadrangles to be built, with a few of the faculty taking their meals
with the undergraduates and each college forming a largely self-
governing unit. This would give many of the advantages of a "small
college with its closer association," and yet allow the young men
to study under the many distinguished professors available only to
a large institution; it would also help the new preceptors to come
into even closer touch with the students.

Wilson talked well; but he was coming into conflict with the
emotions and traditions connected with the clubs and his plans
would require a great deal of money. Within a week Grover
Cleveland was asking some of the other trustees to help make
certain that interest in building a new graduate school should not
be indefinitely postponed; although Wilson felt that a recent bequest of $250,000 was sufficient to construct an excellent building
for the school and that both projects could be carried on together.
Dean West demanded a graduate college located in the countryside
and placed under his personal control. Cleveland gave his support
to Dean West's plan, probably without realizing how impossible
was such a divided authority as the dean proposed. These two
influential men formed the core of a powerful opposition, which
soon became more widespread and more violent.

After presenting his plan of creating small colleges to the trustees,
Wilson left in January 1907, on the orders of his doctor, for a rest
in Bermuda; but he busied himself just the same with outlining a
series of lectures to be delivered at Columbia University. These
were published in 1908 under the title *Constitutional Government*
and showed a greater realization of the powers of the President of
the United States than he had indicated in his earlier volumes. He

now recognized that the chief executive was far more than a mere administrative officer.

On June 10, 1907, Wilson presented the report of the Committee on Social Reorganization which he had typed in person. The plan had the general approval of the other members of the committee and Wilson carried with him the tremendous prestige of his almost uninterrupted successes. He wanted to ask in the report to be allowed to execute this general plan but his friends persuaded him to request only authority to "mature" it. Even over this more modest request there was a lot of discussion in the trustees' meeting and there were various stories about what took place on that occasion.

The report covered every phase of the question of what to do about the club system and demanded a new "social co-ordination" of the university. After accusing the club system of separating the social interests of the students from their intellectual life, Wilson went on to say that "About one-third are left out in the elections; and their lot is little less than deplorable." He spoke again of the spirit of exclusiveness and luxury in the clubhouses and maintained that the only adequate way to deal with the problem was to do away entirely with the eating clubs and form residential quadrangles or colleges for the undergraduates, each with its own halls for dining and relaxation and its own resident preceptors. He wanted the university to "organize her life in such a way that these contacts between the university and the student shall be the stuff of daily habit." The trustees adopted the report and authorized Wilson to do whatever should "seem wisest for maturing this general plan and for seeking the co-operation and counsel of the upper-class clubs in its elaboration."

The clubs themselves were filled just then with students and alumni back for commencement and class reunions and Wilson immediately set out to explain his project to them as fully as possible. The committee report itself came out in the *Alumni Weekly* on June 12 and although the opposition was not very vocal at first it soon gathered force. The faculty gave Wilson its support by a majority created only by the young preceptors; but his opponents among the trustees and alumni tried to justify the club system even by such remarks as "No one can make a gentleman associate with a mucker," and were indignant at the attempt to destroy it.

The new scheme was opposed by many of the faculty, and even his old friend Profesor Hibben discussed "the dangers which attend this plan as regards the vital interests of Princeton." Doubtless Hibben regarded any such violent contention as was aroused by the suggestion as being so undesirable in itself that the issue involved was not worth it; but Wilson always felt that he must fight for what he thought was right, no matter what the consequences. Wilson never forgave Hibben for this stand of his; although at the same time he remained friendly with Henry Van Dyke who opposed the plan as being undesirable in itself, and he later made Van Dyke minister to Holland. He evidently was willing to brook a disagreement in principle but not advice by one of his friends to give up a project because the opposition to it promised to be intense.

The October trustees' meeting was held almost at the crest of the 1907 panic, so that financial considerations were added to other grounds of opposition to the quadrangle plan. The result was that when the meeting opened Moses Taylor Pyne immediately presented resolutions that the action of the June meeting be reconsidered and that the board did not now deem it wise to adopt the recommendations made by the committee. The president was asked to withdraw the plan, with all the trustees except one voting in favor of the resolutions.

This was such a shock to Wilson that he decided to carry his appeal to the alumni, as a prime minister might carry one to the country at large. But it was impossible to arouse much enthusiasm in those dark days of financial disaster for a scheme that would cost an additional $2,000,000. Another blow came when a committee of Wilson's own supporters investigated the club system and reported that membership in the clubs did not seem to lower scholastic standards "nor discourage study in itself."

This put a final end to the argument; but it left Wilson with a feeling of resentment and frustration. He had refused to compromise by agreeing to a reform of the club system or to regard with toleration those who were opposed to him, following some inner urge which frequently seemed to push him forward in an unyielding temper when he felt himself to be battling in a righteous cause.

The students recognized the strong man and the fighter, even when they did not sympathize with his plans. At commencement they sang:

> Here's to Wilson, King Divine,
> Who rules this place along with Fine.
> We hear he's soon to leave this town
> To take on Teddy Roosevelt's crown.

Twenty years later Harkness gave funds to Harvard and Yale which enabled those universities to build quadrangles such as Wilson had fought for, with living quarters, dining halls and recreation rooms, so that the clubs and fraternities at those institutions now maintain little more than a nominal existence. This was what Wilson was working for, but it was obviously impossible to put it through without money and without the co-operation and help of the Board of Trustees.

After this dispute had threatened to tear to pieces the loyal feelings of Princeton men, attention was directed to a new struggle, dealing not with the clubs but with the location and administration of the graduate school. In this contest Wilson's antagonist Dean West was still contending for a school located in the countryside away from the main campus, with himself in charge and making direct reports through the Graduate School Committee to the Board of Trustees. In this position West was supported by the immense prestige of ex-President Grover Cleveland whom he had persuaded to settle in Princeton.

On the surface the dispute was concerned with the location of the graduate school. But this was merely a question of where to place the dormitories and dining rooms, so that there seems no sense to its having given rise so such a bitter wrangle. It is entirely reasonable to believe that the real foundation of the argument lay in the problem whether or not Dean West and the general administration of the graduate school should be subject to the authority of the president of the university.

After West had been made dean of the graduate school in 1901 the trustees sent him to Europe to investigate similar schools there and report to the president and trustees. He came home full of enthusiasm and prepared a report which Wilson read. This was published with beautiful pictures, probably in a far more elaborate form than Wilson had anticipated. Wilson wrote a preface in which he said: "The plans for such a graduate college as Professor West has conceived seem to me in every way admirable." He continued: "In conceiving this little community of scholars set at the heart of Princeton . . ." This phrase showed that he felt the graduate schools would not be very different from any other department of the university. But Dean West wanted a school whose members should eat and live apart, in an atmosphere so elaborate that many of the less wealthy students might actually have been repelled by it. These conflicting ideas might well have been merged into some sort of compromise, but instead the quarrel tore apart both the faculty and the Board of Trustees.

Wilson kept on asking people to give money to the college. Dean West sent forth his beautifully illustrated pamphlet requesting help for the graduate school. Moses Taylor Pyne, who had been the most generous of the trustees and a supporter of West's ideas, gave a big house to the graduate school, and at the same time there came a bequest of $350,000 which could be used to construct dormitories and a dining hall. Wilson had frequently insisted that the school should be located near the center of the university. He had referred to this in his inaugural address; he definitely did not want a separate and almost competitive school to be created, and he had behind him a majority in the Board of Trustees, including Cleveland H. Dodge, David B. Jones and Cyrus McCormick.

In October 1906 West was offered the presidency of Massachusetts Institute of Technology. Wilson was one of a committee which requested him to remain at Princeton, stating that they would consider his loss "quite irreparable," and promised full support for his graduate school plans. Perhaps Wilson was influenced by the fact that West's supporters included Pyne and Cleveland, making a trio of strong, experienced fighters. Wilson, lacking executive experience, probably felt that it would be better not to antagonize these men by letting West depart. But West and his friends believed that by keeping him at Princeton Wilson had given full approval to his plans which he was now eager to go ahead and put into execution; and they had all been indignant at Wilson's attempt to shove the quadrangle issue ahead of the Graduate School.

In early 1908, soon after Wilson's return from a trip to Bermuda and after the quadrangle plan had finally been rejected, the graduate school question came up again. In April trustees supported Wilson's position that the graduate school should be built on the grounds of the president's house and not somewhere off the campus as West, Pyne and Cleveland desired. Early the next year Wilson persuaded the trustees to pass a reorganization plan which deprived West of most of his authority over the school's appointments and curriculum.

In the midst of all these contests the idea that he might go into politics was growing in Wilson's mind, as was realized by those who were close to him; but of course the fight at Princeton left him little time to give such questions his serious attention. These university struggles and the bitterness they engendered were a worry to him; and whatever disturbed her husband was also a matter of concern to his devoted wife. These were the times that she sent him to Bermuda where he met Mary Hulbert Peck and discussed with her the idea of running for governor of New Jersey.

In May 1909, the university received an offer of half a million dollars to be used for the graduate school, if the alumni would match the amount. Attached was a proviso that the buildings should be located where Mr. Proctor, the donor, who was advised by Dean West, might stipulate. The alumni promptly made promises to match the gift and there was $300,000 still available from the bequest of 1906. Dean West had now definitely decided that he wanted the school located out in the country and not "set at the heart of Princeton." This would form a new unit which would involve larger expenditures on maintenance and it would also mean deserting the ideas of a president who had been winning fame for Princeton as an institution of learning.

But what if the trustees refused it? Who ever heard of a university tossing aside a gift of a million dollars? It was a dreadful dilemma for the trustees but they made up their minds to reject it and retain their president. This surprising action shocked and enraged the wealthy alumni who had matched Proctor's gift, and they were made even more angry at the next commencement when an anonymous pamphlet was distributed which assailed the social order at Princeton. This tended to reopen the quadrangle question, but the trustees had no funds available for new quadrangles even if they had desired to build them.

In any case the sporting alumni, who had extra money in their pockets and came back almost annually for football games and commencement, were thoroughly indignant at the rejection of so large a gift and even more incensed at Wilson's reason for it, his protest against the idea that mere wealth should prescribe any part of the conduct of the university. These gentlemen expressed the feeling that the idealists were ready enough to accept money to help them carry out their own plans. So bitterness and ill will were boiling in Princeton that commencement time.

The trustees at first tried to accept the donation without the conditions which were attached to it, but Mr. Proctor declined to take off the strings. Naturally the rejection of such a gift was spread across the headlines of newpapers all over the country. Wilson spoke eloquently in the dispute, insisting that money was attempting to dictate the educational policies of American universities. Theodore Roosevelt was lambasting the power of riches in economic life. This gave Wilson a great audience. The supporters of Dean West had no powerful voice since Grover Cleveland was dead, and this made them all the more furious.

On Christmas 1909 Wilson wrote to Moses Taylor Pyne, who had

86

Exterior of First Presbyterian Church in Augusta, Ga.

Johns Hopkins University Glee Club in 1884. Wilson was back row second from left

Wilson about 1886, while he still wore handlebar mustache.

Wilson family in front of fireplace at Prospect, about 1903.

Wilson and Mrs. Wilson in the garden at Prospect, about 1910.

Probably first photograph of Wilson with Thomas R. Marshall
as candidates, Aug. 7, 1912; notification ceremonies at Sea
Girt. N. J.

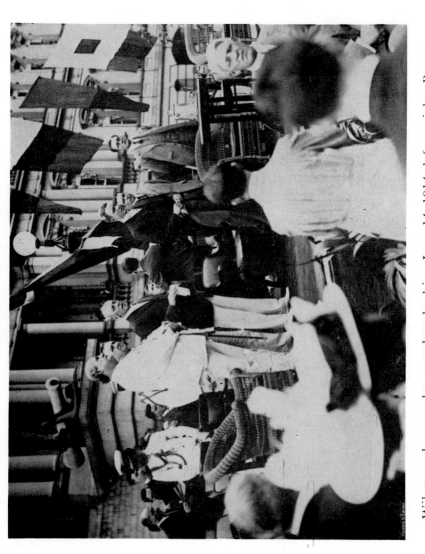

Wilson and some who served under him, June 14, 1914; left to right: Bryan, Daniels, Wilson, Breckenridge Long, William Phillips and Franklin Delano

Wilson's last cabinet-meeting; left to right: Wilson, David F. Houston, Treasury; A. Mitchell Palmer, Attorney-General; Josephus Daniels, Navy; Edwin T. Meredith, Agriculture; William B. Wilson, Labor; Bainbridge Colby, State; Newton D. Baker, War; Albert S. Burleson, Postmaster-General; John Barton Payne, Interior; and Joshua W. Alexander, Commerce.

Wilson and Mrs. Edith Bolling Wilson at door of their home, greeting the crowd calling on Armistice Day, following ceremonies at Arlington.

succeeded Cleveland as chairman of the trustees' Committee on the Graduate School, repeating that he could not "accede to the acceptance of gifts which take the educational policy of the University out of the hands of the trustees and faculty and permit it to be determined by those who gave money," a statement which was broadcast all over the nation.

Perhaps it was not the question of location nor of domination by money that made Wilson fight, perhaps it was the idea of establishing a graduate school under the ideals and administration of Dean West. But the reason he gave certainly made drama, it created an issue which could arouse the American public. And it was an important reason; perhaps after all it was the most important, for the other issues would have made it a mere private quarrel, even though the questions of unity of administration and plain living by the students were also involved in the local problem.

Wilson's opponents accused him of being insincere and interested only in gaining political preferment by posing as a liberal. They pointed to the fact that his whole attitude had been conservative and satisfied with things as they were until he became president of Princeton. Before that he had probably felt that wealth unquestionably ruled wisely and benevolently. Later, his ideas on this had changed, and changed largely because his experiences at Princeton had taught him that many of the possessors of wealth and privilege would not willingly have any of their prerogatives taken away from them; not even in the interests of democracy or scholarship or the community at large. So he had acquired a lasting distrust of the forces which these men represented and a determination not to let them stand in the way of reforms which he felt were necessary to promote a good society.

An important meeting of the Board of Trustees was held on January 13, 1910 in the chapel of Old Nassau, an oak-beamed chamber with marble floors and dark paneling twenty-five feet high, with another fifteen feet to the rooftree. The hall held memories of the battle of Princeton, of Washington, Lafayette and the Continental Congress, of John Adams, Aaron Burr and Madison. It probably appealed to Wilson as the right place to hold his first great battle. For the trustees were divided almost equally between the two factions and Dean West himself was there in the capacity of a committee secretary.

Wilson had intended to propose a resolution declaring that on account of the conflict of opinion over the site the trustees felt compelled to reject Proctor's offer. But Pyne startled the board by producing a letter from Proctor accepting Wilson's proposal that two graduate schools be built. Wilson had made this suggestion to Procter rather casually as he was seeing him off on the train one day, and probably thought no more about it.

The sudden offer almost necessarily brought Wilson around to take his stand upon his other and perhaps more fundamental reason: "If the Graduate School is based on proper ideals our faculty can make a success of it anywhere in Mercer County." Then he drew a copy of Dean West's prospectus from a pile of papers and said, "There, gentlemen, in that book is the real reason why the Proctor gift must be declined. That book contains Professor West's ideals. They are his personal ideals; they are not the ideals of Princeton University and they are radically wrong."

When the trustees asked why he had written a laudatory preface to the volume Wilson replied that he had not seen the book when he wrote the preface. This may have been true; but he did see it later and might then have retracted his preface. Perhaps a truer explanation was that Wilson had not known of the photographs of European schools and architects' drawings of magnificent proposed buildings which decorated the printed volume and which radically changed by their very presence its entire character. Also he had stated in that preface his very definite conviction that it must be a graduate school "located in the very heart of Princeton."

They then asked him why he had made the suggestion to Proctor of two graduate colleges. Wilson said he had made a mistake, that his "friends in the faculty" had "convinced me that the plan was impracticable and unwise." They inquired why had he written Pyne on December 25 that his proposal of two separate colleges had the

88

"hearty concurrence" of his colleagues at Princeton? To this Wilson gave no satisfactory explanation. It is possible that his colleagues changed their minds in that three-week interval or that it was his own friends who opposed it, for that was what he specifically stated. It is also probable that he had made the suggestion to Proctor without proper consideration and with no idea that it would be accepted. On the whole it seems as though even if the statements he made at this meeting were technically true they had a clear appearance of dissembling. Perhaps he thought this was justified as the result of changing the basis of his argument from the minor issue of location to the more genuine one of the control and fundamental character of the graduate school, but many of the trustees accused him of perfidy. Actually the preface stated clearly and succinctly Wilson's attitude toward the school, and he might better have rested simply upon that statement than to have become involved in all sorts of extraneous arguments.

After this meeting Pyne seems to have thrown himself wholeheartedly into the fight against Wilson. He suggested that Proctor should withdraw his offer and Dean West resign, thinking this would force Wilson out; and he compiled a list of statements by Wilson that seemed contradictory. Some of the trustees began to declare that the issue was now "Pyne vs. Wilson."

Procter withdrew his offer on February 6 and four days later the trustees met and accepted the reports of committees of their own body and of the faculty, both of which strongly upheld Wilson's desire for a graduate school located on the campus and closely allied with undergraduate life and studies.

The attention of the public was first called to Wilson's struggle and the graduate school controversy by an editorial in the *New York Times* on February 3, 1910. This was composed by Henry B. Brougham and was largely based on a letter written by Wilson in answer to a request for editorial guidance. It accused the forces of wealth of encouraging "mutually exclusive social cliques, stolid groups of wealth and fashion, devoted to non-essentials and the smattering of culture." But when Brougham asked for more, Wilson

89

sent a much less belligerent reply and showed no desire to press his charges any further, saying that to explain in detail why the editorial was true would require the disclosure of facts and the assertion of matters distinctly detrimental to individuals. Professor Paul Van Dyke went to see Wilson and referred to the editorial as "unquestionably false." Wilson replied that in its coloring it was highly exaggerated but the foundation of it was in his opinion true.

After the February meeting Wilson took a short trip to Bermuda but was back early in March, feeling rested and ready to renew the argument. His opponents had the idea of electing as a new trustee Adrian H. Joline, a railroad director and a conservative New York business man. Wilson set out to present his side of the graduate school controversy to the alumni and incidentally to try to prevent the election of Joline. He spoke in Maryland, Brooklyn and Jersey City; then on March 26 he addressed the Western Association of of Princeton Clubs in St. Louis. Here he met with great enthusiasm and concluded his speech by proposing that the graduate school problem should be referred to the faculty for decision.

In New York he told an unresponsive audience that the graduate school had been in the hands of a single administrator, the dean, without the genuine interest and energy of the faculty to back it. He said that Proctor's idea was to "treat graduate students as they are not treated elsewhere in the country."

When the trustees met again on April 14, the Pyne group was in control and their refusal to let him submit the graduate school question to a meeting of the faculty exasperated Wilson. Two days later he spoke to the alumni at Pittsburgh. Here he accused the privately endowed colleges of giving in to the desires of wealthy students and alumni: "The great voice of America does not come from seats of learning." He added that he had sought "to bring the colleges that I have anything to do with to an absolutely democratic regeneration in spirit." He went on to ask, "will America tolerate the idea of having graduate students set apart?"

This speech was reported in a number of Eastern newspapers. His position had been stated with forcefulness and vigor, he seems

90

to have been aroused to the point of speaking with such boldness by the action of the trustees two days earlier. When he came back from his trip Adrian H. Joline had been defeated. Wilson's interest in politics was shown by a letter he had written Joline three years before regretting Bryan's leadership of the Democratic Party. He had written Mrs. Peck to the same effect, but the letter to Joline later became public and threatened Wilson's ambitions. Meanwhile he regained his confidence and joy in life since the majority of the alumni were cognizant of the issues and seemed to uphold him, while the trustees who supported him could now feel themselves in a strong position.

Then by a sudden blow the entire scene was changed. On May 18 an old man named Isaac C. Wyman, whose father had fought in the battle of Princeton, died and left most of his fortune to Princeton. Ten days later David Lawrence, then a student reporter for the *New York Times*, knocked at Wilson's study and showed him a telegram saying that the estate was ten millions and Dean West was one of the two executors. When Wilson had read the message a second time he became rigid, then white-faced, and exclaimed: "Lawrence, this means defeat. We can never overcome ten millions."

That was the end of his career at Princeton. When Procter also renewed his offer Wilson felt that he had definitely lost the fight and there was no reason for him to remain. The gift later proved to be much smaller than had been rumored, but he accepted his defeat with good grace, recommending that West should remain as dean of the graduate school, and recognizing that the gift "enables us to secure a great graduate faculty." On October 20, 1910, he tendered his resignation as President.

Wilson's achievements at Princeton had been the result of his intense interest in education and his determination to carry out his ideals. He had greatly improved the quality of both faculty and students, he had worked out courses of study which had sufficient unity to orient the students, and he had introduced the preceptorial system to create close contacts between faculty and students. Many new buildings had been erected, a lake had been constructed and

91

the faculty had been expanded. The endowment had been increased and the alumni were contributing $100,000 a year for current expenses.

These were extraordinary accomplishments for the space of eight short years; and when he found insurmountable opposition to his later projects of supplanting clubs by quadrangles and establishing the sort of graduate school he desired, it was not surprising that he sought a place for his services in other fields. Wilson had devoted himself for many years to the study of politics and government, and he had made a name for himself as a college president who was willing to reject gifts of millions in order to avoid domination by the forces of wealth and privilege. As Bryce observed in the *American Commonwealth*, college presidents have much greater national prestige in America than in England; so it was not surprising that politicians were already calling upon the President of Princeton to enter the arena where he had always hoped to find his destiny.

CHAPTER VIII

THE
DYNAMIC DEVELOPMENT
OF WILSON'S MIND

An understanding of the intellectual interests which occupied Wilson's mind during these years of university activities can best be obtained by a discussion and analysis of his writings. The moment of change from the quiet life of Princeton to the larger world of government would seem to be a logical point to insert such an inquiry and to see how he made a reputation with his pen, just as he had hoped to do as an undergraduate. Not only did his publications win him a considerable audience, but they also added to his somewhat limited income.

Wilson's writing began while he was still a student in college, when he published essays on Bismarck and William Pitt in the *Nassau Literary Magazine* and his article on "Cabinet Government" in the *International Review*. The active part taken by him in debating was another indication of his interest in giving expression to the ideas and conclusions which he was formulating as the result of his studies and his thinking. He had opinions which he felt he wanted to present to that part of the public which he was able to reach through these magazines, while he wished for a still larger audience.

It was to be expected that he would be quick and adept in setting forth his theories in clear and pleasing form, since his father had trained him from earliest boyhood to form sentences and para-graphs that expressed his meaning precisely and succinctly. Con-sequently, it was an uncommon essay or book or speech of his which failed to convey his thought easily, gracefully and with vigor. His writings also had some popular appeal because they dealt primarily with men, institutions and events; they did not go wandering off into ethereal regions of philosophy. Idealism was there and breadth of vision, but frequently combined with a desire to improve some specific human institution, whether it was his college, the govern-ment of his country or perhaps later the relation of nation to nation. He almost never dealt in abstract thought or vague philosophizing.

It was by his writings that he first made a name for himself outside of his own college. It was through them and through his speeches that he won advancement for himself in his profession. But above all they were part of him; he quite evidently felt an inner urge to express himself and to tell others what he was thinking. He also wanted to help mould the opinion and thinking of the nation, and these were the means which he had been trained to use. It was largely because of this desire to spread knowledge and an under-standing of history and his theories that he wrote so prolifically for twenty years.

An examination of his more important literary works as well as a number of his lesser ones will convey something of the range of his interests, his abilities and his point of view. In this last connection it is well to bear in mind that while he early recom-mended a radical change in the American form of government by the adoption of the cabinet system, he went on from there to a number of historical works which by their very nature almost precluded him from presenting suggestions for reform, until in 1908 his mature thought appeared in a work entitled *Constitutional Government*. He became a crusader for democracy in collegiate, national and world institutions, but since the literary outpourings of this last phase consisted almost entirely of speeches made in con-nection with his leadership in other activities, they will not be considered in the present chapter. Nevertheless the possibilities for this development and new outlook must have been inherent in his nature all the time, or they probably could never have come to fruition.

The essays, written before his historical works indicated his early interest in the careers of British statesmen and the operation of democratic government. They contained some excellent writing, exhibiting forcefulness of thought combined with clarity of expression. His first published work was an article on Bismarck which appeared in the *Nassau Literary Magazine* in the fall of his junior year at Princeton. He wrote admiringly of the Iron Chancellor's capacity as a statesman as evidenced while laying the foundations for Prussia's future power and greatness, but at the same time he recognized the cruelty and ruthlessness of some of the methods employed. These Wilson was inclined to condone as necessary for Bismarck's larger purposes.

This effort was followed a year later by a prize essay on William Pitt, Earl of Chatham. Here Wilson pointed out that this statesman possessed many petty foibles and weaknesses of character, but that his wise policies won India for the English Crown, built a great empire in the Far East and drove the French from America, thus making possible our own republic. It almost seemed as if he had a premonition of his own fate when he pictured Chatham as "a noble ruin," rising to answer one who had challenged his plan to save his country, and falling, "never to rise again."

The essay on "Cabinet Government in the United States" which was written in his senior year at Princeton and which brought him a big reputation among his fellow students because of its publication in the *International Review* was his first exposition of a theme to which he frequently returned. It was his hope that by this and later publications he could lay the groundwork for far-reaching changes in the operations of the American government. He explained that government by a cabinet whose members were chosen from the legislature would coordinate the work of the two branches of government, give the Executive greater power, and at the same time make the administrative branch more directly and immediately responsible to the will of the people, for such a ministry would have to resign if the major measures it proposed did not meet the approval of Congress. To this proposition was added an intimation which was more fully expounded in his book on *Congressional Government,* of the evils of the committee system in Congress, by which the more important committees, under a chairmanship imposed by mere seniority of service, could kill legislation which was of real importance for the welfare of the country. This sabotage of healthy legislation could be accomplished without the public being fully cognizant of where the responsibility actually lay, since the measures never saw the light of day.

These were big thoughts for a young student to be pondering and his exposition was no less clear than his ideas. It has been said that he probably got his first suggestion from Bagehot as well as from magazine articles by the lawyer and reformer Gamaliel Bradford and others, but there can be no question that he developed this line of reasoning in such a way that it could be easily comprehended and it soon began to command considerable attention. In time this and his later writings even led to the development of a whole school of specialists in government who felt English institutions were worth while studying in order to improve our form of government.

While at Middletown Wilson finished *The State,* one of the most scholarly of his works, but one which tried to cover so much ground that it was little more than a bare outline. After a chapter on the earliest governments, he investigated those of Greece and Rome. Then he discussed with some thoroughness those of modern Europe and the United States. As the book was largely based on the works of German scholars, part of his job was to become master of that language in order to become familiar with the materials he needed. This was perhaps the only one of his writings which was no pleasure to read, not because the thought was abstruse but because the style was dull.

Actually the large bulk of the material made it almost impossible for this book to be anything more than a mere compendium of facts, but he did discover a sort of evolution in the development of each new form of government from an earlier one. He believed that customs were changed by war, imitation, individual initiative and various other circumstances, drawing an analogy here to the ideas of Darwin. He also pointed out that any government always took upon itself certain necessary duties such as the protection of life and property, to which might be added optional duties like public improvements, state regulation of economic life and social legislation, saying of these that "wisdom will go as far as experience admits or times demand." He was inclined to take a middle ground on such matters as the control of monopolies; he trusted free enterprise but believed it should be placed under any restraints which were necessary to make competitive conditions reasonably close to equal.

Toward the end of the book he expressed a belief that democracy seemed destined to prevail everywhere, "ever since the rise of popular education in the last century." This was a faith which stayed with him all through his life. Perhaps it is harder to feel so confident about it today; and yet most of Wilson's logic seems still to hold good, for it is from those areas of the world where popular education has not been properly developed that the threats to democracy now arise.

Wilson was well read in English and American authors and orators. His study of forensics led to an admiration and close study of such representatives of the British Whig tradition as Burke, Bagehot and Gladstone. Edmund Burke had the greatest influence upon him, though Burke was a Conservative. Wilson soon discovered that facts did not always jibe with the ideas of the classical economists, and his thinking always tended to be in practical terms of political policy rather than in abstract theory. In this he resembled Burke, the subject of one of his early essays. Wilson believed that competitive individualism should be tempered by a sense of social responsibility and an approximation of equality of opportunity. The conceptions of free enterprise and of equality were both frequently present in his thought but he usually did not feel it necessary to try to reconcile them.

In his early essay on Gladstone, Wilson also expressed the idea that the world was steadily moving toward less despotic forms of government and in 1887 he predicted a federated democracy for the world. "There is a tendency—is there not?—a tendency as yet dim, but already steadily impulsive and clearly destined to prevail, towards, first the confederation of parts of empires like the British, and finally of great states themselves. Instead of centralization of power, there is to be wide union with tolerated divisions of prerogative. This is a tendency towards the American type of governments joined with governments for the pursuit of common purposes in honorary equality and honorable subordination."

Tennyson had expressed a similar conception in his poem "Locksley Hall" and perhaps it was suggested even by the philosophers of ancient Greece, yet Wilson offered something new when he added "in honorary equality and honorable subordination." This implied an international community founded upon a voluntary but definitely binding limitation of sovereignty.

In a review of Bryce's *The American Commonwealth* which appeared in 1889, he said: " In the first place, no people can be a nation before its time, and its time has not come until the national thought and feeling have been developed and have become prevalent. Until a people thinks its government national it is not national." He also recognized that this a process which can not be forced, just as he believed that "The English alone have approached popular institutions *through habit*. All other races have rushed prematurely into them through mere impatience with habit; have adopted democracy, instead of cultivating it."

The years of study at Johns Hopkins were a great stimulus to the development of Wilson's thought. There he met Frederick Jackson Turner, the historian who emphasized the influence of free land and the frontier upon all American life in making the people unusually mobile, self-reliant and adaptable. There too he saw how the doctrines of the Manchester School of British economists who emphasized free-trade, laissez-faire, and peace led to inequality, unfairness and inaction. As a consequence of this he turned toward a system of historical inductive economics; that is, he began to feel that lessons as to the results of various actions could be learned from the study of history. Largely as a result of this new conviction he changed about 1890 from writing on general literature and political philosophy to current politics and the historical background of America. In addition to writing on these matters he soon began to deal with educational topics and he frequently spoke and wrote to encourage affirmative state action for the advantage of society as a whole.

It was characteristic of Wilson that at the age of only thirty-one he did not hesitate to attack a book on the study of government by the most famous living professor of the subject. Writing for the *Atlantic Monthly* in 1891 he criticized the whole attitude taken by Professor Burgess of Columbia in his new volume of that year. Wilson pointed out that "A state cannot be born unawares, cannot spring unconsciously into being. To think otherwise is to conceive mechanically, and not in terms of life. To teach otherwise is to deaden effort, to leave no function for patriotism." At the same time he showed his own point of view when he went on to say: "The juristic method is the method of logic; it squares with formulated principles; it interprets laws only, and concrete modes of action. The method of political science, on the contrary, is the interpretation of life; its instrument is insight, a nice understanding of subtle, unformulated conditions." This was in accord with Wilson's own writings which tried to show how institutions developed and how they actually worked in practice rather than the mere theory upon which they were based, quite a new attitude toward the subject.

At about the same time he spoke appreciatively of the thoroughness and completeness of the first volumes of Rhodes' *History of the United States* which were just appearing, but he felt that the author betrayed an attitude prejudiced in favor of the North. His own point was that the struggle of the South could in no way be regarded as treason since there was really no nation until the question of sovereignty had been settled by the Civil War itself.

In the essay "Mere Literature" (which gave him the title of a book) he said that this phrase which he used for his title was "a serious sneer conceived by the scientific mind with the implication that a piece of work which is nothing but literature" was of little consequence. The typical scientist, he believed, seemed to regard the creations of the human spirit as only incalcuable vagaries of no importance. Wilson criticized college courses which dissected into little pieces even the very greatest works of literature. He showed how a passage from an eminent writer can make ordinary writing dull and insipid by comparison. He quoted Wordsworth as saying that poetry is "the breath of the finer spirit of all knowledge." His final conclusion held that "Mere literature . . . may keep our horizons clear for us, and our eyes glad to look bravely forth upon the world."

An autobiographical essay called "The Author Himself" appeared in the *Atlantic Monthly* in 1891. Here Wilson pointed out that if an author wanted reputation and some share of immortality he must seek to attain self-reliance, self-government and "a certain aloofness and self-containment." He emphasized the importance of an "originative personality," a definite point of view and "saying things in such a way that you will yourself be recognized as a force . . . in saying them." He ended by declaring that "The rule for every man is . . . to strive to see things as they are, and to be himself as he is. Defeat lies in self-surrender."

In an address to the International Congress of Education held at Chicago during the World's Fair in 1893 he exhibited and analyzed his own habit of reasoning when he praised the use of deduction, that is—judging a fact by a general theory. He said that if the "habit of carrying special cases up into the region of general principles—where alone the real light of discovery burns—be not formed during the period of preparation, it will hardly come afterward, when the special cases crowd fast and the general principles remain remote." He rarely failed to use this method himself all through his life.

This address was followed by a book review of Morse's *Lincoln* in which Wilson deplored the absence of any penetrating study of the forces which shaped Lincoln, since "history underlies statecraft." Then came a discussion of the historical ideas of Professor Goldwin Smith in which Wilson explained the separation of the American colonies from Britain as mainly due to the influence of the frontier. In an essay on "Political Sovereignty" published in 1893 he first used the word "covenant" in his public writings and pointed out that it was not the people themselves but, in America, Congress who governed.

His essay on "An Old Master" dealt with Adam Smith, who was gentle and benign in manner but who failed to see how the principles he expounded would be affected by emotions which were not connected with mere love of gain. For instance, said Wilson, the development and use of markets might be limited by prejudices, lack of imagination, love of home and the opinion of neighbors in any particular case, and the "Old Master" neglected to take these factors into consideration. What men would do in a given case could not be laid down with certainty, like the laws of a chemical reaction, Wilson said. "Men love gain, they sometimes love each other."

Wilson's thinking was much influenced by Montesquieu, Burke and Bagehot. In an essay on the last he recognized Bagehot's ability to peer into the physiology of political institutions and describe them accurately. Wilson demonstrated that Bagehot could speak out freely, by quoting him as writing: "Literary men can say strong things of their age, for no one expects them to go out and act on them." Yet Bagehot was essentially conservative and a believer in the preservation of order as is shown by his comments in *Physics and Politics* on Napoleon III's coup d'etat of 1852.

The essay on Edmund Burke, "The Interpreter of English Liberty," was one of the longest and most enthusiastic of these articles on British statesmen, yet by commenting on the truth of Burke's ideas he enables us to compare his own views with those of his subject. They both felt that the opinions of the people should prevail in order for them to have liberty but Wilson believed that they must first have had long experience with habits of order and self-control. Both thought that morality constituted a standard even above the law, but Wilson's attitude was religious rather than philosophical; he conceived of morality as "right action, action according to individual conscience, justice, truth, and regard for the common welfare." This view was developed later in *The New Freedom* and his vision of the accomplishments of America.

In an article on *"The Significance of American History,"* he went on to emphasize the idea that "The history of nations is spiritual, not material, a thing, not of institutions, but of the heart and the imagination. This is one of the secrets American history opens . . . the play of spirit in the processes of history." Then he developed this further in 1910 when he said the "deepest facts" of history were "the spiritual experiences, the visions of the mind, the aspirations of the spirit, that are the pulse of life." He felt that the history of America was not anything separate, it was "an integral portion of the general history of civilization, a free working-out upon a clear field, indeed, of selected forces generated long ago in England and the old European world, but no irregular invention, no histrionic vindication of the Rights of Man."

The essay on "Mr. Cleveland's Cabinet" published in 1893 gives expression to ideas which are of interest in connection with Wilson's later life when he pointed out that the new secretary of State would be a novice in conducting foreign affairs and went on, "Mastery in such matters cometh not by observation merely. Besides the wishes of the President, he will have only his own legal capacity and his own natural apprehension of right and wrong to guide him. Fortunately our foreign relations are generally simple enough to require little more." This seemed to indicate that he already felt that the President should be in control of foreign affairs and that they should be conducted with morality as a suitable guide. Wilson was an admirer of Cleveland's ability to arouse enthusiasm for the Democratic Party among younger men and he expressed the hope that the party would once more be built up into a powerful organization for progressive ideas.

Wilson himself felt that he had a fault of style which appeared especially in his essays. He said: "The phrasing is too elaborate, has not the easy pace of simplicity. . . . They do not sound as if they had come spontaneously, but as if they had been waited for, perhaps waited for anxiously. The fact is not so. They come fast and hot enough usually, and seem natural molds for my thought. But I am speaking of the impression they make when read." But on the occasions when they did not come fast he told his friend Bliss Perry that he waited for the proper word, waited with his hand over the typewriter instead of pacing about or lighting a pipe as other men did. And if his style suffered at one time from overemphasis and too much decoration, these faults disappeared later in the strength and vigor of his diction when he was President.

His literary artistry has been the subject of various essays, short appraisals, and even has had an entire volume devoted to it. This last is called *The Story of a Style* and was written in 1918 by William Bayard Hale who had earlier written a sort of campaign biography of Wilson which included tales of his subject's boyhood obtained in a few brief interviews. Hale attempted to take Wilson's idiom to pieces, he cited words and phrases which he asserted showed the presence of "aristocratic affectations, learned addictions, symbolism and phonetic phenomena," as he catalogued them. This line of criticism was taken up by Link in his preliminary volume on Wilson, which also put in objections to the use of ornamental and descriptive adjectives. However these adjectives made for vividness and easy reading; and they seldom occurred with any frequency except in the biography of George Washington which originally appeared as a magazine serial.

A fairer estimate, and one by a better recognized authority, was that by Bliss Perry in his essay on "Woodrow Wilson as a Man of Letters." In this study Professor Perry, who served on the faculties of Princeton and Harvard, as well as being for many years editor of the *Atlantic Monthly*, expressed his admiration for Wilson's style. He pointed out not only its clarity and swiftness of pace, the frequency of its "gay and alert" passages, but above all its sincerity.

He said that the phraseology possessed "sentiment without sentimentality, ease without diffuseness, eloquence without declamation." He pointed out that in Wilson's pages there was always "a sort of spaciousness, a consciousness of wide backgrounds and far horizons."

Perry admitted that Wilson's style was subtle and sometimes a bit redundant, repetitious or overelaborate, but he noted that it was essentialy the style of a speaker, addressing itself to the ear rather than the eye, and that Wilson wrote as he spoke, without trying to put himself in a literary frame of mind when settling down at his desk. Perry emphasized that almost all of Wilson's pieces made delightful reading and that during his early career editors of the leading magazines were constantly in competition for his essays, while later in life under the stress of unselfish emotion he was capable of "such examples of great writing as can scarcely be matched in the long history of English prose."

Coming now to Wilson's historical writings, they proved to be far greater in length and more to the popular taste than his essays. Yet they were probably inferior to the essays in literary quality and in exuberance of ideas. It was unavoidable that they should be rougher in texture and less sparkling than the essays which could receive the perfect polish of small jewels. Not only did his historical books bring him substantial sums of money, they also gave pleasure and instruction to hosts of readers. Wilson felt that one great reason for the study of history lay in the help that a study of the past gave to an understanding of the present; and since he bore this constantly in view he was apt to lay emphasis on such things as cause and effect, the springs of human action and the growth of ideas rather than upon men, dates and figures. His histories dealt with leaders, institutions and politics rather than with economics.

He believed that the historian should convey his general views and impressions, that he "needed imagination quite as much as he needs scholarship, and consummate literary art as much as candor and common honesty." He was successful in his effort to attain this ideal and consequently wrote historical books which the public could read and enjoy far more readily than most such volumes.

Wilson grew to maturity in the prosperous years of American business enterprise and energy. There were constant migrations to America from Europe, while the expanding network of railroads enabled the new immigrants to move out to the West and from the farms to the cities. These developments were generally regarded as achievements of capital in building and broadening industry, but at the same time the Western farmers began to object to the domination of the East, feelings expressed in the growth of such movements as the Grangers, Greenbackers, Free-Silverites and Populism.

Wilson did not write much about these movements and forces although he must have been consciously or unconsciously aware of them. However he did speculate on the type of the true American character which he thought was to be found especially in the West. In general he felt that the American spirit was "optimistically progressive . . . hopeful and confident," as well as "neither pedantic, provincial nor fastidious."

While at Johns Hopkins he had become a friend of Frederick Jackson Turner who published in 1893 his famous essay on "The Significance of the Frontier in American History." With the thesis of the dominant influence of the frontier on American life Wilson was thoroughly in accord and he added the proposition that "The Westerner has been the type and master of our American life." He believed that the East was making a mistake in failing to undertake a serious effort to comprehend the desire existing in the West and South for free coinage of silver. To all this he added a plea for the sympathetic study of Southern history.

His *Division and Reunion* was a general history of the United States from 1829 to 1889 which came out in 1893. As general history it showed not only knowledge and a sense of proportion on the part of its author, but also a surprising detachment, political sense, and power of analysis. It was especially good on the development of political thought during the period.

In summarizing the development of the country in the years before 1829 at the beginning of the volume he said that, "for the creation of the nation the conquest of her proper territory from Nature was first necessary," and added, "Expansion has meant nationalization; nationalization has meant strength and elevation of men." After devoting considerable space to the administrations of Jackson and Van Buren from 1829 to 1841, he dealt with the Mexican War, a struggle against an inferior foe which he regarded as an act of "ruthless aggrandizement."

In discussing the Civil War he pointed out that the South had not changed her ideas from the time of the adoption of the Constitution because she had not changed her condition, while the rest of the country had undergone profound changes. "Standing still, she retained the old principles which had once been universal," especially her "belief in states' rights and in the advantages of slavery." He emphasized that her slender economic resources were no match for the North, but he presented, in a style which made easy reading, an excellent discussion of the Constitution and government, resources, army and finances of the Confederacy. The whole work showed detachment and scholarship as well as the strong character of the author. His final judgment was that the United States were not authentically a nation until after the Civil War had imparted "to the national idea diffused vitality and authentic power."

Wilson's *Life of George Washington* was written in a popular vein, which was well suited to its first publication as a magazine serial. The diction was simple and easy; in fact it has been subjected to some criticism as being too colloquial, but it obtained the largest general audience of any of Wilson's books. Moreover it made a real contribution by treating its subject against a broad general background. The book gave a picture of the colony of Virginia in the time when Washington was growing up, emphasizing the differences between the customs and people there and those in New England. It told about the colonists and their occupations, presenting the conditions which made it possible for Virginia to develop so many Colonial leaders as well as subsequent presidents. While the story of Washington's life was graphically told, the people and problems that he had to meet were well presented with vivid pictures of their main characteristics.

With a historian's broad view Wilson showed how his hero's life and character developed and increased in influence among the surprising men and events of his time. The book shows almost too much of its author's own personality and feeling as his father indicated by saying, "Woodrow, I am glad you left George to his own dying in your book." But perhaps this only added to its interest. It certainly carried out Wilson's theory that an author should always express himself in his writings if he desired to increase their power and his own reputation.

Wilson's *History of the American People* was so good that it led the famous historian, Frederick Jackson Turner, to remark that "It is impossible to find in similar compass or by another single author so sustained and vital a view of the whole first cycle of American history that rounded itself out with the nation's completion of the conquest of the West, and its step overseas into colonial empire."

The work was published in five volumes, but contained only about 300,000 words, so it could have been compressed into less, by the use of smaller type, thinner paper and fewer illustrations. Its author followed his natural inclination to discuss important leaders and political events rather than endeavoring to make the book an economic and social history. Perhaps one weakness lay in his very ability to sum things up in quick, effective sentences or phrases which moved along so easily that the ordinary reader might fail to be impressed by their importance or to see what meat had been compressed into them. Yet although more facts and more stories might have struck upon the reader's consciousness with greater effect they would necessarily have made the work far longer.

The proportion and the point of view could scarcely have been improved in a book which covered so many important events over so long a period of time. After the first volume had given a synthesis of the varied living conditions of Colonial days, the second took up the exciting stories of the French and Indian War and the Revolution. The third required a great deal of condensation to cover the first fifty years of the new nation's life, while the fourth carried the narrative to the end of the Civil War with much the same perspective and fairness that characterized the author's *Division and Reunion*. The last volume maintained this spirit of impartial judgment, but showed sympathy with the achievements of the Democratic Party under Grover Cleveland as well as with the expansion of national interests that came with the Spanish-American War.

Constitutional Government was the most important statement of Wilson's considered opinions on political science and government. It consisted of a series of eight lectures delivered at Columbia University in 1907 and was filled with philosophical ideas. Wilson presented a description of how government really worked rather than a mere discussion of theory. He felt that the American form of government could only have come about as a result of the country's past history and he urged that we prepare the Filipinos and others for a similar experiment. He stated that the activities of all public officials ought always be open to investigation. He believed that the President's office was "anything he has the sagacity and force to make it." He spoke of the strain that the office of President put upon a man and recommended that on account of the difficulty of making treaties the President should "establish intimate relations of confidence with the Senate . . . keeping himself in confidential communication with the leaders," advice which he later disastrously failed to follow.

Wilson believed that "The object of our federal system is to bring the understanding of constitutional government home to the people in every part of the nation." In conclusion he emphasized the need to simplify questions for the voters since this would enable them to keep the government responsible to them, and make parties their instruments and not their masters. "A people who know their minds and can get real representatives to express them are a self-governed people."

Almost all his writings dealt with practical affairs but were infused with an underlying spirit of idealism. Most of his subjects were connected with government, history, education and related matters. He never went off into abstract philosophical discussions; and with the exception of that dull tome *The State*, all that he wrote was easy to read. He was extraordinarily prolific; in addition to the works that have been specifically discussed here he wrote many other essays and delivered a stream of speeches upon all sorts of occasions. Few among these failed to hold and arouse his hearers. He spoke to the men of his time decisively and clearly, so that both his writings and his speeches reached an ever expanding audience throughout the nation.

His writing was done almost entirely during the years 1885 to 1902, when his work as a college professor gave him some extra time in vacations and even during the academic terms. Before he went to Princeton in 1890 his publications were political, they dealt with political leaders and the problems of political science. Then came his essays, when his literary style was at its best and leading literary magazines were eager to get his work. In the last period came his three historical works which were longer and written more hurriedly, volumes which brought him both money and popularity. In addition to all this he frequently spoke on questions of religion or education but these remarks were not consciously literary productions nor intended for publication; neither were the great speeches of his later period.

Wilson worked hard at his writing, bringing to it an active and clear mind. Not only was the extent of his production surprising, it was of superior quality; and not only were his books useful in the academic world, but many of them were also read extensively by the general public. His mind was principally engrossed with politics and government, but it touched upon literature, education and life in general. His ideas did not often have any startling originality but they were sensible and well expressed, so that they received the attention of many readers of the best magazines and books. As a critic he was incisive and shrewd. If he was not a gifted portrayer of human life and character, nevertheless his books helped to spread understanding, especially of government. If they set forth the theories of a conservative rather than the militant liberal which he later became, they certainly showed freedom of thought and a wide range of interests. Above all they demonstrated the driving urge to instruct and enlighten which always kept pushing him on toward leadership.

Besides increasing his reputation and influence year by year, the mere execution of this vast quantity of writing and speaking, piled on top of his daily college work, increased the stature of the man. Such an output of material involved an immense amount of work which was not necessary for the physical well-being of himself or his family, so that his firmness and his strength of purpose were tested and developed by carrying such additional tasks through to the end.

The study and seclusion which were involved in these labors also developed the power to look at history and human institutions in a clear light. Through his writings he built up for himself not only some literary reputation, but a will to work, an ability to express himself, and an exceptional breadth of vision.

CHAPTER IX

DESTROYING A POLITICAL MACHINE

When he left Princeton Wilson's life entered an entirely new world, a world of politicians and party bosses backed by great corporations. These had obtained what looked like a stranglehold on the government of the State of New Jersey. Yet against these bosses men were marshaling apparently impotent but vociferous forces. For some time the muckrakers had been busy attacking the railroads, Congress, and Wall Street, until a spirit of criticism was developing upon a national scale. The reformers were looking for leaders and so were big business and the bosses; both sides wanted men who would make good candidates to present to the people, men who combined prestige in other walks of life with an attractive personality.

George Harvey had already announced in 1906 that he felt Wilson was the man for whom he would like to cast his vote for President. In the following year he suggested Wilson's name as a candidate for the Senate from New Jersey; but the Democrats had no chance of winning that year so it would only have been an empty honor; and besides, Wilson thought that the publicity would interfere with his work at Princeton. Nevertheless, Harvey still believed that he was their man, with his illustrious career in the educational world, his facility in speech-making and his pleasing personality.

111

By 1909 Harvey had been made editor of *Harper's Weekly* which he was operating under the aegis of the house of Morgan, so that he was able to use his magazine to mention Wilson again as a Presidential possibility. The struggle for democracy at Princeton soon gave Wilson even more favorable publicity, but to Harvey's mind this college contest did not indicate any particular realization on Wilson's part of the issues involved between the reformers and the bosses. To Harvey, Wilson appeared to be one whom the bosses could control while at the same time he stood at the very top among all the strong men in the educational field.

It was easy to believe that Wilson would be receptive to the suggestion of a political career. All his life he had been studying political science with the realization that at the same time he had been giving himself excellent training to participate in the direction of public affairs. His intimate friends at college as well as his father had some understanding of this; and his feeling was also clearly indicated in some of his letters to Charles Talcott and Mary Peck. He had told a Princeton trustee that if things went badly with him there, he could always find a career in politics and his situation at the University had now been undermined. In view of all this there could be little doubt that he would be ready for the call to public service whenever it came clearly.

The majority of the voters in the New Jersey cities had been organized by political machines which were controlled by bosses, generally Irish and Roman Catholic. The Republican machine had become a tool of the Pennsylvania Railroad, while the Democratic organization received its principal support from other public-utility corporations. There was a great show of fight and unfriendliness between them, but neither of them was really prepared to go against the interests of any of the big corporations which kept both supplied with funds.

The revolt against these machines in New Jersey appeared first from about 1906 to 1908 in the Republican Party. One of its leaders was George L. Record. This revolt was called the "New Idea," and it caused a split in the Republican ranks which gave the Democrats a good chance to win in 1910. At that time their machine was under the control of former United States Senator James Smith, Jr., James Nugent, and Robert Davis, city collector of Jersey City. These were known as the "Jim-Jim" crowd and "Little Bob" Davis, Smith being recognized as one of the most successful bosses of the time. Smith had sent his sons to Princeton, but he had earned such an unsavory reputation by buying sugar shares while the Senate was acting on the sugar schedule that the state legislature had not re-elected him to that body.

One Sunday evening late in June 1910 Harvey gave a dinner for Wilson, to introduce him to Smith and Colonel Henry Watterson, the eminent newspaper editor from Kentucky. Everything was amiable and, according to Watterson, Smith made it very plain that he would not again be a candidate for the Senate. Harvey soon persuaded Smith to support Wilson for governor and arranged dinners at Delmonico's restaurant in New York where Smith's henchmen kept assuring Wilson that the Democrats of New Jersey were eager for his nomination. When pressed to state his attitude toward the leaders of the organization, Wilson said he would be glad to consider their suggestions and to appoint their selections to office if on his own independent investigation he found them to be the best men. The reason the Irish politicians let him get away with this statement without asking anything more definite in the way of a promise may have rested upon a mere good-natured contempt for "the college professor."

Early in July Harvey called Wilson to a conference in New York which was attended by representatives of both the machine and big business. Richard V. Lindabury, an outstanding New Jersey corporation lawyer stated that at this meeting that "No one, I am quite sure, annexed any condition or attempted to exact any promise" from Wilson as to his conduct in office, despite many allegations to the contrary which were published later. On July 15 Wilson announced that if it was "the wish of a majority of the thoughtful Democrats of the State" he would accept the nomination, a mode of expression which offended the Irish so much that extra political barbecues and picnics to pacify them had to be financed from the coffers of the bosses. Two months later the nominating convention assembled with a platform presented by Smith, whose machine worked up a great show of enthusiasm for Wilson although almost none of the members had ever seen him. The reformers, under the leadership of Martin P. Devlin, W. W. St. John and Joseph P. Tumulty, were supporting Frank S. Katzenbach, mayor of Trenton, but they saw the machine rapidly crushing their starry-eyed hope of ending the reign of the bosses. John W. Westcott, who later nominated Wilson for President, made speeches against the highhanded methods being used by the bosses and asserted, "We want a candidate whose wisdom is derived from experience and not from dreams;" but nothing could stop the well-oiled machinery set in motion by Smith.

When the nomination was assured, Wilson drove over from Princeton, dressed just as he came from the golf links in a dark gray business suit and knitted sweater. He immediately addressed the delegates, many of whom were disgusted and none of whom were enthusiastic about this man they did not know. Yet Wilson won this gathering over by his idealism and his sincerity, with the climax of the speech asserting: "The future is not for parties playing politics but for measures conceived in the highest spirit by parties whose leaders are statesmen, not demagogues, who love not their offices but their duty and their opportunity for service."

By the time he had finished, John J. Crandall, who had broken a cane over a Wilson supporter's cranium during the deliberations, was seen shaking his head and yelling at the top of his voice, "I am sixty-five years old, and still a damn fool." For although Wilson had only asserted much the same thing that many a tool of the bosses had said before, he had convinced the hearts and minds of these hard-boiled delegates, reformers and dreamers who knew their politics, that he meant what he said and that he really would lead them in returning the control of the state goverment and the Democratic Party to the hands of the people. He looked like a man who was accustomed to meet and overcome opposition, he looked like a leader of courage and brains.

He also gave an appearance of youth as he began the campaign, and his speech was fluent like that of a teacher in the classroom. He had his father's old servant Dave Bryant come up from North Carolina to tell the Negroes of the New Jersey cities about him. As soon as he got back to Princeton after the nominating convention he issued a statement saying, "It is a humiliating and absurd thing to say that I am a Wall Street candidate for Governor of New Jersey. I never had any affiliation with Wall Street or Wall Street people." And in the next number of *Harper's Weekly* Harvey quoted Wilson as "truthfully" stating that "I have made no pledge and given no promise. Still more, not only was no pledge asked but as far as I know none was desired." One reason for all this emphasis upon the fact that Wilson made no promises in order to get the nomination lies in the fact that it soon became evident that Smith wanted to be sent back to the United States Senate by vote of the New Jersey legislature; so the suspicion arose that Smith had backed Wilson in order to put across a Democratic legislature which would do this for him with Wilson's approval.

But before this question arose the campaign came. A few days after the nomination Smith went to the university president's home in Princeton and when he saw the house and garden he said to James Kerney, editor of the *Trenton Evening Times,* "Jim, can you imagine any one being damn fool enough to give this up for the heartaches of politics?" Wilson explained that his idea was to make one big evening speech in every county rather than going around shaking hands from house to house. This general scheme was adopted, and when the political leaders of Mercer County, where Princeton was located, were admitted to the meeting Wilson followed every suggestion from the experts as to how to treat them, called them by name and made them all feel friendly and comfortable.

The first night of the campaign Wilson addressed three large meetings in Jersey City with speeches attacking the big corporations

115

with effective phrases such as "Guilt is personal." Smith's hench-man Nugent arranged a whirlwind tour and threatened to speak himself in Wilson's name if Wilson failed to meet his engagements. His Republican opponent was capable and honest; and when Wilson offered to meet any Republican in debate, George L. Record, who combined a knowledge of all the issues with great power on the platform, immediately took up the challenge. The Democratic leaders urged Wilson to make no answer to Record, but after waiting a few days the candidate wrote Record that all his dates for speeches had been filled but that he was ready to debate through an exchange of letters.

Since Record could not meet Wilson on the platform he sent a letter full of searching questions, asking whether Wilson was in favor of a direct primary, the fixing of rates for utilities and higher taxation for railroads, a corrupt-practices act to bring about clean elections, and some way of curbing the Democratic leaders such as Jim Smith. Wilson replied unequivocally that he would support every one of these measures which the Republican reformers had been advocating. He said he proposed to break up the domination of the bosses by the selection of men who would refuse to acquiesce in it while lending all their energies to break it up by pitiless publicity. He said that he would not submit to dictation from any persons, "special interests" or organizations in the matter of appointments or policies.

He caused even more of a sensation when, with Smith and Harvey sitting in a box at the theater in Asbury Park a few days after he had offered to debate by mail, Wilson definitely asserted that he did not "want the votes of anyone who thought he would obey a political boss." Smith, thinking this mere campaign oratory, made no effort even then to exact any promise from Wilson. With the support of the Democratic machine and most of the reformers, including even the Republican commuters to New York, Wilson won easily by 49,000 votes.

The new governor's initiation to practical politics and the schemes and methods of the bosses came almost immediately after the election and before he was even inducted into office. Since a Democratic legislature had been elected in the landslide which he had started, the Democrats in that body were now in a position to elect a United States Senator. A preferential primary election had been held to determine who the voters' choice was and although its results were not legally binding upon the legislators one of the planks of Wilson's platform had been the support of direct elections. This proposition would mean that the results of the primary should be followed, although many of the best men had refused to have their name put up for what they thought would be merely an empty and expensive honor. The man chosen in the primary was James E. Martine, who was considered an honest and conscientious man of no great ability.

In the beginning Wilson did not consider Martine well qualified for the post, so that he suggested an outstanding Princeton graduate for the position. It was perfectly obvious that James Smith wanted to go back to the Senate to rehabilitate his name. One reason many of the Democrats were unwilling to stand for the office in the primary was the fear of offending Smith. With the power the boss possessed it seemed almost certain that the legislature would grant him his dearest wish and send him back to the the Senate. Technically and legally, Wilson had no obligation to go to the legislators and tell them what they ought to do.

In view of all these circumstances Wilson at first was inclined to feel there was no reason why he should support the rather inadequate Martine, and many of his influential friends urged him not to interfere. But most of the radicals felt that it was necessary for him to state his position in order to live up to his stand for the direct nomination and election of high officials by the people. Wilson at this time had selected young Joseph Tumulty as his secretary, partly because he was familiar with New Jersey politics. Tumulty advocated support for Martine, while at the same time he influenced his friend William W. St. John to write articles for the *New York Evening Post*, the paper Wilson was accustomed to read. Consequently it was not long before the issue of his duty became clear

117

in Wilson's mind, especially since he had stated that if elected he intended to consider himself the leader of the party in New Jersey.

Once he became convinced that he saw his duty he was not to be deterred from doing it, either by gratitude to Smith or from fear of the machine. He went to see Bob Davis who, although dying of cancer, still controlled the large group of legislators from Hudson County. He was told that Davis had promised to support Smith and felt himself obligated to do so. Nevertheless this visit to their chief went to the hearts of Davis' followers, lessening their antagonism to the actions of the new governor-elect. Then Wilson went to Smith, telling him that he could become the biggest man in New Jersey by giving up his ambition to return to the Senate; but Smith said his health was better now than in July when he had positively stated that he would not be a candidate. He also asserted that he wished to clear his name of the stigma Cleveland had cast upon it in the sugar trust investigations. Smith felt that with the help of Davis he could sway the Democratic caucus of legislators. On December 9, 1910, Wilson put out a formal declaration, saying that so far as he was concerned the preferential primary vote was conclusive and he thought it should be equally so for every member of the legislature. In reply, Smith gave a pleasant message to the press that the campaign had been much too strenuous for Wilson and he now needed a rest.

The fight was bitter but Wilson carried it through, traveling all over the state to give speeches in which his ability to talk convincingly served him well. He summoned before him every Democratic legislator-elect and emphasized to each personally the importance of standing by the Democratic platform, as well as his obligation to the citizens who had entrusted the government of New Jersey to the Democrats after so many years. Wilson not only possessed the prestige of being governor, but his revolt against the bosses, now so dramatically portrayed, was making him a national figure. He cast no epithets at Smith, but in spite of the latter's efforts, including a huge parade and brass band in the streets of Trenton the night before the voting, he did not win the victory; Martine was elected to the Senate, by the State Legislature.

This honor might have gone to Joseph Tumulty, a former member of the legislature, for he was one of those who had been approached about allowing his name to be put on the Democratic primary ballot. Tumulty did not get the job, but he got a more important one when he became Wilson's secretary, for he stayed in that position for all of Wilson's public life. Tumulty was short and heavy-set, with good Irish features and receding hair. He served his hero with fidelity and honesty all those years. In return, Wilson trusted him and loved him while constantly making use of his advice and help. On many occasions Wilson went to others for the knowledge and intellectual assistance he needed, but it was Tumulty whom he relied upon day after day. By accepting a salary of less than half what he had been making as a lawyer and member of the legislature for the support of his large family, Tumulty felt that he would be able to show how a Presbyterian and a Roman Catholic could work together for noble purposes. As a result of this decision he eventually wielded a substantial influence in his country and the world.

Yet it was a strange association, for Wilson was a shrewd but idealistic Scotch Calvinist while Tumulty was a genial, lighthearted Irish Catholic. The new governor and his career became Tumulty's one absorbing interest, while Wilson relied upon Tumulty's loyalty and knowledge of political matters. He also took great delight in his secretary's wit, good-humor and simple-mindedness. Tumulty was more than a secretary, not quite an intimate friend. He also seemed to Wilson a typical average American. "When it is especially important that I be understood, I try out a speech on Tumulty, who has a very extraordinary appreciation of how a thing will get over the footlights."

Since Wilson wanted to put together a program of reform to be submitted to the legislature he called a conference of the reform leaders of both parties at the Hotel Martinique in New York on

January 16 and asked various members to draw up bills embodying the legislation they had in mind. Wilson asserted that there was nothing secret about this meeting nor was there any reason why George L. Record and other Republicans should not have taken part in the proceedings. He said that "Mr. Record is well known to be one of the best informed men in this state with regard to the details involved in most of the reforms proposed." This was a public announcement printed in the Trenton *Evening Times* of January 19 and it seemed to refute the suggestion that Wilson sought to belittle the services of Record on this occasion.

Wilson began his inaugural address the next day by saying: "I assume the office of Governor of the State with unaffected diffidence," and went on to discuss the need for reform in business and politics. Record remarked upon the subdued, not to say sad, behavior of the crowd of important and would-be important politicians who attended. At the receptions that afternoon and evening Wilson said he felt a "constant human interest. All sorts and conditions of people came, men, women and children, and I felt very close to them." In the minds of most of the liberals the inaugural was "a great utterance—great in its thought, great in its simplicity, great in its vision."

With all his high ideals Wilson realized that the state legislature was not so very different from others in the quality of the individual members, so that he decided to push just four extensive reforms. The first dealt with primary and regular elections as well as corrupt practices in general, and was sufficiently drastic to terminate the power of the bosses over elections and party organizations. Wilson took the leadership in the fight to put his measures through, addressing groups of editors, boards of trade and the legislators themselves. Here, he acted like a British prime minister, preparing the legislative program, employing the party caucus to decide policies and even resorting to threats when necessary.

When the bill on elections was introduced in the Assembly by a former student of Wilson's, it was known as the Geran bill. Jim Nugent, still holding the powerful office of state chairman of the

Democratic Committee, appeared at the State House on the first day of the session to lead the opposition to Wilson's reforms, beginning with the Geran bill. After almost having a fist fight with Edward Kenny, the speaker of the House, Nugent told those supporting the bill that none of them would be re-elected to which Kenny rejoined, "I won't stand for any attempt to queer the bill. The Geran bill will pass and don't you forget it." But since he felt that this sort of contention could not continue Wilson commanded Nugent to come to his office on March 20 in order to find out whether he intended to persist in his opposition to the bill. Nugent said he would fight it with all his strength for he believed it was upheld principally by progressive Republicans and "traitorous" Democrats. When Wilson said it would pass just the same, Nugent suggested that Wilson was using patronage to push the bill through. Wilson became angry and showed Nugent the door. Nugent stammered and shuffled toward it, shouting that Wilson was "no gentleman" and he had "always thought he was no gentleman," to which Wilson simply repeated his words of dismissal, "Good afternoon, Mr. Nugent." But a popular story attributed to him the crisp retort, "You're no judge."

The incident led to much enthusiasm among Wilson's followers inspiring numerous editorials and cartoons, including one which showed Nugent flying head foremost from a door propelled by a foot marked "Wilson." The governor said he did not enjoy this at all but that "apparently it did a lot of good." However, the passage of the Geran bill had already been decided upon by a party caucus a week earlier. Wilson's right to attend this meeting was questioned by one asemblyman, but Wilson quoted from the state constitution that the governor should recommend to the legislatures "such measures as he may deem expedient" whenever he felt it necessary. After this was settled Wilson talked for three hours on the Geran bill, threatening at last to carry the fight to the people. On the very evening after his interview with Nugent the Geran bill passed the House by a narrow majority and on April 13 substantially the same provisions were adopted by the Senate. This law required the nomination of all elected officials by direct primary, gave the courts supervision over the choice of election officials and contained the other usual provisions of a corrupt practices act. Votes could no longer be cast in the name of dead men, corporations were forbidden to contribute to campaign funds, and bribery was to be punished, even when it consisted merely of gifts of tickets or liquor. All this made it almost impossible for the bosses and corporations to control the votes or actions of legislators and other officials.

After the Geran law, came legislation controlling the rates and services of public utility corporations which went through easily with Wilson's backing. This was followed by a workmen's compensation law to hold corporations responsible for injuries to their employees suffered while at work. A bill to authorize a commission form of government for cities was weakened because it required approval by too great a percentage of voters, but nevertheless a number of cities began to operate under its provisions. The following year a number of less important reform measures concerning schools and the inspection of food and factories, as well as regulation of the labor of women and children, were enacted, all under the impetus of Wilson's prestige and with his support.

All this time Nugent had retained his position as chairman of the Democratic Committee which made him still the technical head of the party in New Jersey, in spite of the objection that he was always to be found in opposition to the governor and the legislative majority. Wilson did not want to take any active step to put him out. However, on the night of July 25, 1911, while attending a party at Scotty's Cafe in Neptune Heights, with several officers of the New Jersey National Guard at neighboring tables, Nugent rose and said, "I propose a toast to the governor of New Jersey, the commander-in-chief of the Militia, an ingrate and a liar. I mean Woodrow Wilson. I repeat, he's an ingrate and a liar. Do I drink alone?" The story is that he did drink alone while the officers threw their glasses on the floor and marched out. Two days later Nugent publically admitted that he had proposed such a toast with the result that within less than a month a majority of the state committee held a meeting at which they deprived him of his office, temporarily destroying the last remnants of his power.

Meanwhile Wilson's appointments, made with the help of Tumulty and James Kerney, were generally regarded as excellent; while editors all over the country were enthusiastic about the vast body of reforms which had been enacted in one of the strongest citadels of the bosses and big corporations. Wilson had proved himself a capable party leader as well as one who could arouse public opinion sufficiently to gain the co-operation of many Democrats and Republicans alike. He showed that the welfare of the people could be made the guiding principle of a government wrenched from the hands of selfish politicians.

Smith and the other New Jersey bosses had underestimated their man. They forgot that he had learned politics as president of Princeton. He once said that state politics were "child's play" compared to the college variety. Actually, he was fortunate in having had so many earnest advocates stirring up the spirit of reform for several years before he took office.

CHAPTER X

A PROFESSOR'S
PRESIDENTAL CAMPAIGN

Wilson's achievements in New Jersey were blazoned on the pages of newspapers all over the country. He became the hero of many liberals, radicals and progressives, for he had put through the kind of program they were advocating. Its fundamental purpose was to see that those who did most of the hard work of industry should get a greater share of its rewards and benefits. Government was to be given back into the hands of the people; then those whom the people chose as their leaders should see that the workingman was not made to pay excessively for the services of great corporations and invested capital. Theodore Roosevelt had tried to make himself the leader of this movement; but at the same time he had played along with the trusts and big business, so that his sincerity was subject to question.

The election of Wilson as governor, followed by his victory over the bosses and the enactment of his reform program, put him in a position to be one of the foremost prospects for the Democratic Presidential nomination in 1912. Harvey had worked hard earlier to build up an organization to labor toward this end, but the bosses had no interest in supporting a man who made it his purpose to smash poltical machines.

In early March, 1911, Wilson's old friend Walter Hines Page, now editor of *World's Work,* called a meeting to discuss how to build up an organization for his campaign. A New York lawyer named McCorkle was there; but the most important member was William F. McCombs, a cripple who had been born in Arkansas and was one of Wilson's former honor students. He gave the appearance of being smooth and sophisticated. He was described as having "a broad full forehead and a wide disarming smile," with no indication of internal stresses, strains and melancholy thoughts. They raised $3,000 to finance tours through the West after the adjournment of the New Jersey legislature. Meanwhile Wilson made his first speech at Atlanta, where he gained the support of Hoke Smith, the reform governor of Georgia.

Two days later Bryan was to speak at the Princeton Theological Seminary and Mrs. Wilson wired her husband to come back immediately. Wilson no longer felt supercilious toward Bryan, for he believed that the old leader's emotions were on the side of the people and that he had properly pointed out the evils in American society. Wilson on his side had won over Bryan by his fight for Martine and by urging the adoption of an income tax amendment. Bryan came to dinner with the Wilsons the following day. They had a very congenial time together. Wilson found in Bryan a man who had "extraordinary force of personality, and it seems the force of sincerity and conviction." Not long afterward Wilson praised Bryan in public for the first time as one who had "borne the heat and burden of a long day."

Wilson began a western tour with a speech at Kansas City on May 5 in which he advocated the initiative, referendum and recall in government, measures which he had remarked upon unfavorably in his books but which he now felt would work to bring back representative government. Two days later at Denver he sought to show that Christianity was much the same thing as progressive democracy and that he would make an ideal leader of a Christian-social democracy. He went on to Los Angeles and San Francisco where he told a group of conservative businessmen that if they failed to follow the line in politics laid down for them by bankers, the banks would not lend them money for their business. This statement was of course heartily denied by those present but praised by the progressive newspapers of the West. Speeches in Oregon and Minnesota completed his western tour. His balance between progressive ideals and sensible reforms won many people to his banner.

"Sea Girt," site of the governor's official summer residence, saw the arrival and departure of many politicians, governors and interested friends during the next few months. William Gibbs McAdoo, who was president of the Hudson Manhattan Railroad Company which had built tunnels under the Hudson River, came from New York to meet and appraise the new candidate for President. Wilson's duties as governor still occupied considerable time. He complained once that even his Sunday afternoons had to be given over to reviewing the National Guard. He could not continue to occupy the Princeton presidential mansion, so for purposes of economy Mrs. Wilson simply took four small rooms at the Nassau Inn for a few months. Later Wilson bought a house on Cleveland Lane in Princeton and as governor commuted to Trenton.

Now Colonel Edward M. House began to help Wilson toward his goal. House remained his guide, counselor and intimate friend throughout almost all the years of his public life. House had supported Bryan as a leader of the popular cause and he wielded great influence in Democratic Party circles of Texas. Impressed by a speech Wilson made at the State Fair in Dallas in October 1911, he was flattered when Wilson called on him a few days later in the Gotham Hotel in New York to ask him to be on a campaign committee. Although House pointed out that such a committee was likely to be a mere hindrance, he was fascinated by Wilson's liberal and progressive ideas. Wilson was always seeking understanding and here was a man who not only understood and sympathized, but could also offer help.

House was a slender man of about five feet six, whose oval face carried a stubbly mustache above a powerful chin and a mouth, sensitive and yet determined. A gentle voice, kindly eyes that could glow with great enthusiasm, and a rather lofty forehead were among his other characteristics. He was a good and cheerful listener, but perhaps the greatest of his qualities was an imagination of wide scope and vigor. The letters Wilson wrote this new friend show how perfectly the two worked in harmony and affection through the years.

In the actual campaign which was now opening, McCombs showed himself fuller of ideas and enterprise than either House or Page. In October Wilson named him his campaign manager. McCombs lost no time getting in touch with editors and other public men. By December he had set up a branch office in Washington to send out original material to eight hundred daily and six thousand weekly newspapers. McCombs was afflicted with an erratic temperament and domineering personality, but as a smart campaign manager he knew that the best results came from building up an organization and working with the state leaders. McCombs undertook to spread Wilson's characteristic liberalism all over the country.

But once Wilson was in the limelight, a violent campaign of abuse, lies, and conspiracies broke out against him. These onslaughts were so venomous and emanated from so many sources that it was almost impossible to ward them off. Few candidates have had to meet attacks so vitriolic as those delivered by the New York *Sun* and such newspaper supporters of Underwood and Clark as Hearst and Tom Watson.

The New York *Sun* spoke for big business and Wall Street, under the direction of its irascible editor, Edward P. Mitchell, who had opposed Wilson's reform measures ever since early 1911. On December 5 of that year the *Sun* ran a story on its front page stating that Wilson had asked for an annuity retirement grant from the Carnegie Foundation for the Advancement of Teaching. This was a pension to be given for distinguished service after a career of twenty-five years of teaching and Wilson thought himself entitled to apply for it and receive it. When his application went in, the committee had just decided to grant only old-age pensions in the future. His opponents claimed that the application could not be justified, that it was "for indigent teachers and not for indigent politicians," and that the money was "steeped in the blood of

Carnegie's workers . . . while struggling for a decent wage." Most of Wilson's supporters felt it best simply to ignore the incident and its implications. Others called attention to the fact that the criticism came from Wilson's reactionary enemies rather than from his liberal friends. The New York *World* even declared that "if one use of the Carnegie Foundation is to bar retired educators from public life it needs reform" and the feeling was gradually established in the public mind that Wilson had done nothing out of the way.

The next move of the *Sun* was an effort to create a rift between Bryan and Wilson by publishing a letter which Wilson had written five years before wishing "that we could do something at once dignified and effective to knock Mr. Bryan once for all into a cocked hat!" This sentiment had been contained in an enthusiastic reply to Adrian F. Joline, president of the Missouri, Kansas and Texas Railroad, who had sent Wilson a copy of his speech to the directors of the road at Parsons, Kansas, on April 4, 1907, attacking Bryan's recommendation for government ownership of the railroads. Joline was then a trustee of Princeton and friendly with Wilson, although he later took the side of Dean West in the graduate school controversy. Wilson said he had read Joline's address "with relish and entire agreement."

Joline had given copies of the letter to three of his friends with the understanding that they would keep it confidential. One of these must have given it to the *Sun* which published an inaccurate version on January 7, 1912, followed by a corrected version given out by Joline himself ostensibly in the interest of truth. The editor's purpose was clearly to cause a split between Wilson and Bryan. Senator Gore of Oklahoma was one of the many who commented on this, saying Joline "had two designs, both sinister; first—to put Wilson and Bryan asunder, to divide progressive Democrats and conquer them; second—to influence the animosity and resentment of Mr. Bryan's faithful friends and followers and cause them to desert Wilson." McCombs raised the cry of "Wall Street" but all the same Wilson's campaign managers were greatly disturbed.

All this gave Bryan an opportunity to show his large and generous

128

temperament. Luckily he was visiting Josephus Daniels of Raleigh when the item appeared and, although naturally annoyed, his anger had cooled by the time he and Daniels reached Washington for the Jackson Day dinner on January 8, a gathering of very important Democrats. At the dinner Wilson made a short but highly successful speech. As he faced Bryan he said, "There has been one interesting fixed point in the history of the Democratic Party, and that fixed point has been the character and the devotion and the preachings of William Jennings Bryan." He went on: "Let us apologize to each other that we ever suspected or antagonized one another" and show ourselves "at least to have been indeed the friends of our country and the friends of mankind." At this conclusion Bryan put his hand affectionately on Wilson's shoulder and said, "That was splendid, splendid." He and Wilson were drawn much closer together than ever before.

The next attack was an apparently carefully planned effort by George Harvey to put Wilson in a position where he would be open to a charge of ingratitude. The basis for this accusation was that Wilson had gratuitously told his first important supporter for the Presidency that he no longer desired his backing. The incident upon which this was founded occurred on December 7, 1911, but the story did not become known until a week after the publication of the Joline letter. At that time Harvey sent a communication to the newspapers alleging that Wilson had made a statement directly to him that the support of *Harper's Weekly* was affecting his candidacy injuriously.

Actually Harvey, Wilson, and Henry Watterson of Kentucky had held an apparently amiable meeting at the Manhattan Club on that day and as they were leaving Harvey said to Wilson, "I want to ask you a frank question and I want a frank answer," and on Wilson's promise to speak out Harvey said, "I want to know if the support of *Harper's* is embarrassing your campaign." When Wilson replied "I am sorry you asked me that!" Harvey insisted, "Let's have the answer anyway"; to which Wilson felt forced to say, "Some of my friends tell me it is not doing me any good in the West." For a few minutes they tried to figure out some method of making it clear that Harvey was independent of J. P. Morgan and Wall Street, and although they found no way of doing this Wilson felt they had separated as friends.

Harvey tried to use Watterson as his mouthpiece in bringing his charges against Wilson, and to a certain extent he succeeded in getting the Kentuckian involved in the controversy. But the account given to the newspapers by Harvey was actually dishonest, for it did not explain that Wilson's declaration was in reply to a direct and reiterated question by Harvey nor that it was made only at the latter's extreme insistence. These additional facts were finally stated by Watterson in an interview with the Associated Press on January 17 which entirely freed Wilson from any implication of ingratitude. The controversy probably helped Wilson as the New York *World* came out with an editorial on January 19 saying that: "Ingratitude is one of the rarest virtues in public life. 'Gratitude' is responsible for many of our worst political abuses." To Bryan's mind the incident offered a final proof that Wilson changed from a conservative college professor into an active reformer. Bryan later likened the transformation to that of Saul of Tarsus.

This change in Wilson was genuine enough, for he had seen what the bosses and great corporations were doing to exploit the people. But he also came to realize that a liberal position was the way to win votes, and that such a stand might win him a place of power. He never doubted he would use this power for the benefit of mankind. In all these decisions his wife Ellen stood by him and encouraged him to become the leader that she felt in her heart he could be.

Although he had able assistance in his campaign, his decisions were his own. House helped him carry Texas, Josephus Daniels offered the support of North Carolina, and McCombs was an agile and adept campaign manager. Bryan and other men who honestly feared the grinding force of the great industrial machine of big business were behind him. But Wilson had learned the ways of politics and politicians by his studies of government in action. He had gained, too, by his two years in the rough and tumble politics of New Jersey. His study, experience, and penetrating vision, enabled him to pilot his own ship to victory over his rivals for the nomination and election.

His name was already well known throughout the country; while college men were telling what he had done for education, farmers and many liberal-minded business men were looking toward him as their candidate by the early months of 1912. He was called on to make so many speeches that he had real difficulty finding time to carry on his duties as governor.

Almost from the time of the Civil War until the end of the century the forces of privilege and business had been tightening their grip upon the country until the average workingman had little left in the way of ability to direct his own activities and fate. Against this static, stifling system Wilson semed to be the most promising Democratic leader. He was a constructive thinker, he believed in the need for reform and change. His speeches were only mildly radical, but his performance in New Jersey had given proof that he was definitely on the side of the average man and that he was determined to do all he could to make democracy work.

Against Wilson were arrayed forces which had three favorite sons to offer. Champ Clark, speaker of the House, had been all his life in politics. His campaign, with a platform fully as progressive as Wilson's, was now in the hands of a Missouri political machine controlled by David R. Francis, and Senators Stone and Reed. Governor Harmon of Ohio and Senator Underwood of Alabama both had large conservative followings; Tammany and the big New New York State delegation would have preferred either of them to Wilson.

When the convention delegates were chosen these three candidates held between them the great majority of the delegates. Each of them knew that if their delegates were released from their pledges to support a specific candidate many would swing over to Wilson. It was this that made Wilson's prospects good in spite of the fact that nearly half of the delegates were pledged to Clark. Colonel

House was determined to overcome Clark's advantage by seeing that "the Wilson people made airtight agreements with a sufficient number of delegates instructed for candidates other than Clark to the effect that under no condition would any parties to the agreement vote for Clark; there was no agreement as to what would be done after Clark had been eliminated."

The Republican convention had already been held and the conservative Taft had won the nomination over the vociferous and more progressive Theodore Roosevelt, forcing the latter to seek the Presidency as an independent backed by an *ad hoc* party. The Democrats met at Baltimore late in June with most candidates sure of some conservative support but with Wilson completely free from suspicion of reactionary connections. Just before the convention, Bryan sent all candidates a letter of protest against the nomination of Alton B. Parker by the National Committee as temporary chairman. This letter was eccentric and not always to the point but it breathed the spirit of a fighting liberal objecting to the choice of a thoroughgoing conservative for this important post. When Wilson was the only important candidate to endorse its sentiments, the ties between him and Bryan were made stronger than before.

When the convention assembled at the end of June in Baltimore, Bryan still bore about him some of the glamour of the "Boy Orator of the Platte" which he had been called almost forty years before. On those hot summer days he wore an alpaca coat with white vest and clerical necktie; his face was benign, his head like a dome. He stayed and struggled through the steaming hot days of the convention, while Wilson and his family remained in the governor's mansion at Sea Girt. Meanwhile Colonel House had gone to Europe happy in the belief that Wilson would win because his plans were well laid.

Although Wilson had advocated a change to a mere majority, which would have lost him the nomination, the Democratic convention rule still required a two-thirds vote for nomination. The hall held eleven hundred delegates on the floor and almost ten thousand spectators in the gallery. Wilson's ideas had to win acceptance from two thirds of the delegates in order for him to gain the nomination. Of substantial help to him was the spirit of the galleries, so vociferous for liberalism that most of their occupants stamped rudely out of the hall when Parker started his first speech accepting the position of temporary chairman.

The next day came a roll call upon the old rule which required each state delegation to vote as a unit. After a sudden Wilson demonstration the liberal forces won their point, if only by a mere seventy votes out of over one thousand. This change allowed each delegate to vote for whom he pleased, when once the candidate for whom he was instructed saw fit to release his delegates. Wilson and Clark had the support of all the country west of the Alleghenies except the South, while the conservatives held New England and the Atlantic states, a division very similar to that which had split the Republican convention between Roosevelt and Taft. That split and the triumph of the conservative Republicans by what were regarded as "steam-roller" methods had aroused the ire and fighting spirit of the liberals at Baltimore. They were especially indignant at the New York delegation which included Charles Francis Murphy, the suzerain of Tammany, and August Belmont straight from Wall Street. The delegates found themselves receiving many telegrams urging a liberal stand. When a permanent chairman was selected the choice fell upon the progressive Kentuckian, Congressman Ollie James.

Wilson kept in touch with the proceedings from Sea Girt by telephone conversations with McCombs and McAdoo. He seemed to maintain a calm and imperturbable spirit, joining in with his wife's pretense that she would really be glad of his defeat and a chance to relax among the English lakes. Just the same he had to make decisions, many of which were of a crucial nature. At the very beginning Wilson had ignored the advice of McCombs by openly stating that since the convention was dominated by liberals this fact should be recognized in the way it was organized. Bryan helped his cause by introducing a resolution that "we hereby declare ourselves opposed to the nomination of any candidate for President who is . . . under obligation to J. Pierpont Morgan, Thomas F. Ryan, August Belmont, or any other member of the privilege hunting and favor-seeking class." After the resolution had passed by more than four to one, since few wished to put themselves on record as being so obligated, the nomination speeches began and were followed by cheering and parades, with the Wilson demonstration being by far the most prolonged, lasting one hour and a quarter.

After the tenth ballot and on the fifth day of the convention Wilson had to decide if he would follow the advice of McCombs and release his delegates since the New York delegation had gone over to Clark and so given him a majority. It was true Wilson had supported the idea that two thirds should not be required to nominate, but the old rule had been maintained and McAdoo put in a violent protest over the telephone against the release of Wilson's delegates. Wilson was convinced that he need not follow his own theory since it had definitely been overruled by the convention, and so he kept the hold on his delegates. He made the smart move of asking Bryan if the candidates might not be requested to refuse any nomination unless it was made without the help of New York. In response to this Bryan went even further than Wilson had suggested, declaring that while Clark received the support of New York he would vote for Wilson. This made it appear that Clark was the Tammany candidate, which naturally turned more liberals to Wilson.

More votes were cast for Wilson on each succeeding ballot, but now came a final temptation. He was asked for a promise that Bryan would not be his Secretary of State. This was suggested in the hope of winning the support of some conservatives, and he must have felt himself that the Great Commoner knew so little of foreign affairs that he would have been glad to have refused him the post. But Bryan's support had been a great help to him; moreover he had steadily refused to promise offices in order to win elections, and he very wisely refused to make even a negative promise in this case. As his vote increased even the political bosses of Illinois and New

York turned toward him, so that on the forty-sixth ballot, taken on July 2, Wilson obtained 990 votes, more than the required two thirds. The liberal spirit had won.

Now came the electoral contest against the conservatives under Taft and the progressives under Theodore Roosevelt. Wilson talked wisely and sensibly, somewhat academically perhaps, but certainly in a far more temperate manner than Roosevelt. Taft was left behind, with almost nothing to say except a few bitter remarks about both his opponents. Wilson had a tendency to talk in generalities, but he frequently gave his audience a reasonably concrete application of his ideas. He said that the control of banking and currency should be in the elected representatives of the people rather than in the representatives of big business. The Democratic platform had come out for Presidential primaries and the direct election of senators, prosecution of trusts and Federal supervision of public utilities, a tariff for revenue only and an income tax. Wilson's record in New Jersey and in his speeches were calculated to convince the voters that he would redeem these promises, especially as to the two main issues, the tariff and the trusts. On these two points the Rooseveltians seemed weak and uncertain. George W. Perkins of J. P. Morgan and Co. had conferred with Roosevelt, and since that time little had been heard from that candidate concerning any action against the trusts. This "missing plank" naturally became a subject of frequent jibes by Wilson and supporters.

There were, of course, many difficulties for Wilson, including stories about his relationship with Mrs. Peck. Their correspondence continued all through the campaign and gives today the best expression in many cases of his hopes, misgivings and problems. These letters are full of interest as a record of his reactions but no intense emotion for Mrs. Peck appears in them, although some of her letters to him betray a more ardent affection.

A different problem was presented by McCombs whose mistrust and envy, probably increased by the worsening of his illness, aroused the antagonism of McAdoo and many other Democratic leaders. It was only their confidence and enthusiasm in Wilson that

135

kept these important supporters working hard for their candidate when he insisted upon retaining McCombs as his campaign manager and named him national chairman of the party.

A tour of the South and West gave Wilson a chance to present his views with good effect. His early training in oratory enabled him to talk easily and yet have his unaided voice carry to the outer limits of large audiences. Bryan made almost five hundred speeches, and liberals everywhere were won over to Wilson, who at the same time sought to reassure business by recognizing that it was "exceedingly sensitive" and that there must be no "rash or hasty action."

Wilson's sincerity appeared to be vouched for by his record in New Jersey. Roosevelt had attacked the trusts in both of his campaigns but had done almost nothing to get action against them. He had allowed "Uncle Joe" Cannon as speaker of the House to thwart all important reforms. He had been friendly with the leaders of big business and endorsed in the *Outlook Magazine* the high Payne-Aldrich tariff. He had been the great American hero, but the people appeared to have become tired of his incessant activity and talk of the strenuous life. He made a good subject for ridicule, and Senator John Sharp Williams of Mississippi composed the following verse to the perennial candidate:

> I'm twice as great as Washington
> I'm twice as great as Grant
> Because third terms they didn't get
> They needn't think I can't.

Meanwhile Wilson made straightforward speeches in which he outlined something of his plans and pointed to the flaws in Roosevelt's record. He enlarged his circle of friends and acquaintances during the course of the campaign, coming to know and admire Louis Brandeis and Samuel Gompers. When a deranged man shot Roosevelt, Wilson refused to speak until his opponent had recovered. This was not only a generous gesture but also a good political move, as he himself recognized, for he said that "Teddy will have apoplexy when he hears of this."

Wilson took the whole campaign with a casual air, which doubtless belied his real emotions. By ten o'clock on election night it appeared certain that he would win and the Princeton students thronged over to hear him speak from his front porch. He told of his "feeling of solemn responsibility" in facing "the very great task ahead." He had received only 42 per cent of the popular vote but a great majority of the electoral votes. His character and previous career gave promise that a fresh era of liberalism in government was about to begin. Already he was planning his reforms.

CHAPTER XI

PUTTING AN END TO
DOLLAR DIPLOMACY

The new president appeared a little taller and a little lighter than the average man; his face was long with large and luminous eyes, which some found to lack steadiness of gaze. His brown hair was now turning slightly gray with his fifty-six years. He possessed the teacher's easy manner of speaking and an excellent choice of words, so that he seemed able to hold any audience, large or small, to an alert attention. He delighted to talk about important topics and to propound original points of view; in fact, this was his favorite form of fun. He sang well and enjoyed music, although he had no technical knowledge of the art.

In ordinary intercourse he was invariably courteous and agreeable but without the friendly touch and manner that made his father loved. At the time he left Princeton, when the leading citizens came in procession to present him with a loving-cup, he said that when he asked to charge something at a store in that small town the clerk often inquired, "What name, please?" Since the welfare of humanity became the passion of his life, this lack of friendly relations seems to have been due to no purpose of his own; he always said he wished that he could overcome it. Perhaps it was owing to his tense and high-strung nature, to his active mind which did not easily relax and waste time in idle amiable conversation. He had no time nor gift for casual friendships. And perhaps all this in turn was due in some mysterious fashion to his own physical make-up with even his almost constant stomach trouble playing a part. His strict Presbyterian training was also an essential element in his background.

He was no back-slapper, but gave himself to a few intimates. Within his family clrcle itself there was affection as well as understanding. He almost always had several close women friends like Mrs. Mary Hulbert Peck and the wives of various professors. Hibben had been very close to him at Princeton and Colonel House was to become his especial friend and adviser at Washington, while others had grown into his confidence at the university and remained there. From his friends he took advice and help, but he seems to have been unable to tolerate real opposition to his fundamental principles even from those most intimate with him.

When his mind was given an opportunity to work he was tense and alert. Samuel Blythe describes an interview in Wilson's library in the late spring of 1914 when they were discussing Mexico.

> "The President closed his fingers into a sinewy fist. He leaned forward in his chair . . . as a man leans forward who is about to start on a race, his body taut, his muscles tense. . . . His eyes were narrowed, his lips slightly parted." He was expounding his view that liberty must always be attained by forces working from below not handed down from above. He went on, "I say to you that the old order is dead. It is my part, as I see it, to aid in composing . . . differences, so . . . that the new order . . . shall prevail."

He was taking a great step in his life, the greatest step of all. Now he was President of the United States. He had worked and fought to gain the position, but he could not avoid a feeling of apprehension at what he was facing. Before leaving Princeton he wrote, "This is our last evening in this little house and we find our hearts very heavy. We leave familiar scenes which we may possibly never know again, and go out to new adventures among strangers. New adjustments must be made all along the line—a new life must be worked out—a little full of strain and anxiety." And when an old friend and preacher congratulated him, he replied, "I appreciate your good wishes, but had you not better pray for me?"

While the inauguration ceremonies were in progress on March 4 Wilson observed that a wide space had been cleared in front of the speakers' stand. He motioned to the police saying, "Let the people come forward," and this was taken up by his followers as an expression of the spirit of his administration. They believed that he was destined to be the leader of a "New Freedom." There was deep silence during the first portion of his inaugural address and later applause. "Our duty is to cleanse, to reconsider, to restore. . . . Justice, and only justice, shall always be our motto. . . . Here muster, not the forces of party but the forces of humanity. . . . I summon all honest men, all patriotic, all forward-looking men."

The inaugural ball was omitted, to the great disappointment of many, because neither he nor Mrs. Wilson liked social display, which seemed a somewhat selfish reason. But the Bones sisters were there, and Ellen McMasters from Columbia, while his father's old Negro servant, Dave Bryant, was preening himself in the kitchen. The next day Wilson entered upon his duties by giving a statement to the press that he felt it necessary to refuse to see applicants for office in person so that he could devote himself entirely to the business of government and large questions of policy. At ten o'clock that morning he met members of his Cabinet for a conference to "talk about getting started on our way." It was decided that if their nominations had been confirmed by the Senate they should hold their first regular meeting the following day. After talking with several of them individually Wilson returned to the White House, where he found Dr. Cary T. Grayson taking care of a cut on his sister's forehead.

Grayson had been a naval officer assigned as one of Taft's medical advisers and he had met Wilson two days before at a tea given by Taft. He had thought Wilson extremely courteous but "rather formal and cautious" until Taft said his daughter Helen was a student at Bryn Mawr. Wilson then told stories of happenings while he had been teaching there and just before the party ended Taft put his arm around Grayson's shoulder and said to his successor in office, "Mr. Wilson, here is an excellent fellow that I hope you will get to know. I regret to say that he is a Democrat and a Virginian but that is a matter that can't be helped." Wilson did get to know him better very quickly and soon asked to have him appointed as his medical adviser. An intimacy gradually developed which grew into one of the closest and most lasting relationships of Wilson's life. Grayson remained with him to the end.

That afternoon Wilson received more than one thousand visitors. Then he took Mrs. Wilson and his old friend Fred Yates for a short automobile drive around the Washington monument. Crowds were cheering everywhere. Mrs Wilson and her daughters were soon serving tea to thirty guests while the President attended conferences. McCombs was disgruntled over not being invited to join the Cabinet and wanted a statement to "set him right with the country." After dinner for twenty-five Wilson relatives the new executive retired to his private study on the floor above, to his own typewriter and his problems.

In his Cabinet Wilson included almost no distinguished men, probably because he expected to make his own decisions, although it is true that the Democrats had been out of power so long that they had few men of wide experiences in national affairs. In the the case of Bryan, the new President was bound to take into account past services both to himself and the the party. But even though he did not obtain men of great ability, those whom he appointed were not mere political hacks or corporation lawyers, but public servants whom Wilson believed fitted for their posts.

Besides selecting those sufficiently qualified Wilson was inclined to favor men of progressive leanings from the agricultural South and West since he was determined to shift the real control of the government into those areas and away from the conservative, urban, industrial East, asserting that he was seeking "the best men in the Nation" for each post. Wilson failed to announce his selections until almost the date of the inauguration itself.

First of all it was necessary to decide about Bryan, whom Wilson liked and admired, but whose spontaneous exuberance might prove embarrassing. He had to be provided for first of all, since he had

141

been the Democratic leader for sixteen years. Also, Wilson must have realized that, as Mr. Dooley wisely remarked, he would do better to have Bryan "in his bosom than on his back." Because he feared the Nebraskan's rashness as well as his inexperience in diplomacy, Wilson suggested that he go abroad as an ambassador rather than become secretary of State; but Bryan told Carter Glass that he did "not intend to get that far away from Washington." "The Great Commoner" accepted the State Department post as soon as it was offered to him, on December 21. Taking much pride in his new office, Bryan immediately began sending in recommendations of names for different members of the Cabinet and other offices, all of them deserving Democrats.

Even before he left Bermuda, Wilson had decided upon McAdoo for Treasury. McAdoo had been a great support in the campaign, knew the ways of business, and any criticism of him as a mere "promoter" was disregarded by Wilson. McCombs had wanted this office; the evening of the election he hobbled into Colonel House's room at the Waldorf Astoria to remark, "If I cannot be secretary of the Treasury I will take nothing." But he was incapable of working with others and soon after the election Wilson told his family in private that he did not regard McCombs as Cabinet material. When offered the post of ambassador to France McCombs hesitated and sent contradictory messages, but finally refused it.

Josephus Daniels, selected as secretary of the Navy, was a North Carolina newspaperman who had supported Bryan ever since 1896 and had prevented the "Peerless Leader" from breaking with Wilson over the "cocked-hat" episode, but he knew little of naval affairs. Albert S. Burleson was selected to be postmaster general as a "thorough-going politician" who knew most members of Congress intimately, having served in that body for eight terms. Colonel House refused any office, a stand which increased Wilson's confidence in his integrity more than ever. David F. Houston, chancellor of Washington University in St. Louis, and a well-known economist, was chosen for Agriculture. James Clark McReynolds, who had prosecuted the tobacco and coal trusts as special counsel for the government, became attorney general. Franklin K. Lane, chairman of the Interstate Commerce Commission, was chosen secretary of the Interior, largely because he wrote a letter recommending another for that office which showed an intimate knowledge of the problems and business of the department. A. Mitchell Palmer declined the War portfolio because he was a Quaker, so that Lindley M. Garrison, a New Jersey judge, was given that office over his well-founded protests that he was "temperamentally unfitted for the post." William F. Redfield, a manufacturer and former member of Congress who believed in a low tariff, was given the Commerce Department, while William B. Wilson, a former miner who had become a union leader and prominent Democrat in Pennsylvania, was appointed to the new post of Labor. Wilson also decided to retain the faithful Tumulty as his secretary, actually the most important post of all. Except for Bryan the men selected were almost unknown; and only McReynolds, Lane and William B. Wilson had experience which seemed to fit them for the work they were called upon to direct. The expectation was that the President would make his own policies in any event.

At the first official Cabinet meeting on Thursday Wilson established the practice of calling upon the members in turn. The ten men sat around a table in a small room and talked freely together about the affairs of the day. There was no formality or pomp; it semed rather like a group of friends with common interests meeting together under one whom they recognized as their chief. Franklin K. Lane, Secretary of the Interior, wrote of Wilson a few days later, "He is the most sympathetic, cordial and considerate presiding officer that can be imagined. And he sees so clearly. He has no fog in his brain."

The following Sunday Dr. Grayson told the President he must stay in bed for the day to get some rest. Wilson obeyed these orders although with the protest, "You are forcing me to set a bad example to the American people in not going to church." The next day he returned to his desk and sought to find "the best men in the nation" for other important appointments. After trying to get ex-President

Eliot of Harvard and Richard Olney of Boston for ambassador to Britain he chose Walter H. Page, his friend from the old days in Atlanta, who also had the support of Colonel House. When Page later felt he must resign because of the expenses of the office, Wilson wrote Cleveland Dodge of Princeton who willingly put up the needed funds. When Dean Fine of Princeton refused the German post, Wilson gave it to a Tammany man, James W. Gerard; and the President later discovered that those trained in public life were frequently better qualified for office than the inexperienced "good man." In fact the poor information service during World War I was partly due to lack of experience among those in responsible posts, but Wilson was perhaps misled by the thought that he did not want men who had the material interests of individuals in mind instead of the public and moral considerations which he thought ought to control.

At first he demanded to see the entire list of postmasters, intending to go over it name by name. But Burleson assured him that only good, honest men would be appointed, that it did not "amount to a damn who is postmaster at Paducah, Kentucky. But these little offices mean a great deal to the senators and representatives in Congress." He said if the President turns them down "it means that that member has got bitter trouble at home." The result was that before long when Burleson brought him a list of appointments Wilson would smilingly ask, "Where do I sign?" Later when Burleson was subjected to a burst of violent criticism Wilson stood by him most loyally. But under no circumstances would he appoint any of his own relatives, even turning down his brother, who had been well recommended, as postmaster of Nashville. He did nominate Thomas D. Jones, his old friend and supporter among the Princeton trustees, to the Federal Reserve Board, but the Senate distrusted the appointee's connection with the International Harvester Company. He gave a place on the federal bench to Charles A. Woods of South Carolina whom he had met on a voyage to England in 1896 and whom he had left with the joking understanding that when he became President, Woods would be appointed judge. But soon larger problems than mere appointments were demanding action.

When Wilson went into the White House his purpose was to give more power, economic and political, to the people. He wished to improve their standard of living. When problems arose and he faced opposition, his spontaneous appeal was to the people, he relied upon them for support. He intended to put an end to the supremacy of the great corporations and financial institutions over the economic life of the nation, a supremacy which had been maintained ever since the close of the Civil War. As a result of his study of government he believed that he knew how this could be done as well as how to persuade Congress to pass the legislation he wanted.

In his *Constitutional Government* Wilson had, in 1908, presented the theory that the President's "office is anything that he has the sagacity and force to make it." He wanted to push his reform bills through Congress without their being held up by lobbyists or by committees filled according to the seniority principle. A letter to Congressman A. Mitchell Palmer not long before his inauguration stated that a president should be "the leader of his party," a prime minister "concerned with the guidance of legislation" as well as the orderly execution of the law, and also be the spokesman of the nation.

The new President often asked members of his Cabinet to draft legislation which he desired, and if there seemed danger that this would be held up, he was always ready with a message to Congress to speed it on its way. These messages quickly reached the people through the newspapers and if they were especially important he delivered them in person, as had been done by the earliest Presidents. He asked congressmen to think of him not as "a department of government hailing Congress from some isolated island of jealous power," but as "a person . . . trying to cooperate with other human beings in a common service." And Postmaster General Burleson was able to get enough jobs, campaign contributions and other favors to keep the legislators fighting for the President. A group of about thirty young Democrats, which included Franklin D. Roosevelt and Joseph E. Davies, helped to exert pressure when needed. Wilson

145

also started the system of press conferences with talks "off the record" to present his ideas to the people. It has been said that he was able to put through legislation by the combined use of Jefferson's power of persuasion, Jackson's boldness and Theodore Roosevelt's publicity, because he knew how much each of these weapons counted.

"It would be the irony of fate if my administration had to deal chiefly with foreign affairs," said Wilson to E. G. Conklin of Princeton University just before he became President; for his life had been devoted to the study of history and the internal problems of government with almost no attention to the relationship between nations or the difficulties of a nation at war. Yet for several months after taking office his principal activities concerned the affairs of foreign countries. Questions were arising in Asia and Central America, so that he had to deal with unexpected events in Mexico, China, Japan, Panama and Nicaragua. The actions he took were swift and decisive, their results were surprising. They amounted to the abandonment of "Dollar Diplomacy" as it had been practiced by his predecessors.

Almost at once, he made his position clear. His first statement on Mexico was put forth a week after his inauguration and that on China just one week later. Nor were they routine pronouncements. In both cases they announced a complete change of policy from that established in previous plans of the State Department, with the consequence that both bureaucrats and diplomats were displeased and highly critical.

Wilson's idea was to restore moral principles as a guide for his program, which became known as the "New Freedom." At home he wanted to resist the influence of big business upon tariff policy, the control of credit, and exploitation of our natural resources. He was prepared to support the West and South in their revolt against the power of the private interests which controlled the railroads, banks and industries of the country. Now he found that these same great combinations of capital were seeking to dominate the foreign policy of the United States.

146

Trouble was brewing in several parts of Latin America. President Madero of Mexico had been overthrown by Huerta's soldiers and then murdered while in their custody, only two weeks before Wilson's inauguration. When Ambassador Henry Lane Wilson recommended to Taft that he recognize the new administration, all those with financial interests in Mexico strongly concurred. But Taft felt that Wilson should deal with this problem from the start since future decisions would have to be made by him.

At the same time the Republic of Colombia refused to recognize the United States' rights to the isthmus upon which the Panama Canal had been built or to acknowledge satisfaction with a suggested settlement of her claims. The "Giant of the North" was also seeking rights over another canal route in Nicaragua under conditions which would constitute almost a protectorate over that country. Meanwhile England was arguing over the right of other nations to use the existing canal on equal terms with the United States.

After the Cabinet meeting of March 7 had been devoted chiefly to the Latin American problems Wilson appeared on the eleventh with his own typewritten copy of a proposed announcement. This began by stating that one of the chief objects of the administration would be "to cultivate the friendship and deserve the confidence of our sister republics of Central and South America." He went on to say that "cooperation was possible only when supported at every turn by orderly processes of just government based upon law, not upon arbitrary or irregular force." In closing he promised that the United States had "nothing to seek in Central and South America except lasting interests of the peoples," and that he would not interfere with their rights or liberties. But for that very reason he would refuse to recognize Huerta, who had obtained the presidency of Mexico by force and assassination.

Several members of the Cabinet objected that such a declaration would be hasty and that it was not in accord with the usual processes of diplomacy, for Wilson had not consulted his own experts. But the President expressed a feeling that "agitators in certain countries wanted revolutions and . . . he was not going to let them have one if he could prevent it." When he went ahead and gave the statement to the press the next morning, the resulting newspaper comment was almost unanimously enthusiastic. The result of this action was to give him immediately increased prestige both at home and abroad.

The "Six Power Loan" to China next required his attention. Two partners of J. P. Morgan and Company had called on Bryan to ask if the policy of the Taft administration on this subject was to be continued. Byran brought up the question at Cabinet meetings on March 14 and 18, when he declared that the provisions of the loan authorized foreign intervention in the Chinese fiscal administration and even the use of force for collection. That afternoon Wilson gave a statement to the press that the conditions of the loan would "touch very nearly the administrative independence of China itself" and that the result might be a "forcible interference . . . obnoxious to the principles upon which the government of our people rests." He ended by saying that his government would continue to uphold the Open Door, "the only door we care to enter" and we would not employ force to collect this loan.

The popular reaction to this pronouncement was also one of approbation and when the American bankers made the announcement of their withdrawal from the loan it was greeted as a "knockout for Wall Street." The attitude of the Chinese government was shown by its minister, who came to tell of his gratitude, while the Japanese ambassador protested against the message. Six weeks later Wilson welcomed "the new China, thus entering into the family of nations."

Wilson had gone forward vigorously with blows against evils as he saw it, in the same way that he had begun his administration in Princeton and New Jersey. He had rejected cooperation with the other powers when he did not approve their purposes, but he was disappointed because the new government in China did not prove as democratic as he hoped. When faced with armed revolt, President Yuan did not hesitate to resort to high-handed measures which were likened by Bryan to Huerta's methods accompanied by the same justification. So China was one of the first places where Wilson's desire to assist political development in other countries led him into trouble.

This effort to follow moral principles was the keystone of his policies as a President. He approved sending delegates to a world congress for the control of opium in April, indicating by his action that he was not opposed to international cooperation in general. The country liked that, while his action on the Chinese loan by its very boldness and vigor had again shown his determination to make his own policies.

The arguments which arose with Japan were more complicated than those with Mexico or China because they involved the sovereign rights of California and Washington. These states were preparing to pass laws prohibiting the ownership of land by Japanese immigrants, a situation which was explained to Wilson on the day after his inauguration by Ambassador Chinda, but since the federal government was entrusted by the Constitution with control over foreign problems, here was a threatened conflict of authority. Wilson wanted to mollify Japan while at the same time respecting the rights of states to pass any legislation they saw fit with respect to domestic matters.

After Chinda's protest, Wilson went over the question with Bryan, who then wrote a letter to the governor of the State of Washington urging that the ownership of land be made dependent upon something other than race. Since California presented a more immediate problem Wilson got in touch with Senator Works and Congressman Kent of that state, as well as James Phelan, former mayor of San Francisco. When this move brought no results, Wilson sent personal telegrams to Governor Johnson of California and the presiding officers of its Senate and House urging that land ownership might be sufficiently restricted by a mere provision excluding "all aliens who have not declared their intention to become citizens," since the Orientals could not make any such declaration. But the Californians remained set upon pushing through legislation as originally proposed even though Bryan went out there to make a personal appeal to the legislators. The law passed by both houses put the prohibition in definite words limiting the ownership of real property by aliens to those "eligible to citizenship," which eliminated the Japanese.

Ambassador Chinda entered an immediate protest in terms so forceful that the Cabinet agreed "It would be unwise to publish the statement as it would inflame the public." A far more moderate protest came before the Cabinet on May 13, but Governor Johnson telegraphed he could not veto the bill since it did not transgress treaty obligations. Even with the possibility of war Wilson declined to take the aggressive step of ordering a concentration of naval forces at Manila, and when Bryan continued discussions with Chinda, who asked him if the American reply was to be final Bryan's answer was an excellent example of his attitude, "There is nothing final between friends."

Bryan's obvious good will created a friendly atmosphere even in the face of bitterness on the part of Japan. He was like Wilson in desiring large arrangements for maintaining world peace. Both were of Scotch-Irish descent, so imbued with the doctrines of Calvinism as to be Presbyterian elders. Bryan's sincerity as well as the similarity of their fundamental beliefs in old-fashioned ideas of morality held them together, so that subsequently Wilson stood by Bryan when he was subjected to jibes and ridicule. On April 24 they gave the representatives of foreign countries in Washington a plan called "President Wilson's Peace Proposal." The suggestion was that "all questions in dispute, which diplomacy should fail to adjust, should be submitted to an international commission." The idea was that if nations would investigate for a year they would not fight. Britain declared itself willing to sign such a treaty the following January and a total of thirty nations signed within a single year. But Germany refused to consider committing herself, since to sign up would deprive her of the advantages of her military preparedness.

These strong new measures show that Wilson lost no time in taking a firm stand in foreign affairs. He said this country would not recognize governments that came into power by force and assassination. He would not interfere with the internal affairs of other nations merely to protect the interests of American investors and businessmen. He said that good will and friendly negotiations among nations were to be encouraged wherever possible. But with the best possible intentions his judgment was occasionally at fault, and some of his policies were not liked, even by those he wanted to help.

CHAPTER XII

TARIFF AND THE FEDERAL RESERVE SYSTEM

The issues upon which Wilson had made his campaign dealt, not with foreign affairs but with the tariff, the national currency and the trusts. It was primarily for the purpose of reducing the tariff and reforming the banking system to give a more elastic currency that he called for a special session of Congress, to assemble a few weeks after his inauguration.

The need for tariff revision had impressed itself upon him in early manhood. At Princeton he had upheld the view of many Southerners that a tariff which protected the industries of the North so that they could raise the price of their products was unfair to the agricultural South. His oration on John Bright while at the University of Virginia Law School expressed admiration for Cobden and Bright as the leaders of the movement for free trade in Britain. Two years later in Atlanta he had told the tariff commission at a public hearing that he advocated the repeal "of all protective tariff laws" while establishing "a tariff for revenue merely." He continued making speeches on the tariff at various times while he was a professor; and in December 1908 he expressed his dissatisfaction with the existing system by asserting that "The old formula 'tariff for revenue only' has a barren sound to our ears in existing circumstances, because the tariff as we know it is not a system of taxation; it is rather a vast body of economic expedients which have been used under the guise of taxation, for the purpose of building up various industries."

He felt the Payne-Aldrich tariff was a means of granting favors at the expense of the country as a whole.

When he became President, Wilson did not attempt to have all existing tariff protection suddenly withdrawn, "but steadily and upon a fixed programme, upon which every man of business can base his definite forecasts and systematic plans." He wanted to cut down the import duties on over nine hundred articles with special attention to food and clothes. Even before he took office he talked the problem over with Redfield and McReynolds of his Cabinet as well as Oscar Underwood, chairman of the House Ways and Means Committee. He tried to win over the old Democratic leaders like Senator Simmons of North Carolina, who had voted for the high schedules so that his state should get her share and he finally succeeded in persuading this natural choice for chairman of the Finance Committee to support general downward revision.

Wilson set out to persuade congressmen that they were his "colleagues" and that he should have a part in the making of laws. When he broke the precedent of a century by addressing Congress in person both the floor and galleries were crowded with intent listeners, a scene quite different from the empty seats of other days. He said he wanted to show "that the President is a human being trying to co-operate with other human beings in a common service." He asserted that it was "clear to the whole country that tariff duties must be altered" and that we must "put our businessmen and procedures under the stimulation of a constant necessity to be efficient, economical and enterprising, masters of competitive supremacy." When Mrs. Wilson, on the drive home, said that addressing Congress in person was the kind of thing Theodore Roosevelt would have liked to do if he had only thought of it, Wilson laughed and said, "Yes, I think I put one over on Teddy."

The next day he went to a conference with the Senate Finance Committee, breaking another precedent which had held since the time of Lincoln. After a discussion of the problems connected with tariff reduction he told the newsmen, "It is something I hope the senators will permit me to do often. The net result of our conference is that I am sure we will have no difficulty in keeping together on the tariff." Since it was in the Senate that the bill was to encounter its greatest difficulties this co-operation was of great importance. At the same time he had many capable men to help him in the House, with Cordell Hull in charge of drafting the new income tax provisions of the bill.

Radical reductions in the rates on wool and sugar were among the points Wilson seemed to relish fighting for, even coming to a "death grapple with the sugar people" as Secretary Houston put it. Nor did he demand all the credit for himself; when Underwood's work was emphasized Wilson wrote Glass, "If Mr. Underwood or anybody else can displace me by the work they do in the service of the country, they are fully entitled to do so," but it is unlikely that he thought they would. With the help of a Democratic caucus vote in its favor the bill passed the House on May 8, but four months of struggle were still before it in the Senate, where the Democrats had a majority of only three.

Even before the tariff bill was introduced Wilson and his supporters had tried to obtain a caucus of Democratic senators to discuss it, but this proved impossible because all sorts of changes in individual schedules were demanded by such senators as Stone of Missouri, Newlands of Colorado and those from the sugar-producing states. "Lobbyists, and particularly sugar lobbyists were everywhere," reported Houston. "It was impossible to move around without bumping into them—at hotels, clubs and even private houses." Wilson came out with a public statement on May 26 saying that "The newspapers are being filled with paid advertisements calculated to mislead the judgment of public men not only, but also the public opinion of the country itself." This statement held the Democratic senators in line because they did not want to be known as submitting to pressure and it probably saved the bill from mutilation or defeat. Finally on July 7 a caucus declared the tariff bill to be a party measure, while about the same time the newspapers recognized that "one thing is certain,—lobbying in the old sense has been made henceforth impossible in Washington."

Duties were reduced on over nine hundred articles, with iron ore, steel rails, rough lumber, and raw wool placed on the free list. Sugar rates were cut twenty-five percent and were to be removed altogether by May 1916. In a little speech after signing the bill Wilson said, "I have had the accomplishment of something like this at heart ever since I was a boy, and I know men standing around me who can say the same thing."

Next Wilson turned to the problem of giving the nation an elastic currency. He spoke of this as "the second step in setting the business of this country free." Some new system was badly needed. At times money was scarce, as when grain and cattle poured into the Atlantic states from the West and the necessary payments drained away the money supply. At other times its overabundance led to speculation in stocks and commodities, as well as perhaps to overexpansion of industrial plants and products. Wilson felt there should be some way to adjust the money supply to the shifting needs of the country at different times, so that the supply should not be dependent solely upon the size of the national debt.

The question of how this could be remedied was not a simple one. Nor was it one which Congress might be willingly moved to consider all through the hot weeks of summer and on through the autumn. There was no consensus of Democratic opinion nor real understanding at first, such as had existed in regard to the tariff. The problem was recondite, complicated and of long standing. The Populist movement in the West had raised the question thirty years before and Bryan had campaigned in 1896 principally upon the issue of free silver, which indicated that the evils of a static and inelastic currency had long been recognized. In 1897 Wilson had written in the *Atlantic Monthly*, "Nothing but currency reform can touch the cause of the present discontents," while ten years later the "money panic" of 1907 gave many businessmen much distress. It was the fifth time since the Civil War that such a shortage of money had led to panics and business failures, often in periods of prosperity. The bankers wanted a change, but a change to a system where they might control, to which Bryan and the Westerners would never consent. A Gold Standard Act had been passed in 1900 as well as the Aldrich-Vreeland Act in 1908, but neither of them presented any adequate solution of the problem. Moreover, Wilson pointed out to a group of New Jersey bankers in 1910 that "a combination of banks in the City of New York now practically exercises all the powers of a central bank except the power of issue."

In 1911 when a monetary commission report led to the Aldrich plan for a central bank, Wilson pointed out in June of that year that "control of credit . . . is dangerously concentrated in this country," that it was under "the direction and domination of small groups of capitalists who wish to keep the economic development of the country under their own eye and guidance. The great monopoly is the money monopoly." He went on to say that because our system of credit was concentrated in the hands of a few men they could largely control the country's growth and activities, while their own interest was necesarily concentrated on the great undertakings in which their own money was involved. At the same time he recognized that "No man can in a moment put great policies together and reconstruct a whole order of life." And he deplored "reckless attacks" upon the financial system, such as might result from the easy panaceas suggested by some Democrats.

The Democratic platform of 1912 had made no specific pledge bearing upon what should be done but it did assert disapproval of the Aldrich bill and of a central bank. The Democrats had control of House of Representatives even before Wilson's election and early in 1912 they had passed a resolution calling for an investigation of the "money trust." To implement this the Banking and Currency Committee divided itself into one subcommittee to investigate banking abuses and another to draft currency legislation, the second being placed under the guidance of Carter Glass of Virginia. Wilson wrote Glass after the election that he wished "to devote the most serious and immediate attention" to the banking and currency problem.

He also revised passages in *The New Freedom* on currency reform just as it was going to press. This excellent little book was a compilation of his most stimulating campaign speeches, arranged by William Bayard Hale. On page 15 he said: "American industry is not free, as once it was free; American enterprise is not free; the man with only a little capital is finding it harder to get into the field, more and more impossible to compete with the big fellow." And he went on, "The larger kinds of credit are more and more difficult to obtain, unless you obtain them upon the terms of uniting your efforts with those who already control the industries of the country." He felt that any man who tried to set himself up in competition with big business would "presently find himself either squeezed out, or obliged to sell and allow himself to be absorbed." This condition could be ameliorated by anti-trust laws and by an elastic currency under the control of a government board. Federal banks could help small banks provide capital to build up new enterprises which showed promise.

Glass and H. Parker Willis, who was the technical expert of the Banking Committee, called on Wilson in Princeton the day after Christmas, 1912, to discuss the form of the proposed legislation. Glass was stringy and alert, red-headed and excitable, the editor of a small city newspaper, who had been in Congress for ten years. Wilson was propped up on pillows in bed with a bad cold but they talked for two hours. Glass brought with him a plan for setting up regional reserve banks which could extend credit when needed, the whole organization to be under the comptroller of the Currency. Wilson felt they were "far on the right track" but made several shrewd suggestions. Of these the one of greatest importance was that the head of the proposed system should be not the Comptroller of the Currency but "a separate central board." This board with the power to supervise the system could be altruistic. It could see that the money created was used to encourage small business.

The meeting enabled Wilson and Glass to understand and trust one another, so that the President told Glass to proceed with the plan which had been outlined. But even before this, opposition to any proposal which would differ from the Aldrich bill had showed itself. The American Bankers Association had already endorsed the

157

Aldrich bill and the Eastern bankers tried to prevent Glass from being made chairman of the Currency Committee in order to head off any new project. But when Glass went to the governor's office in Trenton on January 30 with a more detailed draft of the proposed legislation Wilson discussed it with "real zest" and with "such a clear comprehension of the problems" that Glass reported himself, in spite of his special knowledge of the problem, as "rather wary of venturing beyond my depth." Wilson promised complete support both for the measure and for the appointment of Glass as chairman of the Currency Committee, since he would be the best qualified leader to fight for the legislation they had drafted.

This legislation undertook to set up the Federal Reserve Banking System, with twelve great banks in different parts of the nation. All national banks were to be members of the system while trust companies and state banks also had the privilege of joining. The entire system to be under the supervision of a Federal Reserve Board at Washington, which had been Wilson's contribution to the actual plan. But Wilson's principal work lay in the job of getting the measure adopted by Congress.

The plan proposed that the Treasury Department could deposit funds in the Reserve Banks when it saw fit, while the member banks were required to keep a certain percentage of their cash reserves on deposit there at all times. The most important provisions were those allowing the Reserve Banks to issue currency as loans to the member banks with the notes of their customers or other acceptable pledges as security. This arrangement would provide a currency "elastically responsive to sound credit," which would help the small businessman to obtain larger loans than little local banks could offer and to do this without being dependent for help upon the great banking houses of Wall Street.

The fight began as soon as information about the provisions of the proposed bill leaked out. First came the attack from the large financial houses of the East, but this was followed later by the objections of Bryan and the radical thinkers of the West. Paul M. Warburg, whom Glass called "the intensest, the most agile and the best trained" leader of the New York bankers, immediately wrote a critical study and advocated a "single central bank of banks." As soon as the bill was printed, its provisions became known all over the country. Senator Owen of Oklahoma, chairman of the Senate Finance Committee, shared Bryan's feeling that the bill gave too much power to the great bankers while the Easterners felt that it did not give them enough. The battle over these questions was to continue for six strenuous months.

It was obviously necessary that the bill should be worked out until its provisions were acceptable to Wilson's own party before it was presented to Congress. This was done in May and early June, which was the time when Wilson was also confronted with a bitter fight on the wool and sugar schedules of the tariff bill. He appeared to be "relentless" and "cold as steel," but he himself felt the need of sympathy and understanding, so that he turned not only to his family but to friends such as Mrs. Mary Hulbert and Colonel House.

McAdoo was so full of energy that as secretary of the Treasury he felt that he should set forth his personal views; he even prepared an outline bill of his own which he believed would pacify some of the opposition. But he showed no "sign of resentment or even of disappointment" when his proposal was rejected by the President, remaining a strong supporter and enthusiastic adherent of Wilson's plan throughout the fight. And while the mere suggestion of the more radical proposal in McAdoo's outline persuaded many of the conservatives that they had better support the administration measure, its recommendations stirred up the Bryan following all the more.

It seemed possible that Bryan would actually come out against the measure. He and Senator Owen insisted that the entire governing board shoud be appointed by the President, while Glass and McAdoo wanted to have some of the members chosen by the bankers themselves. Wilson decided that it must be solely a government board, resting his decision upon the general principle that supremacy must rest with the government and not with any private interests.

But Glass was not satisfied and neither were the bankers, so that

Glass agreed to head a delegation to the White House "to convince the President that he was wrong." This was a reasonably liberal group from the Midwest, with James B. Forgan of Chicago and Festus J. Wade of St. Louis among its leaders. These two began by attempting to be authoritative and masterful. After they had all given their reasons, Wilson, facing these two in particular, asked, "Will one of you gentlemen tell me in what civilized country of the earth there are important government boards of control on which private interests are represented?" After a minute or two of unbroken silence Wilson continued: "Which of you gentlemen thinks the railroads should select members of the Interstate Commerce Commission?" When no one could answer either question, the discussion that remained referred to minor points of the bill.

Wilson also came out for the proposition that Federal Reserve notes should be "obligations of the United States." This had been one of the principal demands of the Bryan group, but Glass was astounded to hear the President come out in favor of it. After Glass had told all the objections, he said how unnecessary it was because there was already so much security behind the Federal Reserve notes. This security consisted of the liability of the private bank together with the double liability of its stockholders, as well as the security which it had received for its original loan, the gold reserve and the liability of the regional banks, the right to refuse any loan and the power to decline to issue notes. He ended by saying, "There is not in truth any government obligation here, Mr. President, it would be a pretense on its face. . . . The suggested government obligation is so remote it could never be discerned." Wilson knew all this, but since he wanted Bryan's support he explained: "Exactly so. Every word you say is true, the government liability *is* a mere thought. And so, if we can hold to the substance of the thing and give the other fellow the shadow, why not do it, if thereby we may save our bill?"

After this decision Bryan came out sincerely in favor of the measure, and he made a statement to the press supporting it on June 23, the same day that Glass was finally made chairman of the

Senate Committee on Banking and Currency. Bryan spoke of the "wise, steady, unrelenting leadership of the President;" while Wilson invited the members of the Currency Committee to the White House for a conference. He presented his ideas on currency reform to Congress that same day, saying: "We should give the businessmen of this country a banking and currency system by which they can make use of the freedom of enterprise and individual initiative which we are about to bestow on them." He asserted that as soon as the tariff reduction was passed, business would have an opportunity for expansion and that this would require larger resources of credit than those then in existence. He felt that these resources should be available to all business upon an equal basis.

The fight in Congress started when the bill was introduced into both houses three days later. Wilson had won Bryan over to the support of the bill, but not all of his followers. In his effort to win them over Wilson resorted to both reason and persuasion. He invited the dissatisfied leaders to conferences at the White House and when Glass became so desperate at the opposition that he threatened to resign, Wilson urged, "Damn it, don't resign, old fellow, outvote them." Bryan gave Wilson strong support, writing to Glass : "I am with him in all the details. If my opinion has influence with anyone . . . I advise him to stand by the President." With this help, a caucus on August 28 made the bill a party measure.

Meanwhile Wilson's family had gone off for the summer to the home of the novelist Winston Churchill in Cornish, New Hampshire, "almost at my command" as he put it. He writes of his loneliness without them, although Dr. Grayson and Tumulty were both with him and he played golf every afternoon to get his mind off troublesome affairs. He was glad to find his leadership "most loyally and graciously accepted," and expressed the hope that this was partly because men recognized that he had "no private and selfish purposes" of his own. When his daughter Jessie became engaged to Francis B. Sayre he found his prospective son-in-law highly satisfactory, and when he went to church in a white linen suit he records that he "created a mild sensation"; adding gaily, "but that of course is what every public man wishes to do, at church or anywhere else." Meanwhile the dramatist Percy MacKaye in a talk with the President at Cornish found in him what seemed to be an ambition to "create a renaissance in America."

Members of the House felt themselves bound by the party caucus and passed the bill on September 18. But the Senators were more conservative and were subjected to a more powerful lobby and in consequence they consented to hear what the bankers on the other side had to say. Everyone was worn down by the heat of the summer and the struggle over the tariff bill; so that the opposition hoped that more obstruction and delay would cause a weary Senate to drop the matter. The bill was condemned by the American Bankers Association, the United States Chamber of Commerce and many local organizations; it was also bitterly attacked by what Representative Stephans called "the subsidized press of the country" and the "propaganda of the money trust."

Congress on its part felt a strong urge toward a "much-needed vacation," but Wilson told the Democratic Steering Committee of the Senate that he was opposed to any adjournment for more than three days at a time. Although he was called a "dictator in the White House," his own view was that "They are using me; I am not driving them." He felt that the Senate had to be "led and stimulated," which seemed to him so unwarranted that he feared he would "lose his patience and suffer the weakness of exasperation." But in spite of his attempts to pacify its members, such prominent senators as Reed of Missouri, Hitchcock of Nebraska, and O'Gorman of New York were so restive under his leadership that about the middle of October the bill appeared to be in real danger of rejection. The strain was telling on the President so much that a friend wrote Colonel House that he "was shocked to see him looking so wan. The change since January last is terribly marked."

But during the third week of October Wilson's personal discussions with senators suddenly began to have a beneficial effect so that both O'Gorman and Reed came out with interviews favoring the bill. Bryan, McAdoo and House were also doing their best to help it. Although Frank A. Vanderlip of the National City Bank of New York presented to the Senate committee an entirely new bill on behalf of the Eastern bankers, Festus J. Wade and most of those from the West came out in support of the President's measure. The November elections went strongly in Wilson's favor, greatly increasing his prestige; and while the unusual maneuver of a Senate caucus was unable definitely to commit the entire party to the bill, it did decide that there should be no Christmas holidays for that body unless the bill was passed by December 24.

The final attack came from Republican Senators led by Root and Lodge, who set out many reasons for their opposition. Then many amendments had to be dealt with and defeated, while another attempt at delay was overturned by the decisive stand taken by the President. On December 19 the bill passed, 54 to 34, with every Democrat supporting it, and after brief conferences between the two houses it went to Wilson for his signature four days later. He made quite a little ceremony of signing it using four gold pens and jokingly saying that he was "drawing on the gold reserve." He then presented pens to Glass, Owen, and McAdoo with a little speech.

As soon as the new system could be set up, banks, large and small, came into line and were quick to assert their willingness to join. These included many state banks which were not required to do so. Secretary Houston expressed the feeling of the country when he wrote Wilson four days after Christmas that it was "the first clear-cut piece of currency legislation we have had." He went on to quote a director of the First National Bank of Boston as saying that "sentiment in Boston had absolutely altered." Ten years later the *New York Times* epitomized the opinion of the nation toward the act by saying "without it the United States might have been swept along with Europe into depreciated paper money" in the war years, going on to point out that its passage was accomplished only by "powerful and unyielding pressure from the White House."

When even Republicans tried to take credit for the measure as only an outgrowth of the "Aldrich plan," Wilson consistently pointed out that "the heart of the Aldrich plan was a single central bank. . . whereas the heart of our system is. . . a body appointed by and responsible to the government." He had put through a system of currency which was elastic and could be controlled by the government. This currency could constantly be made to conform to the legitimate needs of business. This achievement, together with the reductions in the tariff which he had engineered, was an effort to curb the privileges and powers of big business and Wall Street. He felt that well-protected industries would no longer get rich at the expense of the rest of the country and new enterprises could now get the money which they required to grow.

CHAPTER XIII

MEDDLING
IN MEXICO

The next problem which Wilson had to face arose in Mexico. So once again he was swept away from dealing with the domestic reforms which he had at heart and forced to pay particular attention to foreign affairs. Here he was confused and never quite seemed to make up his mind whether to stay out of internal Mexican affairs or to intervene.

But before those matters became urgent he had three weeks of rest and recreation starting just before Christmas 1913. He spent these weeks of triumphant satisfaction at Pass Christian on the Gulf of Mexico and they were perhaps the happiest of his life. His most important internal reforms had been adopted largely because the impetus of his initial attack had carried all before it, just as it had done at Princeton. But he did have some other reforms in mind, measures which were important and logical enough in his own reasoning but which were not grasped nor appreciated by the public at large. Next upon his own agenda was an anti-trust campaign for which he was even then preparing a speech to Congress.

An extraordinary willingness to accept his leadership for the moment seemed evident upon all sides. Taft generously said he rejoiced to see the party in power "fulfilling its promises," while a British journalist asserted that Wilson's prestige "stood at a higher point than any President has reached in our time." Thomas Fortune

Ryan stated that "the whole country is proud of President Wilson," while even a violent Progressive Party newspaper recognized that he had "exhibited a capacity for leadership" which "had not generally been considered possible." But this was the peak; and never again in peacetime was he to receive such universal acceptance and praise.

Wilson himself wrote one of his friends that he wished he could believe that his administration was "reviving the optimism and ideals of other men as it has been fortunate enough to revive yours." He went on to say that "the heart of the country is so sound and its sense of justice so clear" that he felt as though he could see "the light that shines upon the road ahead of us." His relations with Congress and his Cabinet were altogether friendly, Bryan was happy with his peace treaties, Lane was making plans to develop Alaska while McAdoo and Houston were working out the organization of the new Federal Reserve System.

At Pass Christian all the President's family were in good health. When they came back to Washington January 12, 1914, he was looking better than in several months with a fresh elasticity in his step and a ruddy glow in his complexion. Ellen Wilson also came back with what appeared to be new strength as well as an active interest in all her husband's activities. But things changed very quickly. Conditions in Mexico got rapidly worse. At the same time there were questions about a revolution in Haiti and what should be done about the tolls on the Panama Canal. Perhaps it was worry over these matters that caused Ellen Wilson to fall in her room on March first, struck down by some malady from which she never completely recovered.

The Mexican crisis had been building up for a long time, ever since Wilson's inauguration. From the moment when Huerta seized the supreme power by force, at the same time seeing to it that the former president Madero, who had been trying to introduce some economic reforms, was assassinated, large mining interests had been urging Wilson to recognize Huerta's government so that business could proceed as usual. But most American newspapers expressed dissatisfaction with the explanations of the murder put forward by Huerta, while many Mexicans were suspicious and ready to rise in rebellion against the new regime. Wilson said he desired to look out for the welfare of the Mexican people rather than American interests in metals and oil. He said, "My passion is for the submerged 85 per cent of the people of the Republic who are now struggling toward liberty." In fighting for them he got himself into trouble. On March 11, 1913, Wilson had announced that co-operation with Mexico was "possible only when supported at every turn by the orderly processes of government based upon law, not upon arbitrary or irregular force." By the end of the month a revolution by a party of men calling themselves the "Constitutionalists" and headed by Carranza, governor of the state of Coahuila in northern Mexico, had broken out against the Huerta administration. The European countries had quickly recognized Huerta largely because they felt this would help preserve order and consequently their property and material interests. They regarded Wilson's reluctance to do so as mere impractical idealism, but he continued to think of the struggle as one in which the poor were trying to throw off a yoke imposed by the great landowners almost equal to that of feudalism. It was largely because of this idea that he maintained a policy of "watchful waiting."

A committee representing American copper and oil interests recommended recognition provided Huerta agreed to call an election at an early date, but Wilson believed that the dictator was not to be trusted. Feeling he did not have enough information about the situation, Wilson dispatched two special emissaries, William Bayard Hale and John Lind, to Mexico City. On June 14 Wilson sent a document to the ambassador requesting an early election with Huerta not a candidate, along with a general amnesty. On August 4 Wilson asked for the resignation of Henry Lane Wilson, who had been President Taft's ambassador to Mexico, because he was not in sympathy with the new policy of refusing to recognize the Huerta government.

Huerta had been described as "a short broad-shouldered man

. . . restless, vigilant eyes . . . tireless Indian perseverance. . . . They say the more he drinks the clearer his brain becomes." He was undoubtedly ruthless and dissipated; he was referred to as "the old Indian" in Mexico City. He even talked to his friends of marching an army to St. Louis without opposition. Wilson privately called him "a diverting brute" and expressed "a sneaking admiration for his nerve." On August 27 Wilson addressed Congress saying that the country should "exercise the self-restraint of a really great nation which recognizes its own strength." He urged Americans to leave Mexico and said he would place an embargo on the shipment of arms across the border.

Huerta claimed to have the support of twenty-two of the twenty-seven states of Mexico as well as an army of 80,000 men with which he could easily put down Carranza's revolt. He asked Wilson to ignore the revolution and send an ambassador to his government. But on October 10, just before the election, he displayed the real character of his rule by marching soldiers into the Assembly, arresting a hundred deputies and proclaiming himself dictator. At the general election on October 25, 1913, in spite of his promise not to be a candidate, Huerta was elected president of Mexico.

From this day forward Wilson began to work directly for the overthrow of Huerta. The day before the election he had told the students of Swarthmore College he hoped that in this hemisphere "nowhere can any government endure which is sustained by blood or supported by anything but the consent of the governed." He always had the optimistic hope that the "opinion of mankind," to which he frequently referred, could actually be used as a weapon. He pointed out that self-interest sometimes separates nations, but that we seek a "spiritual union."

Since England, France and Germany recognized the superior importance of American interests in Mexico and respected the Monroe Doctrine, they urged Wilson to take measures to protect foreign lives and property in the midst of these disturbances. Wilson had wanted to maintain his policy of "watchful waiting" but he found that this became more and more difficult.

He failed to realize that his candidate Carranza was really a stubborn, conceited conservative who had shown no interest in the welfare of the people until he found it to his advantage to pose as an agrarian-liberal revolutionist. To Carranza's help came Francisco Villa, more honest but less respectable, who was both a swash-buckling bandit and a social reformer. Other leaders like Zapata, Orozco, Alvarado, and Obregon also hoped to fight their way to the top in the prevailing anarchy.

In spite of the disorder, which could perhaps best have been suppressed by the recognition of Huerta, Wilson on November 1 gave notice to foreign governments that he felt it "his immediate duty to require Huerta's retirement from the Mexican government." Sir Edward Grey, the British foreign secretary, adopted this view and the British and some other European governments also advised Huerta to give up his power.

But Huerta just sat there. It did not seem as though the British were really helping to get him out since their minister in Mexico, Carden, demanded that Admiral Craddock should indicate British support by calling on Huerta in full uniform. Leaks in the Cabinet, perhaps inadvertent ones by Secretary Lane, soon made Wilson become more reticent in discussions there and at press conferences, so it began to appear that he was trying to solve all his problems without help. Republicans led by Representative Gillett of Massachusetts began to criticize Bryan and the administration for failing to take action to settle affairs in Mexico. Finally on February 3, 1914, Wilson decided to raise the embargo on arms and gave his open support to Carranza.

But in spite of this help to Carranza, the disorder in northern Mexico seemed only to increase without leading to any active steps toward the overthrow of Huerta. A British mining man was executed by Villa and most Europeans seemed to consider Carranza's "Constitutionalists" as mere brigands, so that a London financial paper referred to President Wilson's new policy as "American aid to assassins." When Mexican bandits crossed the border and killed a Texas citizen, Governor Colquitt wanted to send state Rangers to punish the slayers. But in spite of all these disturbing incidents Wilson stuck to one point. Huerta must go.

Then in the spring of 1914 came a sudden threat of war. On April 9, 1914, a boatload of American sailors from the U.S.S. *Dolphin* landed at Tampico to get gasoline. A Mexican officer with a squad of well-armed soldiers arrested all seven of the unarmed sailors, including two who had remained in the launch. The group was marched through the streets of Tampico followed by the jeers and hoots of the crowd. A superior officer quickly released them and General Zaragoza, commander of the Huertista forces in the town, sent his regrets. He stated that the colonel who had ordered the arrest was simply following instructions to prevent boats from landing at the warehouse dock and did not realize that he was acting contrary to the rules of war.

But arresting the two men who were in a boat flying the American flag "is a hostile act not to be excused," said Admiral Mayo, who demanded a more formal apology from General Zaragoza accompanied by a salute to the American flag. Huerta disavowed the act of arrest but refused to salute the flag, arguing the obligations of international law and courtesy. When Admiral Mayo was instructed to prevent possibile fighting around Tampico between the two Mexican factions, Huerta entered a formal protest, but he did nothing about the salute. Eleven warships and three cruisers of the Atlantic fleet were ordered to Tampico. Two other minor incidents which served to increase ill feeling between the countries were the intentional delay of an official dispatch from the State Department to O'Shaughnesy, secretary of the American Embassy, and the so-called arrest of an American mail orderly at Vera Cruz.

Wilson probably deplored the action of Admiral Mayo but felt it necessary to support his demands. When Huerta continued to refuse a salute, the President appeared before Congress on April 20 and asked approval for the use of "the armed forces of the United States" against "Huerta and his adherents." This was given two days later; but before that, at about two-thirty on the morning of April 21, a wireless message from Admiral Mayo gave the report that a German steamer bearing machine guns and ammunition for Huerta's troops was due at Vera Cruz at ten that morning. After a short consultation by telephone with Bryan and Daniels, Wilson ordered the American fleet to "take Vera Cruz at once." Daniels reported that this decision was taken because it was felt that not only would the arms strengthen Huerta but they might even be used later against American boys. There was no certainty that any bloodshed would result, but the action began by a bombardment of the arsenal and custom house of Vera Cruz. This was followed by a landing of sailors and marines under the protection of fire from the fleet with consequent fighting through the streets of the city. Wilson had not foreseen any loss of life from this operation but eighteen Americans and about sixty Mexicans were killed. General Funsten was then ordered to hold the subjugated city.

Although this was a clear act of war by the United States, Wilson denied any such intention. His unwillingness to recognize its implications was shown when he replied to a "Dear old Tommy" letter from his boyhod friend John D. Bellamy saying "never haul down the flag," with a stern "Dear Sir" note of rebuke; so terminating another friendship. His hand had been largely forced by Admiral Mayo, but another reason why he abandoned his policy of "watchful waiting" was his feeling that if he permitted Huerta to attack our citizens and set our government at defiance without being punished, our moral influence would no longer be able to exert any effective pressure toward getting an honest government in Mexico. But this armed invasion of Mexican soil gave such offense to Carranza that he was never again willing to exhibit any faith in the policies of the United States, even though American policy had been determined by a desire to aid him. European and Latin American governments felt that the United States was embarking upon a career of conquest which might lead to domination of the whole New World, in spite of Wilson's statements that America desired no foot of foreign soil; and the attitude of the press and public from New York to California was largely one of disapproval for a policy which had made the situation more complicated and sacrificed American lives merely for the empty satisfaction of punishing a dictator who had declined to salute the flag.

In many later instances Wilson gave evidence of ability to be patient and calm in the face of insults to American honor, even those emanating from recognized and responsible governments. This hasty seizure of Vera Cruz seemed out of tune with our protestations and out of proportion to the provocation. The immediate effect of the incident was to call forth an offer of mediation by the representatives at Washington of the "ABC" powers, Argentina, Brazil and Chile, an offer which Wilson accepted gladly and even eagerly. Huerta accepted the proposal "in principle" but Carranza was too close to achieving supreme power to co-operate. It soon appeared that while the South American republics had only contemplated mediating relations between the United States and Mexico, Wilson desired them to participate in a settlement of the internal affairs of Mexico. On May 20 the mediators opened a session at Niagara Falls which lasted six weeks. When the final agreement was drawn up it included a protocol which recommended that a provisional government should be established by negotiations between Huerta and Carranza.

Wilson wanted the mediators to go far beyond this. He even demanded a "settlement of the agrarian land question by constitutional means" in an article in the *Saturday Evening Post* of May 23, 1914, going on to say "there is no people not fitted for self government." He said his desire was to help humanity. Standing by the coffins of those who had fallen at Vera Cruz he spoke with emphasis: "We have gone down to Mexico to serve mankind, if we can find the way. We do not want to fight the Mexicans. . . . A war of aggression is not a proud thing in which to die."

All this time the President was beset with other difficulties. In addition to Mexico and the campaign for the legislation which he wanted, he had to deal with serious strikes in the mining districts of Colorado. He wrote to Mrs. Hulbert on May 10 that "There literally is no time to call my own; I must simply steal what I use for this purpose." On the next day he led the parade down Fifth Avenue in honor of the sailors killed at Vera Cruz, disregarding anonymous letters threatening his life if he came to New York. He spent that evening with Colonel House and read poems to him for nearly an hour—Wordsworth, Matthew Arnold and Keats.

He demanded that any provisional authority which was set up in Mexico should be not neutral but "actually, avowedly and sincerely in favor of the necessary agrarian and political reforms." He also believed that "the success of the Constitutionalists is now inevitable" and asked how their triumph is to be "accepted and established without further bloodshed?" He mistakenly thought Carranza to be honest, although he recognized the rebel to be a "very narrow and rather dull person." In spite of Wilson's support Carranza's followers were reported by an American commissioner at the conferences as harboring a "deep-seated fear of the United States and its suspected plans for the annexation of Mexico and Central America." Huerta resigned on July 15, 1914, and on August 21, Carranza took over the government. But the Mexican situation was by no means settled, and the problems presented by Carranza and Villa over the next few years were little less serious than those Wilson faced from the Huerta regime. Pancho Villa even conducted raids into New Mexico, in retaliation for which Wilson ordered General Pershing to take the bandit "dead or alive." But an overconscientious regard for the wishes of Carranza, who desired to restrict the operations of the American force, nearly cost the lives of all its members and finally forced it to return without its quarry.

Wilson had gone into the Mexican problem with what he probably felt to be the best intentions. He had refused to recognize a dictator who had gained the supreme power by force, followed up with murder. He had honestly sought to bring about an agrarian reform by which the ownership of the land should be taken from the large holders and given to the peasants. But all the Mexicans resented his interference and when Carranza came into power he took no more genuine interest in land reform than Huerta had done. So the principal result of Wilson's well-meant interference was to create ill will and fear of the United States in all Latin Amercia, a fear that was not entirely dispelled by his ready acceptance of mediation. Nor did he accomplish the reforms in Mexico he had in mind. In this instance it seemed as if good intentions had resulted only in arousing fear and resentment in those he wished to help.

Along with the Mexican problem came the question of tolls on the Panama Canal. The building of the canal had started in 1901, at the same time that the Hay-Pauncefote Treaty guaranteed that the ships of all nations should use the canal "on terms of entire equality." Yet in the face of this guarantee, the Panama Canal Act of Taft's administration exempted American ships employed in coastwise traffic from the East or Middle West to California from the payment of tolls. It was expected that the waterway should be opened for traffic in 1914 and on December 2, 1912, Britain officially protested that any exemption of tolls would be a violation of the treaty.

Although this exemption had been approved in the Democratic platform Wilson dug thoroughly into the problem, helped by an "illuminating discussion" with two Republicans, Elihu Root and Joseph H. Choate, both well versed in foreign affairs. He came to the conclusion that this exemption ought to be repealed. In this he was supported also by Ambassador Page in London, who reported that the English felt the exemption was dishonest and who expressed his own opinion that: "We made a bargain—a solemn compact, and we have broken it." This view was supported by such men as Andrew Carnegie and Oscar Straus but opposed by some who said that the canal "built and paid for by the American people must be used primarily for their benefit" instead of resorting to "bootlicking Great Britain."

Before delivering his formal message to Congress requesting repeal in March 1914, Wilson prepared the way by inviting the Foreign Relations Committee of the Senate to meet him at the White House on January 26. A number of Republicans proved to be in favor of repeal while such Democratic senators as O'Gorman, Newlands, Vardaman and Bristow expressed themselves as being opposed. Wilson's message maintained that "exemption constitutes a mistaken economic policy from every point of view and is moreover in plain contravention of the treaty with Great Britain." Asking for complete repeal, Wilson followed up by giving his support to a bill introduced in the House by T. W. Sims a few days later. The debate in the House became so active that thirty-eight speeches were made in one day and most of the senators went over to hear the discussion. Champ Clark came out against repeal, but Bryan swayed many Democrats with his assertion that "our country shall not mar the glory of a great enterprise by doing anything that would raise a question as to the nation's honor in its dealings with foreign nations." McAdoo took up the cause, while Burleson called up many old friends in the House the day before the vote was taken.

After passing the House 247 to 162 the fight moved to the Senate, where the debate was hardly less vigorous. Wilson was so glad to receive help from Republicans that he called up Senator Lodge to thank him for his speech and for what he had said in support of the administration's position. The bill passed on June 11 after several weeks of debate. After passage it was generally approved by members of both parties and was received in England as convincing evidence of America's good faith.

Wilson also tried to settle a long-standing dispute with the Republic of Colombia, from which the Panama Canal zone had been taken in 1903. In May 1913 the Colombian Minister asked that the dispute be arbitrated, but Wilson stood out for "direct negotiations." By September the negotiations made clear that Colombia wanted an expression of regret, as well as an indemnity, preferential treatment in the use of the canal and a boundary settlement. Wilson offered $20,000,000 in full settlement but Colombia insisted on an expression of regret and $50,000,000. A compromise treaty was proposed in the following spring with an indemnity of $25,000,000 and the inclusion of the word "regret." Since this word seemed to reflect upon acts of the administration of Theodore Roosevelt it aroused much Republican opposition and the treaty was not ratified until April 20, 1921, after Wilson had left office and with the expression of regret omitted. But all the while Wilson maintained a cordial attitude, assuring the Colombians that full justice would be done and that "the real interests of all American countries lie together and not apart." These generous tactics helped win friends for America abroad.

Wilson would have liked to extend his generous policies by granting self-government to the Filipinos and, although he felt that "they must earn it as we earned our own liberty and independence," he received so many petitions requesting him to free the islands at once that he sent Professor Henry Jones Ford of Princeton there to investigate and stated that in any case all steps taken by the United States would be in preparation for ultimate independence. He decided that Filipinos should constitute a majority in the executive commission at once, and later in the legislature, hoping that this would give the island leaders a chance to prove their political abilities. Although Taft and some of his own Cabinet thought that Wilson should have moved more slowly, the Filipinos were delighted by what seemed to be a long first step toward self-government.

It seems curious that Wilson did not take any definite stand in favor of self-government in Cuba where the problem would have been much more easily solved than in Mexico. But perhaps it was because he had always maintained that self-government could only operate properly when the population had enjoyed a long period of freedom, and Cuba had belonged to Spain until 1900. When he wrote his essay on Cleveland in 1897 he seemed to accept with approval a materialistic basis for our interests in Cuba. In a speech at Trenton four years later he said we fought "to give Cuba self-government," but how "shall we be sure that Cuba has this blessing?" In 1903 he asserted that "We kept faith with Cuba," which again seemed to indicate that he felt we had given Cuba self-government in spite of the Platt Amendment to the Cuban Treaty of 1901. He evidently did not consider American guidance and occasional assistance as being limitations on sovereignty, at least when the help was accepted voluntarily. But his attitude seems inconsistent with his usual ideas concerning the relations of the United States and her near neighbors. It may be explained on the ground that we were bound to feel a special responsibility to help and protect the island which we had so recently freed from Spain.

Another surprise appeared in a treaty with Nicaragua proposed in February 1913 with Wilson's approval, since it contained a protectorate clause modeled on the Platt Amendment. When Salvador and Costa Rica protested, he said that "conclusive assurances" should be given that "no protectorate is contemplated." Actually he evidently still envisaged some sort of protective assistance to Nicaragua similar to that accorded Cuba, but for some reason he did not seem to recognize that this was an infringement of Nicaragua's sovereignty or a source of any danger to her neighbors.

In his dealings with all the Caribbean states Wilson tried to procure for them the financial assistance which they needed, and he would probably have been willing to do this without interfering in their own governmental arrangements; but this proved almost impossible. The nations needed funds from outside to develop their rich natural resources and yet they were rarely able to set up governments sufficiently stable for bankers to be willing to lend them money. The result was that virtual protectorates were set up over Haiti as well as Nicaragua during Wilson's administration, both largely on the model of those which had been already established in Cuba and Santo Domingo. American bankers would furnish money to maintain the smaller country's finances while American officials were put in charge of the custom houses to see that repayment was assured. This was not an ideal solution of the problem and some foreign countries suspected that it was merely a subterfuge for extending American domination and control. But Wilson said he adopted it with the honest purpose of helping the smaller countries and denied any idea of seeking to extend the power and influence of his own country. It probably seemed to him the only practicable plan under the conditions which then existed.

In 1917, in order to make the Caribbean safer for his country Wilson succeeded in purchasing the Virgin Islands from Denmark for $25,000,000. Theodore Roosevelt had tried to obtain them at the time the Panama Canal was constructed, but had not been successful. The acquisition of this archipelago, consisting of three islands of some importance and numerous smaller ones, was made possible by wartime conditions.

Wilson's policy in Mexico set a durable precedent. By refusing to recognize Huerta and taking active steps to oust him, this country asserted that it would, under certain circumstances, refuse to recognize as legitimate the government of another country. Such a refusal was to be considered justified if a foreign government had seized power by force, even though this had been done with a semblance of following the will of the people. British practice still observes the older rule of recognizing and dealing with a *de facto* government; but many years later Presidents Truman and Eisenhower followed Wilson's lead and refused to recognize Communist China.

CHAPTER XIV

TRUST BUSTING AND
PROPOSED REFORMS

Wilson turned to an attack upon trusts and monopolies in January 1914. His purpose was primarily to maintain free competition. This was the third great feature of his domestic program and it was the most fundamental, for it struck directly at the worst evils of corporation power, which had been indirectly assailed by his earlier measures concerning the tariff and the currency.

He presented his views to Congress on January 20, but as early as 1907 in a speech at Norfolk, Virginia, he had talked about "the elaborate secret manipulations by means of which some of our so-called 'financiers' get control of a voting majority of the stock of great railroad or manufacturing companies, in order to effect vast combinations of interests or properties." In 1912 he had directed attention to the dangers liable to result from such interlocking control by pointing out that "what we are afraid of . . . is such use of corporations as will be in restraint of trade; that is, such use as will establish monopoly." When he became President he realized that his general ideas must be clothed in specific and detailed form, so he went for advice to Louis D. Brandeis of Boston and other experts, wiring Brandeis in September: "Please set forth as explicitly as possible the actual measures by which competition can be effectively regulated." Both men believed that above all free competition must be preserved.

The message to Congress of January 20, 1914, recommended legislation to strengthen, clarify and supplement the Sherman Antitrust Act of 1890 in order to reform "an industrial system which holds capital in leading strings, restricts the liberties and limits the opportunities of labor, and exploits, without renewing, the natural resources of the country." He asked for " a common effort to square business methods with both public opinion and the law" in order to put an end to friction between government and business. The Sherman Act was vague in much of its phrasing so that it required constant appeal to the courts for its interpretation. To stop this and add new restraints, Wilson proposed measures which were called "the five brothers," similar to the "seven sisters" laws he had put through in New Jersey. They included such things as the establishment of a Federal Interstate Trade Commission to investigate and control methods of business; the prohibition of interlocking directorates; a clearer explanation of the terms of the Sherman Antitrust Act; the prohibition of unfair practices in business competition; and the regulation of the issue of railroad securities. Wilson maintained his pressure and exerted his leadership in much the same fashion as in the tariff and currency campaigns and he now had so much prestige that any opposition was quickly overcome.

Since they knew that some such action was to be expected even before his speech to Congress of January 20, J. Pierpont Morgan, George F. Baker and other financial magnates announced on January 3 their intention of withdrawing from the directorates of many corporations in which they held an interest. When finally enacted Wilson's measures boiled down to the Federal Trade Commission Act passed on September 26 and an amalgamation called the Clayton Act, after H. D. Clayton of Alabama, chairman of the House Judiciary Committee. The proposal for the regulation of the issues of railroad securities was indefinitely postponed after the outbreak of the European conflict in August, because it was feared that such restrictive legislation would hamper the roads in carrying out the increased burden put upon them by the war.

The Federal Trade Commission which was set up consisted of five members appointed by the President with power to investigate and report on trade, to lay down general rules and to ask for injunctions. Since it was intended to aid business with its investigations and advice, it could demand reports from corporations and also ask for additional antitrust laws. That a group of impartial economic experts should be established to assist both the corporations and the courts constituted a sound idea.

The Clayton Act proved to be a patchwork which contained a multitude of details, frequently unnecessary, conflicting, and even harmful. Too many people had a hand in concocting it and it dealt with such varied subjects as unfair trade practices, interlocking stockholders, dishonest railroad financing, the legal status of trade unions and the use of injunctions in labor disputes. Any corporation was forbidden to absorb another if this would result in a monopoly, and unfair forms of business competition were not to be permitted. Before this, rivals had often resorted to various methods to freeze out a competitor, including price-cutting, rebates, buying secrets through bribery, setting up bogus corporations and suggesting that a competitor's products were worthless.

An important provision of the Clayton Act stated that "the labor of human beings is not an article of commerce," so that labor and agricultural organizations should not be considered illegal combinations or conspiracies in restraint of trade under the antitrust acts, nor were strikes or boycotts to be regarded in violation of the law. Samuel Gompers, as the representative of organized labor, had long been demanding this with such effect that similar provisions had been included in a rider to an appropriation bill which was vetoed by President Taft. In talks with Wilson, Gompers pointed out that human rights and interests were involved in labor organizations; so when a similar bill with the same rider was presented to Wilson, he signed it on June 23, 1914, despite violent protests even from his supporters. From this time forward Wilson was regarded as a friend of labor, and it was only to be expected that the same ideas should be written into the new antitrust legislation for which he was responsible.

Wilson's principal achievement in connection with the tariff, currency and antitrust bills was the way in which he pushed them through Congress. None of them was really new in conception, and only the currency bill has remained substantially unaltered since that time. Wilson himself said in his message of January 1914 that "These are not new things, but old and now familiar." What is remarkable is the way in which he kept Congress working at them. He had no constitutional right to prevent the adjournment of Congress, but except for a short Christmas recess, he kept both houses in continuous session from April 7, 1913, to October 24, 1914. His influence is clearly to be seen in all the bills, for the details were constantly submitted to him for his approval or disapproval. In January, 1914, *Harper's Weekly* reported that "Mr. Wilson is the whole thing at this juncture, he dispenses the high and the low and the middle justice. He has suffered no rebuff in putting into effect his plans and his ideas. The processes of government reflect his will." Or, as Wilson himself previously expressed it, "The Presidency is an office in which a man must put on his war paint."

By these provisions business had been made substantially fair and free. The main driving force of Wilson's "New Freedom" ended with the passage of the Clayton Act. It turned out that business had a hard time digesting so many reforms; but they did accomplish the purposes for which they were framed. Wilson himself was soon occupied with the numerous questions raised by the outbreak of the European war in August 1914. But this diversion of his interests did not seem too detrimental to domestic affairs, since not only he but also the Progressives believed that nothing more needed to be done now that freedom of competition had been established. As it turned out the economy soon had to adapt itself to war conditions which led Wilson almost to encourage mergers into large corporations so that finance, labor, production and distribution could all be more easily subjected to the governmental controls needed in war times. But the measures to create free competition remained on the statute books to be available on the return of peace.

Another problem presented to Wilson was a strike of coal miners in southern Colorado which began in September 1913. A battle between the militia and miners at Ludlow on April 20,1914, led to the burning of the strikers' tents with the death of eleven children and eight adults. When Governor Ammons asked for help, Wilson sent two thousand regular troops to Colorado who were still there at the time of the fall elections.

The elections showed the reaction against the party in power frequent in midterm balloting. But this reversal was magnified in this case by the vigor of Wilson's reforms which led to protests from many diverse quarters. New England objected to the tariff, big bankers disliked the decentralization created by the Federal Reserve Act, while the laws against trusts were labeled "amateurish" and "undigested," or else criticized for the advantages given to labor. Others complained that the South had too much share in the government. Poor business conditions which had prevailed almost since Wilson took office were blamed by the Republicans upon the President's new legislation. Progressives had lost interest in Theodore Roosevelt and were returning to the Republican camp to such an extent that their party vote was cut to less than half of what it had been in 1912. With such varied grounds of complaint against the Administration and with the Republicans regaining so many votes, it is little wonder that the Democratic majority in Congress was drastically reduced.

Wilson was interested in some minor reforms beside these important ones, which he succeeded in putting through before the European War interfered with further changes at home. The 17th Amendment was adopted, providing for the direct election of Senators, but both Wilson and Congress necessarily had their time taken up more and more with foreign affairs. They also felt that measures which might be desirable in peace times were frequently likely to disrupt too greatly an economy which was being subjected to the unusual strains of war.

Prohibition was regarded by Wilson as a "social and moral" issue which should properly be settled by the separate states or even individual communities. This position was in accord with the Southern theory of States' Rights; it had not only been set forth by him before his election but was advocated by him at all times as the proper method of handling the problem. He did not believe that prohibition should be made a party issue in either national or local politics, and during the war he did not want any permanent legislation passed which a large portion of the people might resent. Since he looked upon prohibition as a necessary aid to the conservation of food in wartime, he was opposed to the 18th Amendment and to the Volstead Act, which was designed to enforce it and was passed over his veto after he was unable to procure an exemption for "light wines and beers." Since the problem itself was not left to the states and local communities, he believed that the burden of enforcement should be laid upon them so that local sentiment could at least decide how strictly the law should be enforced. If his suggestions had been followed prohibition in America might have been a more successful experiment than it was with an attempt at nation-wide enforcement.

Woman suffrage was also first regarded by Wilson as a local question. But during the war he came to feel that women had earned the right to vote, and moreover that a true democracy ought to make no discrimination among its citizens. He expressed these views to the Senate on September 30, 1918, saying that to the peoples of the world in general "democracy means that women shall play their part in affairs . . . upon an equal footing with men." He followed this up with cables to senators from Paris so that after two defeats the 19th Amendment finally passed on June 5, 1919. He then pressed some of the reluctant states to ratify, especially West Virginia and Tennessee, so that the adoption of the Woman Suffrage Amendment was in part due to his efforts.

The idea of the conservation of natural resources was presented by Wilson in his first message to Congress. He urged a policy of "positive conservation," by which the national domain could be made use of by private individuals or corporations, with ownership still remaining in the government. He felt that certain areas could be leased and that these ought to be large enough to allow profitable operation without inducing monopoly. He felt that navigable streams could be leased for the development of water power. He recommended that land be sold to returned soldiers in the hope that this would give the nation a backbone of solid farmers. He not only opposed a general opening up of forest regions in the West to general settlement but also recommended establishing national forests in the East. He felt that conservation of the forests could be made more effective by arrangements for fire protection and the construction of roads.

Even with his belief that tariff should be primarily for revenue, Wilson realized that the change to that basis must be gradual in order not to upset established business enterprises. Although he would permit protection for "infant" industries he wanted to encourage competition and give only such protection as would "balance the difference in cost at home and abroad, including an allowance for a difference in freight rates." Before America entered the war he recognized the need for a tariff commission which could give expert opinions on rates, without having any control over policy. The income tax, included in the Underwood bill, later became the chief source of federal revenue, instead of import duties. Its constitutionality was established by the Sixteenth Amendment not long before Wilson took office.

Wilson opposed increasing tariffs both before and during the World War, except on products of dyeing and chemical industries which required building up when imports from Germany were cut off. After the war he objected to any increase of tariffs even to prevent the "dumping" of European goods or to aid agriculture. He sought to help Europe get on her feet by advocating tariffs which would encourage international trade. His stand was always for a low tariff whenever it was practicable.

Wilson's desire to help labor became clear in the Clayton and Adamson Acts. Then during the war it was vitally necessary to help the Allies with products of our factories, so that in order to keep them operating at capacity it was only natural for Wilson to accede to any of the workers' demands which seemed reasonable. These included a shorter working day and an extension of collective bargaining. The War Labor Board was carried over into the period of readjustment after the conflict and Wilson called two conferences of labor, capital and the public; but when they failed to come forth with any creative ideas he began to demand the "genuine democratization of industry." Since he did not interpret the meaning of this phrase, businessmen were afraid to make the large plans for the future which might have helped to increase employment. His humanitarian instincts led him to oppose any restriction on immigration, although more workers would reduce the bargaining power of labor. Consequently, Wilson was not very effective in his efforts to settle the problems of labor and capital.

Great changes had come in Wilson's life in his first two years as President. He and his family were taken from the small-town environment in which they had always lived, for he had commuted from Princeton even when governor, and were thrust into the very center of the national scene at Washington. His years as a professor had given him ease and confidence upon his feet, as well as a ready flow of effective speech. But he had learned little about people and how to deal with them during those decades of college teaching. Now he had become not only an administrator but a leader of his nation, a nation before which lay new and unprecedented problems. He had vision and idealism, but he was handicapped because he was surrounded by a strange and different kind of men, diplomats and politicians, men whose decisions were often based not on facts which would appeal to a professor but on intuition and emotion.

His daughters met the new life with vim and spirit, with joy in all the new advantages they now had for meeting young men of some importance in the world. Their parents rejoiced in watching them; and they proved themselves to be natural, sweet and sensible young women. Two of them married during those first two years and Margaret, the eldest, was frequently away on pursuits of her own choosing.

The different environment of Washington was hardest of all for

Ellen Axson Wilson. She was artistic and temperamental, so good an artist that three of her paintings, entered anonymously, were selected for showing by the New York Academy of Art, a triumph which made the entire family happy for weeks afterward. But her quiet nature was disturbed by the cares and obligations that surrounded her. She did not like society and was so temperamental that she would often sit through a large part of her own dinner parties without speaking. Standing in the doorway her last night in Princeton one of her old friends said to her: "You will stand at your husband's side at many parties of this kind in Washington." Ellen Wilson cried, "I won't do it; I won't do it."

The plight of the poverty-stricken and neglected whom she saw in the big city tore at her heart. She had wisdom, gentleness and a lack of sophistication which made the stately flurry of society especially distasteful to her. She did her best to help her husband, but the strain of all these conflicting burdens bore down upon her. He tried to spare her from many of his problems, pounding out long letters on his typewriter at night to such friends as Colonel House, Mrs. Peck and James Kerney of Trenton, instead of confiding in her as had always previously been his custom. But he could not keep knowledge of all his problems and decisions from her. She worried over the danger of a war with Mexico, which would send young men to die as a result of her husband's orders. Crushed by the weight of worries and responsibilities which she had no spirit to meet and affected with a serious organic ailment, her strength ebbed away during the spring and summer of 1914. Just before evening on August 6, with her hand resting in Wilson's she whispered to Dr. Grayson, "Promise me that you will take good care of my husband." Then, without ever having been told about the war in Europe, she died, leaving the President without her comforting care and love.

Yet even then he must have derived some consolation from the thought of the reforms he had put through. Undoubtedly his greatest contributions to the liberal cause and the triumph of progressive ideas lay in his powers of leadership. Theodore Roosevelt had talked like a progressive but had frequently failed to take any action or assert any leadership. When vital projects were on the fire Bryan had deployed his wonderful oratory but had been in no position to accomplish much, nor is it likely that he would ever have shown sufficient balance to gain the support of most thinking citizens. But Wilson considered himself the leader not of a party or a group but of the whole American people. He felt that this duty was laid upon him by his election as President and he fulfilled it as few Presidents except the very greatest have ever done. He gained a triumph in his crusade for democracy at home.

In all his domestic policies Wilson had tried to carry through measures which would help the people as a whole. He had played a great part in lowering the tariff and creating a currency which could be adjusted to the needs of the business community. He had aided free enterprise by attacking the trusts and various unfair practices. He wanted prohibition to be a local issue, he became a convert to woman suffrage, he advocated measures to preserve America's natural resources and he sought to improve the condition of the workingman; and these sound and liberal ideas were enacted into law largely because of the vigor of his leadership.

CHAPTER XV

FAILURE TO PREPARE
FOR WAR

Wilson was probably surprised by the outbreak of World War I. Most of his observers seem to have been completely unaware that any European catastrophe was imminent, so that even the State Department lacked proper warning. Early that summer Colonel House had written from Europe that the peace of the world had never before been on so sound a foundation. When Wilson's ambassadors and representatives observed the nervousness of European foreign ministers they reported it with amused contempt. So it was not likely that the President, busy with his domestic reforms, and worried about his wife, could have foreseen that a cataclysm was about to engulf the Western World.

House had gone abroad in May hoping to marshal the Great Powers in support of a policy of peace. He had some sort of indefinite scheme to unite England, Germany, France and America in works of good will and the limitation of armaments. The good will was to be exhibited primarily in helping develop the backward regions of the world, a project which might readily have been diverted into a cloak for exploiting them and their inhabitants. House saw the German Army at manoeuvers and described the performance to Wilson as, "Militarism run stark mad"; but a luncheon with the Kaiser led him to the strange belief that all this military force might be devoted to a grand alliance to outlaw war.

Wilson seems to have taken none of these reports as seriously as he might and wrote his friend a casual line: "I hope you are getting a lot of fun and pleasure out of these things."

But after the murder of the heir to the Austrian throne by a fanatical Serb in the streets of Sarajevo on June 28, 1914, and Austria's invasion of her southern neighbor on August 1 led Russia, Germany and France quickly to declare war, he realized his error. And when England entered the conflict a few days later because the German war machine had cut through neutral Belgium on its way toward Paris with complete disregard of treaty obligations, and because of her own commitments to France, he knew America was the one great remaining neutral country. And so on August 4 Wilson sat beside the dying Ellen as he wrote in pencil an offer to act as mediator to get the warring nations to meet together and discuss their differences. However, his offers were rejected by all the belligerents; this may have been either because they were too vague and general in their terms or because they were put forward through intermediaries instead of being presented in person.

Later that day Wilson issued a formal proclamation of neutrality which he based on Washington's proclamation of August 22, 1793, and the Neutrality Act drawn up by Jefferson the following year. Wilson followed this on August 19 with an appeal to the American people against arousing the passions of a population which was "drawn chiefly from the nations now at war, and contained the utmost variety of sympathy and desire," saying that a division into hostile camps would be "fatal to our peace of mind." He then made the almost impossible demand that "The United States must be impartial in fact as well as in name during these days that are to try men's souls. We must be impartial in thought as well as in action. . . . My thought is of America . . . a nation that neither sits in judgment upon others nor is disturbed in her own counsels, and which keeps herself fit and free to do what is honest and disinterested and truly serviceable for the peace of the world."

Wilson was here recommending an attitude which ignored the military and political problems of the war, and he took no steps to prepare the country to enter the war later if that should become necessary. He was keeping the nation out of war, partly from a love of peace and partly in the hope that by remaining neutral he could help some day to arbitrate the entire conflict. Also it must be recognized that isolation had been the traditional role for America up to this time and that he was deeply grieved by his wife's death on August 6.

It quickly became evident that if America did become involved in the war it would be upon the side of England, France and Russia. This led to a rather curious collection of champions of peace. Many of Irish and German descent were moved by traditional hatred of England, some Yankees remembered the Revolution and the War of 1812, isolationists and pacifists urged that the country remain neutral. Farmers and cotton planters felt that the British blockade was interfering with the sale of their products. Many of the farmers were members of the Democratic Party and advocates of reform, people whom Wilson might regard as his natural supporters, but there were also those who had no sympathy with his reforms but admired French culture or felt that the success of their business ventures was dependent upon an Allied victory. Yet many supporters of aid to the Allies were moved by principles and not by profits. Ex-President Eliot of Harvard indicated the threat to world peace which would come with a German victory and pointed out that it was not economic rivalry but mutual fear among the Great Powers that had been responsible for the war. House quotes Wilson himself as saying in the first months of the war that "If Germany won it would change the course of our civilization and make the United States a military nation."

As head of the most powerful neutral nation, Wilson had to listen to protests from both sides. The Kaiser complained of the use of dumdum bullets by the Belgians, while the French and the Belgians called attention to cruelties inflicted by the enemy army. Wilson would take no stand on either issue. He wrote the Kaiser on September 16 "as one friend speaking to another" that to make any move would be a "premature" act, "inconsistent with the neutral position of any nation, which, like this, has no part in the contest." Theodore Roosevelt also said of Belgium: "We have not the smallest responsibility for what has befallen her." This appeared in the *Outlook* for September 23, but a few months later the author asked to have the words deleted from textbooks where they had been quoted, asserting that he had written them only in order not to embarrass the President. Yet in spite of these appeals for neutrality the people of America could not feel neutral; conflicting feelings irritated one another, while the supporters of both sides heaped propaganda upon those who were in authority.

Meanwhile an economic crisis had arisen because of the obstacles which had been thrown in the way of exports of various foods, especially cotton. Wilson and McAdoo recommended a "cotton loan fund," the construction of merchant ships by the government and measures to see that cotton should not be declared contraband. In spite of Wilson's exhortations, especially in a Jackson Day speech, January 8, 1915, that the shipping bill should be passed, Congress adjourned on March 4 without having taken any action. This seems to have been the first real setback to Wilson's tide of success as President, and it was a precursor of resistance such as he had eventually met at Princeton and Trenton.

Soon Wilson shifted his emphasis from mere neutrality to the assertion of America's rights and privileges. These were to be defended, even in the absence of any desire for prizes or territory. The warring nations were all seeking clothing, food, raw materials and munitions, so that those individuals who had wares to sell made a profit almost overnight. The British sought to keep American goods from the Central Powers by a blockade, which could not be very firmly established because of the German submarines. Frequent new Orders in Council, issued without consulting the United States, enlarged the list of contraband articles which could be seized if on a voyage to a belligerent from the ten included in the Declaration of London of 1909 to a total of forty-two. They also seized articles billed for neutral countries around Germany, with the contention that these goods were intended finally to reach a belligerent. The State Department on December 26 contended that this behavior "exceeded the manifest necessity of a belligerent nation, and constituted a restriction of the rights of American citizens on the high seas," and suggested that a continuation of this policy might lose England the good will of Americans. Wilson wished both to maintain our rights and to warn the British, but the note was friendly in tone. He obviously did not want to go to war over technical infringements of property rights.

He took a sterner view when the actual lives of Americans began to be endangered. This threat came from Germany and first appeared in the form of an announcement on February 4, 1915, that she was establishing a "war zone" around the British Isles, within which her submarines would sink any and every ship. Since such vessels sometimes flew the American flag, there was danger that even neutral ships might be torpedoed. On February 10 Wilson demanded that German submarines observe the old rule of visit and search. He followed this ten days later by requesting both England and Germany to stop using submarines and mines except around harbors and to cease seeking safety by the illegitimate use of neutral flags. He also asked England to permit the transport of food into Germany provided it was not to be used to feed her armies. When England refused this proposal on the ground that it would simply make other food available for military use, the German ambassador, Von Bernstorff, sent a scolding note to the newspapers asking the American people to "stop the exclusive exportation of arms to one side." Wilson replied by personally dictating a note which pointed out that by international law all belligerents had the right to purchase munitions in neutral countries.

Germany replied to Wilson's note by embarking upon a policy of terror. After a warning in the newspapers, signed "Imperial German Embassy," that British ships were liable to destruction in the war zone, a submarine torpedoed the *Lusitania,* a British vessel, without warning off the Irish coast on the afternoon of May 7, 1915. Over 1,000 people were lost, including 114 American citizens. The *Lusitania,* was within her rights in carrying ammunition and was not armed. Wilson might have been able to lead the country into war by a resounding message, but most of the population west of the Alleghenies was not ready to enter the struggle, and it is also possible that he did not want to become an ally of the Western powers. So instead, by an exchange of notes, Wilson succeeded in persuading the German government to announce on September 1 that its submarines would not sink any more passenger liners without warning. At the same time Germany apologized for the destruction of the British steamer *Arabic* in August.

A few days before the *Lusitania* was sunk Wilson used the phrase: "There is such a thing as a man being too proud to fight." Tumulty advised him to remove it from the speech and House wrote that "Page and all of us are distressed." Wilson had not realized that it would be quoted by itself, and that the next sentence did not particularly change the meaning by saying: "There is such a thing as a nation being so right that it does not need to convince others by force that it is right." The phrase led to a storm of criticism; and it is possible that the unfortunate sentence encouraged the Germans to believe that even after the torpedo had struck the big liner Wilson was bluffing and not prepared to fight. Bryan also seems to have suspected that Wilson was not in dead earnest, for he even asked the President to send an unofficial letter telling the Germans not to be too concerned over our official pronouncements, which Wilson naturally refused to do. The secretary also insisted that Wilson should agree to arbitrate our disagreements over the conduct of submarines with Germany and he refused to sign the second *Lusitania* note. He then resigned his portfolio with apparent good humor, but he later openly criticized a number of Wilson's policies. He was succeeded as Secretary of State by Robert Lansing, an able lawyer, but a man without any broad policy or vision. McAdoo tried to excuse the appointment by saying, "He was the best material at hand, he could put diplomatic notes into proper form and advise on international law, and the President had determined for the future to be practically his own Secretary of State"; while another member of the Cabinet merely remarked, "What he [Wilson] wanted was really a high-class clerk."

At the same time Wilson's thoughts were turning in another direction. He was uxorious; his nature demanded a wife; and in the spring of 1915 he suddenly fell in love. He behaved almost as though he were a boy again. Always one to feel a great need for feminine sympathy and companionship, he suddenly found it in Mrs. Edith Bolling Galt, sprightly, gracious, gay and beautiful, descended from Pocahontas and John Rolfe of old Virginia. She was both charming and sensible. Wilson met her toward the end of March and asked her to marry him six weeks later. She felt they must not be in too much of a hurry, so that the engagement was announced in October and they were married just before Christmas at an evening wedding in her small house. Soap and perfume, books and mineral water, cakes and candies were among the gifts which came from all over the land.

The bride was in her early forties and possessed a reputation for style and charm. Franklin Lane described his daughter's delight in a new evening cloak by saying she felt that "Cleopatra and the Queen of Sheba and Mrs. Galt had nothing on her." Edith Bolling gave Wilson the unswerving devotion of a strong-minded woman. She had had some business experience as director of her former husband's jewelry business since his death in 1908 and she had no hesitation in expressing definite opinions on many subjects. But because of her feeling that Wilson was always right, it unfortunately became her custom to urge him to follow his own opinions rather than ask counsel of others or be moved by considerations of prudence or concession. She took the place of his old friends, and Colonel House was never again so intimate in the White House. She believed herself alone able to provide help and strength, as well as such gaiety as was possible in the years ahead.

During 1915 the Allies began to run out of dollars with which to buy supplies. Unless Americans were permitted to make loans to the British, they would soon be unable to make any further purchases here, with results which would be disastrous for both econo-mies. McAdoo said the granting of credits to the English of at least half a billion dollars was "absolutely imperative." Bryan's statement early in the war, made with Wilson's consent, that "loans by American bankers to any foreign nation at war are inconsistent with the spirit of neutrality," was now embarrassing. However, the Germans had been able to sell ten million dollars' worth of short-term bonds that spring. On September 7 Lord Reading and a British commission talked to Wilson at the White House. They convinced the President that economic conditions were such that a loan was unavoidable, with the result that a contract between the British and American bankers was arranged on October 15.

A few months later popular opinion veered definitely against the Germans. It was found that German spies and agents were operating in the United States on a large scale. Cases of sabotage were dis-covered, and the German foreign secretary, Zimmerman, boasted that in the event of war "five hundred thousand trained Germans in America would join the Irish and start a revolution." Von Papen and Boy-Ed were indicted for a plot to wreck the Welland Canal in Canada and it was proved that Dr. Dumba of the Austrian Em-bassy had planned to disable American munitions plants. Ships con-tinued to be sunk, Nurse Cavell was executed by the Germans in Belgium and indignation grew against the Central powers.

At the same time Ambassador Page took a strong stand by con-sulting with Sir Edward Grey on ways to moderate all causes of dispute and ill will between England and America. Wilson's acqui-escence made it possible for the British to maintain the blockade in which we subsequently joined them, although Page was constantly saying that he was concerned with standing up for our rights as a neutral. Ambassador Gerard soon found his status in Germany to be "a present object of concentrated hate," and Von Bernstorff noted that, "nobody in Germany believes in the impartiality of the American Government."

Meanwhile Wilson did little to improve our Army and Navy. Theodore Roosevelt, Senator Lodge and General Wood were all violent advocates of preparedness, with Lodge especially raising the issue throughout all of 1915 and Wood pouring vituperation upon the President. Wilson finally gave Wood permission to recruit and train officers at Plattsburg and elsewhere, but he himself seems to have felt that no preparation was necessary. The Navy was being enlarged under Secretary Daniels, with young Franklin D. Roosevelt as his assistant, but the Army could put only about 50,000 men in the field after taking care of the regular army posts and coast defenses. Wilson was threatening Germany but he had little to back him up. He toured the Middle West telling the people that peace might have to be abandoned in order to uphold our honor, but Bryan followed after him with appeals for peace, even though all Wilson asked for was a "continental army" of volunteers which was to be trained for only "very brief" periods each year. This volunteer force was to be increased to about 400,000, still too small to be of consequence; and although he stated that these volunteers ought to be brought under federal control, Wilson still declared himself open to suggestions. Lindley Garrison, capable and nettlesome, resigned because of this lack of action on the President's part, and Newton D. Baker became secretary of War.

A new problem arose early in 1916. On February 10 Germany announced that enemy merchantmen armed with guns would be treated as belligerents. Since British vessels had been armed for some time, Wilson felt it necessary to send a telegram to all the belligerents on February 16, 1916, stating that "there was no present intention to warn Americans to refrain from traveling in belligerent merchantmen armed solely for the purpose of defense." When Jeff McLemore of Texas introduced a resolution in Congress the next day which would warn people against such travel and this was followed by similar action by Senator Gore, it amounted to a revolt against the President's leadership. Wilson moved fast by asking for an immediate vote on the resolution in a letter to the House Committee on Rules. He argued that "the report that there are divided counsels in Congress in regard to the foreign policy of the Government is being made industrious use of in foreign capitals."

197

Within ten days both resolutions had been tabled by a substantial vote and Wilson's position of leadership in Congress remained intact.

When the Sussex carrying passengers across the English Channel was sunk without warning on March 24, Wilson sent a strong note which was really a mild ultimatum to Germany. While battles raged at Verdun and the Somme, Germany gave assurances that this sort of submarine warfare would be abandoned. This promise was not broken for almost ten months. Wilson and his wife celebrated this concession with a game of golf, a trip to the circus and a week-end cruise. It was Mrs. Wilson's constant effort to provide the President with relaxation, which often included visits to the theater three times a week in order to keep him going when the strain of maintaining neutrality was severe.

All this time Wilson had been thinking of himself as a possible mediator among the nations and on May 27, 1916, he for the first time came out for "an universal association of nations to maintain inviolate the security of the highways of the seas" and "a virtual guarantee of territorial integrity and political independence." It seems clear that these statements expressed his deep convictions, and Senator Lodge in an earlier speech at the same meeting also advocated "an international league or agreement or tribunal for peace."

A few days after this, the Presidential campaign opened with the Republican and Progressive conventions in Chicago. When Roosevelt refused to lead the Progressive Party, it broke up into those who voted for Republican candidate Charles Evans Hughes and those who went over to Wilson. Wilson's campaign was based primarily upon his liberal legislation at home and his record in foreign relations. The slogan, "He kept us out of war," probably never received Wilson's official approval; but that issue was firmly established as the platform of the Democratic convention when Governor Glynn of New York said in his keynote speech, "It does satisfy the daughters of our land," and Senator Ollie Jones, the permanent chairman, maintained that "Without orphaning a single American child" Wilson had secured "an agreement to American demands." Finally Bryan expressed his gratitude to "a President who is trying to keep us out of war."

In the summer of 1916 Wilson found time to come to the help of the farmers. Even the war and the Presidential campaign had not diverted his mind entirely from domestic reforms. Both farm owners and tenant farmers were making money and wanted to buy land of their own. In order to provide them with the needed cash, banks were now established in each of the Federal Reserve districts under the Farm Loan Act, all of them to be supervised by a Federal Farm Board. These banks were prepared to provide tenants who wished to buy their land with loans at reasonable rates. In the process they would help the purchasers appraise the farms before acquiring them. Provision was also made for Farm Loan Associations whose membership would consist of borrowing farmers.

Wilson next turned to the difficulty raised by the railroad brotherhoods. They were demanding an eight-hour day and threatening to strike. The Clayton Antitrust Act prevented the use of compulsion against unions and when Wilson recommended arbitration the unions declined. Just before the strike was to have started Wilson asked Congress to pass the Adamson Law. This established the eight-hour day as well as authorizing the fixing of railroads rates by the Interstate Commerce Commission. Wilson wished to include a prohibition of strikes in the measure, but Congress insisted upon passing it without this provision.

The Presidential campaign was far more dignified than the preceding one, both sides promising to seek peace with honor. Wilson's domestic legislation was recognized by the Republicans as so excellent as not to be susceptible of attack. Both candidates endorsed woman suffrage and both were accused by President Eliot of "truckling to labor." But the Republican candidate, Hughes, had little of interest to say. He talked about appointments and patronage without raising any big issue. He showed timidity by refusing to attack the hyphenates until the very end of the campaign, whereas Wilson early replied to an Irish sympathizer, "I would feel deeply mortified to have you or anybody like you vote for me." Hughes never showed himself capable of taking any such stand or of administering any such rebuke.

The plan of Wilson's campaign was drawn up by Colonel House. It was designed primarily to concentrate on the wavering votes in the wavering states. This meant that the party managers would expend little effort on the states east of the Mississippi and north of the Ohio. Vance McCormick became the campaign manager; Bernard Baruch and others had been able to persuade McCombs that he was too ill to assume such a burden. Bryan went on a speaking tour in the Western states; Daniels traveled as far as Kansas and was able to persuade Thomas A. Edison to give his support, along with the remark, "They say Wilson has blundered. Perhaps he has, but I notice he usually blunders forward." Henry Ford told Daniels that he was opposed to campaign contributions but after Daniels agreed that this was often a corrupting influence he asked about legitimate publicity. Ford then said he would make sure that the arguments for voting for Wilson were "presented in papers of large circulation in the pivotal states."

Maine went heavily Republican in September and Tammany turned against Wilson. But Hughes was unable to arouse any enthusiasm and it was said that he just coughed when asked what he would have done when the *Lusitania* was sunk. On election night Hughes went to bed thinking he was President, but the returns from California had not yet come in. The Republican managers had ignored Governor Hiram Johnson and they lost the whole election when they lost his state by a little more than 3,000 votes. Wilson in his casual way refused to seem excited when his daughter brought the news to him the following morning.

By the end of 1916 Wilson had kept America out of the war for more than two years. He had hoped at first to become a mediator in the conflict; but his overtures had been constantly rebuffed and both sides had shown an ever-increasing inclination to infringe upon the rights of neutrals. For those rights Wilson had steadfastly contended.

Germany had now come to threaten not only the property but even the lives of American citizens.

He had not only tried to maintain our rights as a neutral but also obtained the passage of further domestic reforms. He had been very slow in realizing the need for military and naval preparedness; and he had been re-elected partly on his record and partly because of the ineffectiveness of the opposition. But now Germany was about to renew her submarine warfare and her armies were coming close to victory over the Allies. Wilson still clung to the belief he had expressed early in the conflict that such an outcome would be intolerable because it would impose the necessity for militarism not only upon Europe but upon America as well; but he had taken almost no steps to prevent the disaster and the election made no difference in his attitude. He went on trying to preserve America's position as the one great neutral. He did not for a while even seem to lean obviously toward the Allied side.

After saying in October that the war had been brought about "by nothing in particular" he went on in December to remark that "if you relied upon their public declarations the objects which the statesmen . . . of both sides . . . have in mind in this war are virtually the same."

So once again he renewed his efforts to bring about a peace, this time merely by asking the contestants to state the specific conditions which they would propose in order to end the war and establish a lasting peace. This amounted to a demand for peace associated with an appeal to the conscience of mankind. But the statesmen on both sides, fearing that they would face a revolution if they offered peace without large rewards for the sacrifices made by their people, presented terms such as might have been imposed after a great military success with their armies victorious.

On January 22, 1917, a week before the German terms were announced, Wilson presented his own proposals to the Senate. He said he was "seeking only to face realities," when in truth the Allied peace terms he had already received in reply to his request were quite different from those he was suggesting. He wanted a community of power with reduction of armaments, government by the consent of the governed, and "a peace worth guaranteeing." He believed its principle must be "equality and a common participation in a common benefit." He said he was convinced that "only a peace between equals can last." Worst of all, in the eyes of the Allies, he concluded: "It must be a peace without victory."

On January 31, Germany not only announced her drastic peace terms but also declared to our State Department that she would commence "unrestricted" submarine attacks the next day. Even back in October Wilson had expressed the feeling that "The war now has reached such a scale that the position of neutrals sooner or later must become intolerable." That position was rapidly descending upon him, for the Germans not only revoked their promises and defied his protests, but they extended their threats to include the sinking of neutral merchant ships which seemed to be headed for an Allied port. They would graciously permit one United States passenger ship per week to go through the war zone, provided it was illuminated and clearly marked.

Tumulty noticed when he put the dispatch on the President's desk a clamping of the strong jaw as Wilson said "This means war." House reported that the next morning "the President said he felt as if the world . . . had begun to go from west to east and that he could not get his balance." He still wanted to stay out of war in order to save Europe afterward, but he referred to Germany as "a madman that should be curbed." On February 3 he announced to Congress that diplomatic relations with Germany were being severed as of that moment, but said that nothing except "overt acts" could make him believe that she intended to carry out her threats. There was a demand for a coalition Cabinet but Wilson refused to consider it, replying: "They will not get in. . . . The nominal coalition in England is nothing but a Tory Cabinet."

Then on February 25 the British announced that they had intercepted a note from Zimmerman, the German foreign minister, urging Mexico to make an alliance with Germany and offering her Arizona, Texas and New Mexico as a reward. Such a scheme aroused the Western states, together with all American citizens. But Wilson was still hoping for peace and was still worried about the lives of American soldiers. He shut himself up. He would see practically no one.

Now, at last, he did demand measures of defense and even of attack. He asked Congress to authorize the arming of American merchantmen. A filibuster in the Senate held up the measure, and at the same time killed other desirable legislation. The President expressed the conviction that "A little group of wilful men representing no opinion but their own have rendered the great government of the United States helpless and contemptible." On March 5 he armed the ships on his own authority. He sent Admiral Sims to confer with the British naval authorities. Yet the Allies were oppressed with the imminence of defeat; submarines were busy, the French Army was threatened with mutiny, and on March 15 the Czar of Russia abdicated. The need was great and immediate; and besides there was no longer any great autocracy lined up on the Allied side. Wilson advanced the date for the opening of Congress from April 16 to April 2.

On Saturday night, March 31, Wilson sat in his bathrobe typing his war message. Yet even then he could not willingly take such a step. He called Frank Cobb of the New York *World* to help him talk out his decision. Cobb arrived at one o'clock the morning of the second. Wilson appeared to him almost "uncanny" and seemed to feel that he might have done still more to avoid war. The enormity of the decision led him to say that "he'd never been so uncertain about anything in his life." He felt that he must ask for war. "But do you know what that means? It would mean that we should lose our heads along with the rest and stop weighing right and wrong." He expressed complete confidence in his country's strength, saying that "A declaration of war would mean that Germany would be so badly beaten that there would be a dictated peace, a victorious peace." But he still reiterated his hesitation because "Once lead the people into war and they'll forget there ever was such a thing as tolerance."

Criticism of various sorts has been heaped upon Wilson for his conduct in those years of American neutrality which ended that day. Not only many Americans of German birth but some well-known historians have said that Wilson did not act properly because he was not neutral in his own attitude. Professor Charles Tansill asserts that Wilson's bias in a pro-Ally direction was well known and says he was "by birth and upbringing distinctly British." Tansill's book *America Goes to War* is largely devoted to a development of the theme that Wilson set himself to turn American opinion against the Germans.

On the other hand James M. Beck blamed the absence of anti-German feeling upon the "spineless" policy of the President, whom he accused of playing for three years "the part of an insincere coward." Both of these points of view were of course widely held among substantial and vociferous elements of the American community at large; and there is some truth in both of them.

More justifiable is a line of criticism which holds that Wilson did not do what he could to prepare the country for the fact that it was likely to enter a great and serious war. If he had taken more adequate steps himself and also urged the necessity of doing so upon others, he could have built up the Army and Navy and so have made the conduct of the war far more efficient and the impact of American help more immediate. Franklin Roosevelt did much more effective work in this regard; Wilson's failure to do so cost the Allies and his country dearly both in men and money.

CHAPTER XVI

A CAPABLE
WAR PRESIDENT

Wilson's call to arms was issued on the misty evening of April 2 at eight-thirty o'clock. After his qualms of the previous night he had definitely made up his mind, so that he seemed to have no hesitation left. All that day he was well guarded. He performed some routine duties and played a little golf but there can be no doubt that his mind was on the speech he had decided to deliver. At dinner with his family he did not allow the conversation to touch upon the the question of war. Yet immediately after his meal he drove slowly to the Capitol with an escort of cavalry. Other troops also guarded him amid the crowds that were packed around the building, illuminated by indirect lighting that evening for the first time.

As he ascended the rostrum to face the houses of Congress, his face was tense and white. With a voice pitched low by deep feeling, he presented the situation that confronted the nation. He declared "the recent course of the Imperial German government to be in fact nothing less than war against the Government and people of the United States." He spoke of the sinking of "hospital ships and ships carrying relief to the sorely bereaved and stricken people of Belgium," . . . "acts committed upon the seas where no nation had right of dominion and where lay the free highways of the world." In the face of this violation of the rights of humanity, he announced, "There is one choice we cannot make, we are incapable of making: we will not choose the path of submission." At this there was a burst of applause, led by the old Confederate veteran, Chief Justice White.

Wilson then set forth his interpretation of America's purpose and suggested a League of Nations. "Our object is to vindicate the principles of peace and justice in the life of the world. . . . A steadfast concert for peace can never be maintained except by a partnership of democratic nations," he declared. He called for an increase of at least 500,000 men in the army, to be "chosen upon the principle of universal liability to service," and then announced the fighting slogan, "The world must be made safe for democracy."

When the applause for this battle cry had died down, he proclaimed: "We shall fight for . . . democracy, for the right of those who submit to authority to have a voice in their own government." Then he went on in a lower key: "To such a task we can dedicate our lives and our fortunes, everything we are and everything that we have." And he concluded: "America is privileged to spend her blood and her might for the principles which gave her birth and happiness, and the peace which she has treasured. God helping her, she can do no other!"

The cheers rolled on even while he was leaving the platform and he smiled at some of those who crowded around him; but he was sad too with the realization of what he had been doing. Fifty years before, Tommy Wilson had swung on the parsonage gate in Atlanta to see the ragged and war-weary soldiers of the defeated Confederacy come home. Their farms and homes must be rebuilt, their lives remade, while there were those who never would return. Tommy had long since changed to Woodrow, the thoughtful boy into the stubborn man, but he was all the more aware of the many evils brought about by war. So, as he rode back to the White House with Tumulty, he could not help exclaiming, "Think what they were applauding! My message today was a message of death for their young men. How strange it seems to applaud that!" But in his declaration of war the nation was behind him. The people had been ready to fight before the President was; they were willing to pour out their blood at his call, if that was neded to stop the Kaiser's armies.

Colonel House spent the remainder of the evening with the Wilsons, where he noted an atmosphere of relief at the end of the period of suspense. After a quiet discussion of the day's events Wilson read aloud, instead of the usual poetry, a clipping presenting a European estimate of himself. When House suggested that "the President had taken a position as to policies which no other statesman had yet assumed," Wilson expressed an understandable surprise, thinking, "Webster, Lincoln and Gladstone had announced the same principles."

Four days later Congress officially passed a Declaration of War against Germany at three o'clock in the morning, with only six senators and fifty members of the House voting against the measure. Wilson was having lunch with his wife and his cousin Helen Bones when the resolution was brought in for his signature. The division in the country was about in the same proportion as that which occurred in Congress, with the war fever soon well-fed by recruiting drives and the draft. Meanwhile Wilson was given powers larger than anyone could handle, so that he quickly turned them over to other individuals, boards and commissions, many specially created for this purpose. He felt that these temporary agencies were not only essential to do the work but that it was also desirable to prevent this extra authority being given to permanent government bodies. He noted to one Cabinet member that he had observed "an extreme reluctance on the part of government departments to relinquish any powers which had once been granted them."

All through the war the President worked hard, often from six in the morning until after midnight. Eight days after the declaration of war Mrs. Wilson had to take a day off in bed. When Wilson came to her that evening he read a paper he had just prepared asking for the co-operation of American industry. When she asked if he should not include the railroads he replied, "I had forgotten them. My brain is just too tired to act." So his wife packed him off to the theater with his daughter Margaret and Helen Bones for a brief relaxation. He seemed to Mrs. Wilson like a different person on his return. When Admiral Grayson recommended that he take more exercise he said he would try horseback riding and to encourage him, Mrs. Wilson suggested that she too would like to ride. Next day she was asked to be ready to ride at five o'clock with Dr. Grayson and her husband. So a new form of recreation was added to the President's routine.

Little had been done to convert the nation to an arms economy before the declaration of war. Secretary Daniels had built up the Navy, while some of the rest of the war program had already been planned by an advisory commission to the Council of National Defense which had been set up in 1915. But that was about all. Wilson now appointed key men to be the heads of various new boards. Bernard M. Baruch was put in charge of War Industries, Herbert Hoover of Food, Edward M. Hurley of Shipping and Harry Garfield of Fuel. George Creel was given authority over war propaganda as chairman of a Committee on Public Information, while the administration sponsored an Espionage bill to prevent the dissemination of information useful to the enemy. These board heads, placed in control of various aspects of the economy, were designated as the "War Cabinet." They met every week in Wilson's study where they could have an informal discussion of their various problems.

The choice of eminent men who were well-known and trusted did a great deal to maintain popular confidence in the Administration. It was generally acknowledged that the men selected for these key positions were among the best available, that they were honest, soon learned their jobs, and were able executives. Little criticism was directed against them even by those whose activities were necessarily curtailed, or diverted from their course, as a result of the War Cabinet's various directives. Wilson appointed General Pershing as commander-in-chief in Europe and stood behind him and his staff in all their decisions.

Other surprising achievements in the conduct of the war were accomplished under Wilson's leadership. The country was aroused for the first time to thinking on a world scale and tremendous "Liberty Loans" were successfully floated. In no previous war had there been so little graft in the handling of public money, nor had the health and welfare of troops ever been so well preserved. The death rate among the soldiers was cut down to little more than one fifth of what it had been in the conflict with Spain.

One of the greatest victories Wilson enjoyed in his relations with Congress came when he won the members over to the passage of the Selective Service Act. A clear majority of both houses had been in favor of only a call for volunteers at the time of the declaration of war, so that Wilson almost alone had to persuade the reluctant members to accept the principle of universal liability to military service. Congress, however, did hold out for the exemption of conscientious objectors, a provision which Wilson thought was undesirable because it might lead to fraud and injustice; but in obedience to the law nearly ten million men registered for the draft on June 5.

The passage of this act had been made more difficult by the activities of Theodore Roosevelt. Two months before the declaration of war the ex-President had written Newton Baker asking permission to raise an infantry division of volunteers plus a cavalry brigade to serve in France. Then on April 11 Roosevelt came rushing into the White House, offered Tumulty a commission along with a slap on the back and disappeared in Wilson's study to expound the details of his plan. After the question had been given consideration by the military authorities, Secretary Baker told the ex-President that there was no place in the American forces for volunteer armies or untrained strategists. At this Roosevelt privately complained that "The one real arch offender is Wilson; if our people were really awake, he would be impeached tomorrow."

Wilson might have far more easily permitted Roosevelt to have a division to play with, except that he had no desire to endanger the lives of American soldiers with an inexperienced commander. The passage of the Selective Service Act by the House on April 29 was even held up for two weeks in the Senate by an attempt to attach a provision granting Roosevelt the right to raise four volunteer divisions. Finally a compromise was reached, making the acceptance of these divisions optional with Wilson. The decision had already been left with the secretary of War, who was convinced that the former President was by no means qualified for such a command merely because of his participation in the Spanish-American hostilities.

Trouble also came from General Leonard Wood, who had for a while been Roosevelt's candidate for President in 1916. Wood was the top-ranking major general, he had been the chief proponent of preparedness, and he expressed the belief that when it came to a question of assigning him to active service in France, "They would never dare hold me back." But the existing General Staff believed he lacked real ability, while Pershing definitely stated that he would not serve in France if Wood were there. So Wood did an excellent job training soldiers at home.

This granting of full power to the General Staff left Wilson strength to turn to other things. But his absolute refusal to reveal that the decision had been that of the Army's high command rather than his own forced him to bear an undeserved imputation of using the Presidential power for political ends. This erroneous impression helped to pile up resentment and ill will against him.

The many other problems which claimed Wilson's attention were also a tremendous burden. Almost immediately after the United States entered the war urgent requests for aid poured in from France and England. Both needed loans and large amounts of credit so that they could make further purchases of arms and ammunition in this country. Since submarine warfare was placing England in danger of starvation, all American vessels which could help cope with the U-boat menace were sent to sea, and new freighters were built as quickly as possible. A system of priorities in the shipment of freight on the railroads soon had to be established with the approval of the President, and the public became accustomed to wheatless and meatless days as well as to the rationing of sugar and coal.

Wilson also had to take charge of American military planning. General Pershing was sent to France with a few men to work under Marshal Foch, while longer range plans were required to provide for the training and transportation of the American Expeditionary Force. American performance has been called inadequate in the effort to give the Allies enough planes to dominate the air. But in most matters Wilson provided even more assistance than could have been expected. He helped tighten the blockade by joining the British in the performance of many things which he had protested against before; and on their recommendation he enlarged the list of contraband to include everything possible, with no distinction between absolute and conditional contraband. He refused to allow any vessel to refuel in American ports if its activities might benefit Germany and he ordered the Navy to scatter mines all over the North Sea, so that vessels approaching any German port were in danger of being sunk.

Although Wilson hoped that Americans would "all speak, act and serve together," the suffragettes were parading in the streets vociferously demanding votes for women, and more strikes than usual broke out in spite of the new boards which had been created to settle labor disputes. Wilson informed an A. F. of L. convention in November 1917 that all possible methods of conciliation and settlement must be tried before work was held up. He told a group of manufacturers that theirs was "a contribution that costs you neither a drop of blood nor a tear," and on the whole he felt labor was "reasonable in a larger number of cases than the capitalists." Prices had been raised on many articles to what Wilson considered an exorbitant degree, while shipping rates on freight had been increased without regard to the fact that war-risk insurance took care of the extra dangers. When he heard a demand that it was necessary to pay very liberal and unusual profits in order to "stimulate production," he asked if the businessmen felt that they must be bribed to make a contribution when men everywhere were depending upon them "to bring them out of bondage." Price controls and excess-profit taxes were never even considered, but the President tried to keep costs of the war down as well as he could.

Although Mexico was seething with unrest and Japan was causing trouble by claiming special rights in China, Russia created a still greater problem when the Czar abdicated on March 15, 1917. This at first seemed to improve the moral position of the European Allies, since none of them were any longer great autocracies, and Wilson immediately instructed Secretary Lansing to recognize the new government, which he hoped would continue the war. A mission headed by Elihu Root reported after a visit that German propaganda was undermining the Russians' will to fight so that the Army was falling to pieces and the "socialistic element" was increasing its influence. Most of the old divisions of the empire were seeking to break away from it, while even in Petrograd and Moscow the Bolsheviks had to ally themselves with terrorists in order to maintain their power. The Germans had taken over the Ukraine and the Turks were marching into the Caucasus.

Most Americans criticized the Bolsheviks not so much because they were Communists as for their failure to maintain the war against Germany. But Lenin believed that peace was essential for the spread of Communism even if it meant letting the Germans keep the Ukraine and furnishing them with supplies. The French were especially bitter against the Bolsheviks on the grounds that they had repudiated their foreign debts, were offensive atheists, and were brutally suppressing opposition at home. Both the French and British suspected that Lenin was a mere agent of Germany and they wanted to intervene without any invitation from the Russian leaders themselves. They said that one excuse for intervention was to prevent seizure by the Germans of the extensive war supplies which had been furnished by the Allies and were in storage at Murmansk. Another was the saving of 50,000 Czechoslovak soldiers who had enlisted to fight the Germans and were now being threatened by the Bolsheviks.

Neither Ambassador Francis nor Root's mission was any real help to Wilson in making his decisions on Russia. In his hope that a democratic government could be established there, he failed to realize that the people were too inexperienced in all political matters to give it any chance to work. He tried to appeal to the Russian masses in a message to "the people" of Russia on March 11, 1918, but he could only send it through the Congress of Soviets. After conveying thanks for his sympathy, the Bolshevik leaders responded with the hope that all nations including the United States would soon "throw off the yoke of capitalism" so that they could "establish a socialistic state of society which alone is capable of securing a just and lasting peace."

Russia withdrew from the war by the treaty of Brest-Litovsk on March 3, 1918, but when the other Allied governments protested the treaty Wilson refused to join them. Since he wanted to preserve a spirit of friendliness with Russia, he tried to regard her as still a co-belligerent. But there was a constantly growing demand for intervention in Russia both from the Allies and from far-seeing persons in this country. Both Foch and Balfour wanted to keep alive the eastern front against Germany, so they sought to have Wilson send a few troops to Murmansk to indicate American co-operation. But he could not know for certain whether the Russians wanted help in overthrowing their Bolshevik rulers or would resent outside intervention.

In July 1918, Wilson finally decided that we should help the Czechoslovak soldiers in Siberia protect themselves. He also gave in to wishes of the Supreme War Council by sending some soldiers to Murmansk, but he hated to do this, and agreed only because he had refused so many other Allied requests. When the British general in northern Russia tried to use the Allied troops there and in Siberia to open a new eastern front against the Germans, Wilson was bitter over the "utter disregard" of the provisions he had attached to the sending of American troops. The end of the war in November turned the attention of all the Allies to more immediate problems. Wilson had tried to be just and fair, and to do as far as possible what the Russian people desired. But he had pleased few. Brandeis regarded these concessions to the Allies as Wilson's first great mistake, while most of the Allied leaders felt he had maintained too stubbornly his own point of view. So he really satisfied no one with all the effort and thought he had applied to the Russian problem.

The development of Bolshevism under Lenin and Trotsky, together with the question of how to deal with this uprising of the proletariat, worried Americans in 1917 far less than the course of the war. Britian had introduced tanks into trench warfare, pushing the Germans back in Belgium early in the year, but a change came in October 1917 when Austrian troops pushed back Italian reserves of older men all the way from the Isonzo River to the Piave, only a few miles from Venice. They smashed the Italian army at Caporetto and in November the collapse of Russia freed forty additional German divisions for service in the west, giving the Central Powers a definite numerical superiority along that front.

The Germans then felt they were ready finally to knock out the tired armies of France and Britain as soon as spring arrived. Hindenburg started an offensive in March 1918 which broke through between the French and British armies. Before long the tremendous gun "Big Bertha" was dropping shells on Paris, and Europe was crying for help. Wilson sent messages to Pershing urging every effort to help stem the tide, and in the end it was the added assistance of American troops that stopped the drive.

CHAPTER XVII

THE "FOURTEEN POINTS" AND GERMANY'S COLLAPSE

Even before the German advance was stopped near Paris, Wilson had begun a campaign for victory upon the higher front of men's minds. Here he gained one of his greatest successes, one of the surprising achievements of the spirit and mind of man. By an appeal to a universal sense of justice, by a promise of fair dealing, he drew the imagination of many Germans away from thoughts of conquest and toward a desire for peace. It is true that the attraction of his offer was increased because the naval blockade of Germany was reducing its people to a semi-starved condition, the German Navy was bottled up and disgruntled, and the German Army had met forces which were able to prevent any sudden sweep to victory. Yet with the collapse of Russia one of Germany's greatest antagonists had fallen and it seemed possible that additional food from the Ukraine would strengthen the German position, at least enough to gain a stalemate.

Wilson started his campaign in December with a speech at the opening of Congress which specifically asked for a peace of "generosity and justice." More cheers came for his request for a declaration of war against Austria, but he continued his discussion of the proper terms of peace in another address before Congress on January 8 when he enunciated his Fourteen Points, "the only possible program as we see it."

Wilson had begun four months earlier to dig out the background and the facts upon which this speech was based. It was then that he had requested Colonel House to gather together a group of experts to investigate the most vital questions concerning peace, so that he could see what America's stand should be. This group of specialists calling themselves "The Inquiry" were under the supervision of Sidney Mezes, president of the College of the City of New York and brother-in-law of House. These men, learned in history, economics and government, continued their work right up to the time of the Peace Conference. The idea was to enable the President to speak with authority and knowledge upon many intricate aspects of world affairs, but their recommendations were frequently subject to charges of prejudice and unfairness.

Since claims of the other Allies had to be considered, House was sent abroad as the American representative at the inter-Allied council. Lloyd George and Balfour let him know that Britain wanted all the German colonies in Africa, a protectorate over Arabia, Palestine for the Jews and an independent Armenia under American protection. While Trotsky appealed for an end to the conflict and the British called for intervention in Russia, Wilson was working out a statement of American objectives. He almost decided to abandon any public announcement after Lloyd George made a magnificent speech before the Trades Union Congress along the same lines as Wilson was thinking; but the recent publication by the Bolsheviks of secret treaties made before America entered the war made the British leader's rostrum a precarious pedestal from which to talk about ideals. It took the character and sincerity of Woodrow Wilson to win the mind and heart of the world.

So great was the appeal to the masses of Germans and so influential were Wilson's words in the winning of the war that subsequent dictators in Germany and Russia have been careful to seal the frontiers of their countries against foreign ideas and propaganda. Wilson had given them an example before they came to power of what great effect an outside voice calling upon reason and justice could have upon their followers. He was right when he once referred to the American Declaration of Independence as a "whip for tyrants."

The "Fourteen Points" speech on January 8, 1918, began by calling attention to the danger that "unless justice is done to others it will not be done to us." Wilson then stated his Fourteen Points clearly in little more than a thousand words. The main principles can be stated still more briefly if not so completely as follows:

1. Open covenants of peace openly arrived at.
2. Absolute freedom of navigation upon the seas.
3. The removal, as far as possible, of all trade barriers.
4. Guarantees that armaments will be reduced.
5. Adjustment of colonial claims based upon the interests of the populations.
6. Evacuation of Russian territory and leaving her unembarrassed for the independent determination of her own political development.
7. Belgium must be evacuated and restored.
8. French territory evacuated and restored. Alsace-Lorraine to France.
9. Frontiers of Italy on lines of nationality.
10. The peoples of Austria-Hungary should be accorded autonomous development.
11. Rumania, Serbia and Montenegro evacuated and restored.
12. Dardanelles opened to ships of all nations.
13. An independent Poland with access to the sea.
14. A general association of nations to guarantee independence and territorial integrity to all nations (—to Wilson the most essential point of all).

He went on to annouce: "For such arrangements and covenants we are willing to fight and to continue to fight until they are achieved." This seemed to be an assurance for the world of peace, free trade, and just frontiers, with guarantees against aggression, an end to hatred and to armaments. All this with a League of Nations, the strength of America and the integrity of her President to help make it come true.

The speech aroused great enthusiasm. Lodge and Theodore Roosevelt, the *New York Times* and *Tribune* extolled it; and so did others in letters and telegrams from all over the country. Although Britain was worried over Point 2 which advocated freedom of the seas and Italy feared to lose the rewards promised her in the Treaty of London, most of their people approved. The Germans doubted the sincerity of the other Allied statesmen, but they did not question the honesty of Wilson. Copies were distributed on a large scale among the populations of Germany and Austria, where the leaflets did much to destroy the morale both of the fighting forces and the people at home.

Wilson probably deliberately tried to drive a wedge between the German people and their leaders, for he declared that "We have no jealousy of Germany's greatness and there is nothing in this program that impairs it. We grudge her no achievement or distinction of learning or of pacific enterprise. . . . We wish her only to accept a place of equality among the peoples of the world—the new world in which we now live—instead of a place of mastery." On September 27 he again asserted that America would fight to the finish against the "military masters of Germany" who had "shown themselves to be devoid of honor or humanity."

Wilson added at least thirteen more points in later speeches, but some of these were repetitions, so that the total came to about twenty-three. There was to be no bartering of peoples, legitimate national ambitions were to be satisfied, arbitrary power was to be destroyed, international dealing should be honorable, territorial adjustments were to be made in the interests of the peoples concerned, and the peace was to be just and enduring. But while the American people and newspapers were generally enthusiastic about the points it is probable they did not really understand and approve them. Certainly the greatest editorial acclaim greeted those which promised severe treatment for the Germans.

Consequently troubles and disasters loomed ahead for this idealistic program. Wilson should have realized that even the American people were not supporting him, that there had been at the start a great sentiment for a limited-liability war, for the idea that America should quit once her rights were acknowledged. This did not seem to indicate any fundamental willingness on the part of the country to remain involved in world affairs once victory had been won. The American people were more interested in "licking the Kaiser" than in remaking the world after this main purpose had been accomplished. Wilson had keyed up his own country and even the people of Europe to hope for a better world; but a reaction was inevitable, a reaction against the sacrifices which the peace that Wilson pictured would entail.

Nor was there much that Wilson could do toward winning the Allies to support his views. He could scarcely drive a bargain with them when entering the war. Any concessions or agreements made by the Allies then would have been obtained under duress and they would probably have felt quite justified in not living up to them.

So far as American opinion is concerned it was probably unfortunate that Wilson insisted that America was only an "Associate" of the other powers, and not an "Ally." He evidently did not want to become involved in the secret treaties and schemes for aggrandizement which motivated most of the other nations. Yet it would probably have been easier, if he wished to win a continuing involvement of America in world affairs if he had joined the Alliance of European nations in time of war rather than trying to initiate such an action in time of peace. Perhaps it should have been done while people were at a high pitch and ready to work together, not after the coming of peace had led almost everyone, except Wilson himself, to fall back from their high ideals of co-operation and mutual helpfulness.

Wilson did not let up in his efforts to inspire the Allies and demoralize the enemy. Defeats and danger in the field of battle turned slowly during the summer into prospects of victory. But even before this Wilson continued to point out the terms of peace, terms which insured victory but were still marked by generosity and justice.

On February 11 he replied to a new declaration of German war aims by stating four additional points, which were largely an interpretation of certain of the original Fourteen. Two months later he reversed his former pronouncements that force never settled anything. Instead he called for "Force, force to the utmost, force without stint or limit, the righteous and triumphant force which shall make Right the law of the World." This appeal was issued just after he had replied to Lord Reading's appeal for more troops on the western front with the definite promise: "Mr. Ambassador, you need say no more. I will do my damnedest."

On July 4 Wilson gave an address called the "Four Points" speech in which he depicted on "one side the free peoples of the world; who were opposed by an isolated friendless group of governments who seek no common purposes." He demanded the "reduction to virtual impotence" of "every arbitrary power" that would "of its single choice disturb our peace." This might have reminded the German rulers of his Flag Day speech the year before in which he insisted that to get a favorable peace the Germans would have to set up "a government accountable to the people themselves." Already he was thinking of himself as the champion of all peoples who sought to set up democratic governments.

Other points suggested in this speech demanded "the reign of law" and that standards of morality such as prevailed in private life should be followed in relations between nations. He also wanted a peace arranged "upon the basis of . . . free acceptance . . . by the people immediately concerned." These last terms were such as might be acceptable to the Germans, even though the one which sought to interfere with their form of government could scarcely be to the taste of their rulers.

All this time Wilson remained in comparative isolation as he was unable to enjoy any general talk even with the most intelligent men. When Bliss Perry suggested to the French ambassador Jusserand that he should stop by the White House some evening "and talk Wordsworth" with the President, the diplomat replied, "He doesn't want to see any of us." Wilson kept both himself and his country aloof, so that it was impossible to come to any exact agreement with our Allies upon the terms which should be demanded for peace.

Yet his seclusion was that of a scholar rather than a bureaucrat. He frequently appeared before the public in casual and unpretentious ways, with none of the trappings of dictatorship. Every Sunday he walked to church with Mrs. Wilson and he was even seen once at Manhattan Transfer in his private car holding a skein of yarn for her to wind. He was sympathetic with those who came to him for help and understanding in their personal problems. After he had interviewed the representatives of some of the persecuted minorities from Austria-Hungary he was moved almost to tears. Masaryk described him as "actually incandescent with feeling," an "intensely human person." And he still enjoyed a joke, as was shown when Dr. Grayson made him wear a white glove to avoid infection in a burn on his hand and he wrote his daughter that he felt as though he should be "handling things."

Nor did he as yet show any special evidence of conceit. He prohibited the Muscle Shoals Dam from being named in his honor and he wrote the officers of Cambridge University who were conferring a degree upon him that he was unable to see how he had ever done more than follow the plain path of duty. When Mrs. Wilson was accused with utterly no foundation of being pro-German and he was reported to have taken the nation into war for the profit of the great corporations his feelings were lacerated, but he tried not "to take the malignancy too seriously."

The question of boundaries promised to be less difficult than some of the other problems, except where Wilson's ideas conflicted with the promises made to Italy in 1915 to gain her help in the war. But when it came to more general ideas such as freedom of the seas, open covenants, the removal of economic barriers and the making of an association of nations, there were sure to be discouragements. When a British general inquired in a loud voice of Mrs. John W. Davis the wife of our new ambassador, what she believed to be the meaning of freedom of the seas, she replied she feared she knew little about it, but believed it "had something to do with mixed bathing, hadn't it?" The next day her apartment was filled with flowers from the embassy's enthusiastic staff.

Wilson had not neglected the actual physical conduct of the war even while waging psychological warfare with his speeches. He gave the Allies all the financial help they needed so badly, and used the American Navy to help the British enforce their blockade of German ports. Nor did he hesitate to send troops to France, increasing the small task forces of 1917 until they became an Expeditionary Force of almost two million men by the end of the war. Both he and Pershing wished to keep the American armies in a sort of unit with their own officers and staff, rather than permitting them merely to be used when convenient to bolster weak spots in the French and English lines as Marshall Foch desired. The final result of this argument was a compromise which no one regarded as very satisfactory, but which worked reasonably well in practice.

The great German assault which began March 21, 1918, rolled forward to within about eighty miles of Paris. Things began to look very bad for the Allies until more and more American forces were sent in to help hold back the Teutonic flood. Finally in the latter part of July the Allies began an offensive of their own, sparked by the American victories at Château-Thierry and Belleau Wood. By the end of August, General Ludendorff recognized unmistakable signs that the tide had turned and that the only course now open to the Germans was to pull back their forces and give up hopes of decisive victory. At the same time the blockade of Germany by the British fleet was bringing the people face to face with famine; while Wilson's ideas had been permeating their minds until they were just about ready to withdraw their support of the war. This effect of Wilson's speeches had been foreseen when he and House were talking together in the summer White House at Magnolia, Massachusetts, about "organizing Liberal opinion to break down the German military machine."

The prospect of peace brought problems far more intricate than those of war. Even the preliminary negotiations involved so many governments with so many diverse interests that it seemed almost impossible to come to any agreement. But Wilson was ready to take the initiative. He felt that he could make proposals which might be accepted by all concerned, and against any who did not willingly accept them he was ready to use coercion through America's financial power. But of course the difficulty remained, that if a surface acceptance was forced upon his Allies as well as his enemies they would be unwilling to abide by the agreement when the power of coercion was removed. Germany was too broken to resist, but the Allies were in no such condition. Each nation was determined to satisfy its individual interests with little regard on the part of its leaders for Wilson's idealism.

In September, Wilson talked about a League of Nations and what would be a proper price to pay for peace. He berated militarism and autocratic governments and called for a peace of "impartial justice in every item." When he again promised that economic barriers between nations should be removed as far as possible, he found himself forced to modify his stand in order to mollify his own countrymen. He did this by stating that tariffs could be of any height provided they did not discriminate between countries. Yet Wilson felt there was no avoiding the fact that any continuing acceptance and enforcement of all the points which consisted of broad general principles must be dependent upon the establishment of some sort of league of nations.

About the middle of September, Austria suggested a compromise peace and on the 27th the Bulgarian armies surrendered. That evening in a speech for the Fourth Liberty Loan at the Metropolitan Opera House, Wilson again called for a peace of "impartial" justice in every item" while promising that "the United States is prepared to assume its full share of responsibility for the maintenance of the common covenants and understandings." Meanwhile Germany's field marshals were demanding an immediate end to the fighting. On October 6 the new chancellor, Prince Maximilian of Baden, sent a request through the Swiss Legation to Wilson that he call a conference for the purpose of arranging an armistice on the basis of the Fourteen Points and his speech of September 27. At the same time it was evident that the Germans were not counting on any sort of real surrender; if they could not gain peace they hoped to gain time.

Wilson was very pleased to receive this message which seemed to place the power of negotiation entirely in his hands. Confidence in his determination to bring a peace of justice and forbearance had made it natural that the Germans should appeal primarily to him for a settlement which would accord with those ideas, and it was clever of them to take the unusual step of trying to include peace terms in a request for an armistice. They did not refer to his "Four Point" speech of July 4 which demanded a "reduction to virtual impotence" of "every arbitrary power" nor to his Flag Day speech of 1917 which asserted that Germany must have a government "accountable to the people themselves" if there was to be any true basis for peace.

Many people were dissatisfied with the course the negotiations were taking. Senator Lodge and others feared that the German peace feelers were merely a trap into which the President would fall, especially since he did not seem to desire the complete destruction of Germany. Lodge immediately denounced any negotiated peace or any sort of peace that would satisfy the Germans. Meanwhile our Allies felt that they should be consulted, and ex-President Taft as well as many other Republicans agreed with them. But Wilson ignored them and after two days had his answer ready, asking the Germans to be more specific and demanding the removal of enemy troops from Allied territory. When the Germans sank another passenger ship, the *Leinster* without warning on October 12, their secretary of State remarked of this new affront to world opinion, "That sort of thing is terribly exasperating." Meanwhile Wilson's reply, couched in mild terms, avoided the possibility of stirring up German sentiment for continuing the war. Yet it did make clear that the President wished to know whether the request for peace came from "the constituted authorities of Germany," indicating that he was fully conscious of the strength of his own position.

When Tumulty told Wilson on his way in to dinner on October 12 that his terms had been accepted, the President was so pleased that he scribbled a note for House saying, "tell Mrs. W." But disappointment followed a complete reading of the note for it demanded a mixed commission to supervise the evacuation of Allied soil, which Wilson emphatically informed House was not satisfactory. He was not willing to treat with Imperial Germany unless she was so beaten that she would accept *any* armistice terms. In his reply Wilson indicated that Allied officers would arrange all the military conditions and also pointed out that the existing German government was an arbitrary power which could disturb the peace of the world and therefore according to his "Point Four" speech must be reduced to impotence.

German newspapers screamed that this attempt to dictate their form of government was far beyond "limits of the endurable," but Wilson had still not presented his enemies with any issue which could rally the German people to continued resistance. Still hoping that Wilson might give him such a weapon Prince Max informed the President on October 21 that Germany's parliament or Reichstag had been entrusted with the government of the country including the power to make peace or war. Now for the first time Wilson brought these matters before his Cabinet and sent Colonel House to Europe to confer with the statesmen of Britain, France, and Italy. This was just a few days after House had told Lansing that Wilson was considering going to the Peace Conference in person.

In his third note Wilson bluntly asserted that "The United States cannot deal with any but the veritable representatives of the German people . . . if it must deal with the military masters and the monarchial autocrats of Germany . . . it must demand not peace negotiations but surrender." The German soldiers were worn out with fighting and now the German people were encouraged by this note to demand the abdication of the Kaiser. Consequently the Germans sent a gentle reply asking for "a peace of justice" and the Kaiser abdicated on the night of November 8.

Some of the Allies later accused Wilson of forcing them into an armistice of which they did not approve. It was seventeen days after the negotiations started that he turned the decision over to them.

During all that time he had conducted the negotiations without even consulting the Allies. His purpose probably was to put the Allies into a position where they would be obliged to follow a program based upon the Fourteen Points.

While the military leaders were drawing up armistice terms House was consulting with the diplomats in Paris, trying to force the Fourteen Points and Wilson's interpretation of them upon the Allied statesmen. Lloyd George objected to the demand for freedom of the seas in wartime, since it would deprive Britain of her greatest weapon, the blockade. Clemenceau and Orlando had other objections on behalf of their countries. House hinted that Wilson might have to make their objections public, a statement which he reported "had a very exciting effect upon those present." At the same moment Wilson was cabling House that if anyone sought to nullify his influence he would "speak of it to all the world."

By the end of October the German troops were reeling backward, and on November 3 Austria replied to a demand for immediate surrender by accepting an armistice. Discussion of the terms for Germany included a British agreement to review the problems of freedom of the seas in view of the submarine threat and Clemenceau's insistence that reparations should include "any future claims or demands on the part of the Allies." On November 7 word came to America from Brest that an armistice had been concluded and before it was proved false bells clanged, whistles roared and crowds of citizens rejoiced. Although the rumor was premature, still that very night German emissaries crossed the western front to offer surrender in a railroad car in the woods of Compiègne. On Monday, the 11, at five in the morning, the Armistice was signed under the authority of Friedrich Ebert, provisional head of the new German republic, and six hours later the fighting ceased.

CHAPTER XVIII

THE DIZZY PINNACLE
OF HUMAN FAME

For about two months after the Armistice Wilson was hailed by the masses of people everywhere as the hope of humanity and many of their leaders felt the same way. Henri Bergson, the French philosopher, sent a message to him, "Tell the President he is our Pope. Where we used to look to Rome for spiritual leading, now we look to Washington." And Clemenceau had written him a year before that "You set us such a magnificent example that we need only follow you." He became for a moment the accepted moral leader of mankind.

Wilson's great idea, his great contribution to the future peace of the world, was his plan for a League of Nations. This was to provide a means for the use of force, the combined force of many nations if necessary, to compel peaceful settlements and prevent war. It was this idea plus his efforts to bring about a peace of equity and justice, with "open covenants openly arrived at" and "the self-determination of peoples," which Maximilian Harden had in mind when he said that "Only one conqueror's work will endure, Wilson's thought."

From a worldly standpoint, the summit of Wilson's glory came at the moment when the German surrender brought the Allies the victory he had done so much to win. Yet his supreme effort for peace and the welfare of humanity lay in the future in his continued

227

struggle for a just peace and a League of Nations. This fight had just begun.

From the peak there was perhaps no other way to go but down. Some authorities have felt that in October 1918, when his battle for lasting peace entered its most serious phase, they were able to perceive some failing of his powers. This condition became clearly evident after his breakdown at the Peace Conference, but, it was not perceptible to most of his contemporaries in those October days just before the final victory. Justice Brandeis, whom Wilson had appointed to the Supreme Court, believed that he noticed a weakening at an even earlier date, but Professor Thomas A. Bailey has gone exhaustively into the evidence and places it in those last weeks of October 1918.

Bailey believes that from October "we see a different Wilson"; that no longer was his judgment so clear, and that he began to make decisions and undertake actions which, though understandable, were later proved unwise. He aroused unnecessary antagonisms, and tried to force his will upon others, to an extent which excited their resentment and anger. All this simply put needless obstacles in the path of his plans for lasting peace.

Nor did he any longer sufficiently delegate authority. During the war he had made use of the help of many able men and maintained a serenity of spirit which made it possible for him to play golf and attend the theater even during the darkest days. But from now on he seemed to want to do everything himself; he wore himself out with impossible burdens. This change of method may have been due to what he felt to be the supreme importance of the problems involved; but the results were disastrous to his always precarious health.

If there was a change in Wilson, what caused it? Professor Bailey suggests that it may have been "the strong wine of victory" going to his head. Or that perhaps "the responsibility of remaking the world" which Wilson felt lay largely on his shoulders was too great a burden for him to bear. At any rate, his mind and nature became too intense. He tried to do too much work himself. He may even have been constantly in danger of a collapse. After this October his judgment was frequently at fault and he became hard to work with, suspicious of other people's intentions. The rapt concentration of his mind and nature seemed to be given full rein until they broke him.

It might even have been that he suffered a slight stroke or some other physical attack in those last victorious autumn days. The work, the excitement, the necessity for making decisions vital for the welfare of the world may have carried his intense spirit and his frail body to a pitch they could not endure. It is known that often a man suffers a stroke or other physical injury so slight that he is actually unaware of its impact upon himself, although his wisdom and his reasonableness are unalterably impaired. Something of the sort seems to have come upon Wilson at this time, a physical shock, a weakening of his mind and nervous system.

A definite sign of this weakening in Wilson's judgment came in his appeal to the people just prior to the Congressional elections of November 1918. On October 25 he asked the voters for a Democratic majority in both houses of Congress by issuing a statement to the press. Mrs. Wilson records that when she found him composing the statement on his typewriter she said: "I would not send it out. It is not a dignified thing to do." But Wilson said he had promised and could not honorably withhold it. This promise had been given at the earnest solicitation of many congressmen and officeholders who feared for their positions. The issuance of the appeal had also been urged by such astute politicians as Burleson and Tumulty. They pointed out that Theodore Roosevelt and President McKinley had made similar solicitations during the Spanish War.

But now Theodore Roosevelt and other Republican leaders expressed great indignation. The appeal was a direct and outspoken request for the election of a Democratic majority to both houses. Wilson recognized that such an appeal would be unseemly in ordinary times but he said that this was a "most critical period." He explained that he did not question the patriotism of the Republican statesmen who had supported the war loyally, but that they had tried to embarrass the Administration. He explained, quite truthfully, that the Republican leaders were "pro-war" but "anti-administration." And especially he urged the importance of convincing Europeans that he had the support of his own people at home.

The vote gave the Republicans a small majority in the House and Senate. Their Senate majority was obtained only by the seating of Truman Newberry as Senator from Michigan instead of Henry Ford. Newberry and over one hundred others were later indicted for unlawful expenditures to obtain his election and he was subsequently forced from his seat; but his temporary hold upon it made Lodge the chairman of the Foreign Relations Committee during this critical period. It was not true that the vote was a genuine repudiation of Wilson's leadership, since his tenure of office was not in question. People probably voted their dislike of taxes, rationing and all war restrictions, and the elections also gave them a chance to vote local prejudices and to express general dissatisfaction. If Wilson's leadership had seemed to be in question many of them might have voted quite differently. It was in fact not a genuine vote upon his policies, and it is quite likely that the vote would have been the same if he had not made the appeal. But the fact that he had issued the appeal made the action of the voters appear more like a repudiation of his administration than it really was and it undoubtedly hurt his prestige abroad. Premier Hughes of Australia indicated this when he said Wilson "had no claim to speak even for his own country," much less for the world.

It has been said that Wilson "lost the peace" for lack of "preparedness" on his part. It is true that it might have been well to have more discussion of war aims before the Peace Conference opened and that Wilson might have brought himself into closer relations with the Allied leaders. A very considerable groundwork had been laid for the conferences which were to open at Paris, but this was done almost entirely by the Allies among themselves without the participation of America.

The most definite and detailed part of this groundwork consisted of the secret treaties which had been made among the Europeans concerning the division of spoils in case of victory. Most of the treaties dealing with the redistribution of German territory paid little attention to the wishes of the populations concerned, but they were made to gain allies when allies were needed. Nor had the secret treaties been considered vicious before Wilson launched his criticism of them. Italy had been promised territory in the Alps and on the Adriatic, while Japan had been told she would acquire the German Pacific islands north of the Equator. Both British scholars and the group of Americans called "The Inquiry" sought to make a careful survey of all the territorial problems involved and were prepared to submit recommendations.

Not only were these problems complicated, but some sort of league or association of nations seemed likely to be helpful in enforcing and interpreting almost all provisions of the pact, except territorial changes which could be carried out almost immediately. Englishmen like Lord Bryce, Sir Edward Grey, prominent members of the famous Fabian Society and General Jan Smuts, had come out for the creation of such a league, and Lloyd George had included the idea among his recommendations in January 1918. A skeleton form for a league charter had been devised by a committee headed by Lord Phillimore; while Léon Bourgeois became associated with a movement of the same sort in France.

Wilson also had his own plan for a league, and most Americans at the moment were definitely in favor of establishing some such permanent organization. Support came from the American Peace Society, the World Peace Foundation and the World Court League, all actively spreading propaganda for the idea. Men high in Republican Party circles, such as Taft and Root, had been advocating a League of Nations; and Senator Lodge had taken the same position when he had shared the platform with Wilson in 1916 before the League to Enforce Peace.

Now, just a week after the armistice, Wilson announced his

intention of going to Europe to attend the Peace Conference. His first problem was with the diplomats of Europe. He must cope with France's Clemenceau, England's Lloyd George, as well as Italy's Orlando and Sonnino. Even before the armistice he had sent Colonel House over to meet with them and discuss the problems of postwar Europe. Perhaps he had made up his mind to go across himself as an arbiter of peace even before America entered the war. It evidently appeared to him important that he should go now to help make certain that the peace treaty was drawn up in accord with what he regarded as American ideals.

It has been said that this decision to go to the conference was the great mistake of his career. There were good arguments against his going, but there were also some excellent reasons why he should go. Perhaps his decision was made even more certain when House cabled from Paris that many unnamed Americans hoped the President's influence and prestige would not be endangered by his going, and added that both Clemenceau and the English felt the same way. Since Clemenceau had also expressed the opinion that no head of a state should be active, Wilson wired back: "I infer that French and English leaders desire to exclude me from the conference for fear I might then lead the weaker nations against them. . . . I play the same part in our government that the prime ministers play in theirs."

Many leading Republicans were furious about his going and kept dwelling upon the idea that he had just been repudiated in the Congressional elections. Even some Democratic senators felt that he should stay in America and revitalize the party. They argued that his trip was unconstitutional and unprecedented, while others said the Constitution did not prohibit the President from leaving the country and the times dictated his decision. Still other critics pointed out the problems of domestic reconstruction which needed his attention. Wilson felt these could wait, the reconstruction of the world could not. Unfortunately for him, he paid little attention during his absence to reports which Tumulty continually sent him on the trend of public opinion.

Wilson knew little of Europe and her statesmen at first hand, and although he possessed an extraordinary background of training in history and government, the problems were too varied and complicated for any one man to master all of them. It is not entirely true, as J. M. Keynes has hinted, that the foreign diplomats were able to "bamboozle this old Presbyterian," for he had studied the problems more thoroughly than most. Frequently he was to be found on all fours studying an ethnological or geographical map. Although he endangered both his moral ascendancy in Europe and his political strength at home by going to Paris, he took the stand that the task was so important that to evade it would have been immoral. He probably went from a sense of duty, but it is hard to believe that he was entirely free from a desire for self-glorification.

The common people everywhere seemed to be relying upon him to go, and he averred that a failure to do so would have been a betrayal of both the living and the dead. He regarded himself as the predominant spokesman of the allies; and the Germans had sought peace upon the basis of his Fourteen Points. The threads to be woven together appeared too numerous and varied to make a simple problem which could be settled from a distance, like that which faced President McKinley after the war with Spain. When Wilson came home for a mere month in February 1919, he found on his return to Paris that Lansing and House had yielded ground on many points which had to be rewon. There can be little doubt that he succeeded in incorporating many of his ideas into the peace treaty better than could have been done had he stayed at home.

Not only did he feel it his duty to go, but his decision may have been wise, when all the conditions are taken into consideration. These include the complication of the issues, his desire to stand up for the interests of his country, for justice and for the welfare of mankind; the expectation of the masses everywhere that he would go; the greater effectiveness he could have when he was present;

233

and his realization that the problems presented needed serious study. There is no assurance that he would have dealt with the Senate any more effectively if he had stayed at home, although he undoubtedly could have kept in closer touch with public opinion.

He believed he could bring the idealism of the New World to the council tables of the Old; that America was looking forward, while Europe was looking backward to her history, her traditions and her problems of former years. He was convinced that America wanted a peace of justice, while the European statesmen wanted security, with some additions to their territory and some compensation for their countries' losses. He desired a League of Nations, while Clemenceau put his trust in an old-fashioned balance of power. The freshness and hope of the American view point was to be brought by the happy warrior to a weary and disillusioned world.

Having decided to go himself, the question arose whom he should take with him as the other American delegates. His selections brought bitter trouble to him later on. Like each of the other great Allied powers, the United States was to have five commissioners, and it was his prerogative to choose them. He selected Colonel House, Robert Lansing, Henry White and General Tasker H. Bliss to go with him. Taft called them "a cheap lot of skates" and others referred to them as Wilson's "errand boys." Now the Republican leaders became still more violently indignant and they had something definite about which they could complain.

Wilson had a perfect legal and constitutional right to go and take with him whomever he wanted as the United States Commission. He had to choose Lansing, even though he had always in effect been his own secretary of State. House knew the European statesmen personally which was an advantage; General Bliss showed an unexpected grasp of economic and racial problems as well as of military matters, and Henry White was one of the outstanding career diplomats of our foreign service. But, except for Lansing, they could have been taken along as advisers and have been just as useful, while some senators might have been given the official positions so that they could help obtain for the final treaty the necessary two-thirds vote in the upper house. Editorial writers suggested Thomas J. Walsh of Montana and Philander Knox of Pennsylvania, a Republican who later became one of the severest critics of Wilson's treaty.

Root, Taft and Hughes were also possibilities among the Republicans who might have been taken along to appease the opposition. But these three were all men who were accustomed to making their own final decisions on policy and two had run against Wilson for the Presidency. Probably he felt that the harmonious working together of the group would have been more difficult if he had taken any one of them, which may well have been true. Yet it was in the end deeply unfortunate that he did not invite any outstanding leaders of the Republican Party which was definitely in control of the Senate. By doing so, he might have been able to gain their support and perhaps that of their party in his fight for the League, instead of making almost all Republicans resentful.

In his speech to Congress two days before sailing he failed to tell exactly why he was going or what kind of a peace it was that he wanted to bring home. It would have been better if he had been specific in outlining his purposes, but he felt that he had already set forth his ideas and he had always been one college professor who hated to repeat himself. He pointed out that "The peace settlements which are now to be agreed upon are of transcendent importance both to us and to the rest of the world." He said our soldiers had "consciously fought for the ideals which they knew to be the ideals of their country; I have sought to express those ideals." And he probably expressed his genuine feeling when he stated that "It is now my duty to play my full part in making good what they offered their life's blood to obtain."

Wilson sailed December 4 on the *S. S. George Washington* with high hopes of remaking the world. He left amid the shouts of the people on the shore; but he was not in a conciliatory mood. On shipboard he gathered his experts together and informed them that the other statesmen at Paris would not truly represent the wishes of their people, that only the American delegates would be disinterested, so that it was their duty to represent all mankind. Quoting Josiah Quincy, he said he intended "to do this pleasantly if I can, disagreeably if I must."

Wilson's arrival in Europe marked the moment when he became the idol of the masses everywhere, the recipient of the utmost in human adulation. He landed in Brest December 13 to the accompaniment of Presidential salutes, cheering sailors and shouting Frenchmen. The next morning he rode through the streets of Paris, packed with all the people they could hold, along the Seine, across the Place de la Concorde and up the Champs-Elysées. Never had the French accorded a king or emperor a more tumultuous reception. Banners were welcoming "Wilson le Juste." People were giving tongue to a swelling idealism which may well have led Wilson to believe success for his ideals was within his reach. Yet he must have realized something of the difficulties, for it was only a few days earlier that he had told George Creel that "People will endure their tyrants for years, but they tear their deliverers to pieces if a millennium is not created immediately."

From Paris, Wilson went to England, where he stayed at Buckingham Palace and made a speech at his mother's birthplace, Carlisle, near the Scottish border. But his welcome was far less enthusiastic than in France, and he was so busy talking about the new world which he envisaged that he neglected to give any adequate praise to the British soldiers and sailors who had done so much to win the war. This was neither tactful nor properly appreciative of their achievements. It was widely resented, as was his refusal to see the devastated areas of France lest his mind become inflamed by an exaggerated hatred of the Germans.

He went to Italy where he was enthusiastically cheered by the populaces of Milan and Rome. But the government officials feared his influence with the people; they felt that his obsession with the idea of the self-determination of nations would cost their country Trieste. When tremendous throngs waited in Rome to do him homage, his procession was rerouted to avoid them, much to his indignation.

236

To the Italians and to all of Europe he was perhaps less a person than a symbol, a symbol of joy over the end of the war and of the hope of an enduring peace. Never had a man, except perhaps the Roman emperor Augustus nineteen centuries before, stood in such a position, a position where all the world saw in him the prospective creator of a united peaceful world. Augustus had succeeded in fulfilling those expectations; but Wilson had no similar vantage point of unquestioned power from which to work.

CHAPTER XIX

THE LEAGUE OF NATIONS IS BORN

Wilson's problem was to bring into existence the just peace for which he had worked and a League of Nations to enforce it. He had made good use of his moments of power and influence just before the armistice to picture such a peace to the whole world. As head of the richest and least exhausted belligerent, there were a number of things he could do to persuade the other Allies to accept his ideas and he was ready to use these potentialities to the utmost. But he was now faced with the intricate difficulties involved in working out specific treaty terms with the statesmen of other countries as well as getting both these agreements and the League of Nations approved by the American Senate.

Above all he was determined to have the League of Nations incorporated into the Peace Treaty. He had pondered this question for three years until he had become convinced that a League was essential to maintaining the peace for which the soldiers had fought. As the conference proceeded he was even more convinced that the League was needed to reconcile the various conflicting national interests and demands. Many of these questions would take time and study to decide and a permanent force to keep them settled. The European nations felt that military and economic matters should be arranged first. Wilson wanted his principles, which had formed the basis of the armistice, to be followed in all aspects of the settlement. The French had submitted a plan for the conference which put the League last on the agenda, while Wilson demanded that it be dealt with first because he felt that it could help decide difficult problems.

The European statesmen delayed almost a month after Wilson's arrival in Brest before beginning the formal deliberations of the Peace Conference, and it did not meet in its first full session until January 18. Although Wilson was criticized by his enemies for this delay, it was none of his doing. Insofar as it was done on purpose it was probably arranged by the European diplomats so that the populations of Europe might become accustomed to Wilson; the politicians felt that when the eagerness of the people's first enthusiasm subsided they would no longer keep him on the pedestal that gave him so much influence.

It seemed likely that their ardor would be cooled not only by the mere passage of time but by all sorts of other disputes and difficulties which were becoming constantly more pressing. Food was scarce almost everywhere in Europe, France feared a revival of German militarism, while almost all of the Allied statesmen dreaded the spread of the Bolshevik revolution. America sent food over by the shipload but the hungry nations quarreled over its proper distribution. Some of the Allies made special efforts to prevent any of it from reaching the almost starving Germans, who needed it most of all.

The rulers of Europe were convinced that once peace had come the old hatreds and greeds would soon begin to take hold of their peoples. Worst of all was fear, fear and the desire for revenge against the beaten Germans. Lloyd George, for example, after saying on Armistice Day that "We must not allow any sense of revenge, any spirit of greed, any grasping desire to override the fundamental principles of righteousness," was swept to re-election only a month later upon such slogans as "Hang the Kaiser" and "Make Germany pay the whole cost of the war."

The danger which lurked in Russia, in the doctrines and slogans of the Bolsheviks, frightened Wilson far less than it did the other statesmen. He had all along been loath to interfere in the internal affairs and government of Russia. Yet the peril was there, and the other diplomats were quick to recognize the appeal which Communist propaganda could make to unhappy and poverty-stricken masses. Only by prompt action taken just in time could Germany be saved from the domination of the new ideology. Wilson too foresaw the danger of revolutions springing from the growth of Communist ideas, and warned Americans against such foolishness; he felt that the speedy conclusion of a peace treaty would do much to stop all dangerous trends.

But speed was rendered impossible by the multiplicity of questions as well as the great diversity of points of view. The four main leaders, Wilson, Clemenceau, Lloyd George and Orlando, were not having a wonderful time dictating the course of the world. Their assistants and advisers and underlings were not dancing and flirting and intriguing like the diplomats assembled at the Congress of Vienna one hundred years earlier. All sorts of people were besieging them with entreaties and complaints, friends of Ireland and Armenia, Jews and Moslems and a hundred other groups of peoples, sects, and special interests. The British filled five hotels with their staff, and thirteen hundred Americans were busy at the conference. It would take time and much hard labor to achieve any sort of agreement in the midst of this chaos. Since thirty separate Allies had to be satisfied, it is doubtful if progress could have been rapid even if Wilson had not rejected the program for the conference proposed by France, which was intended to speed things up, but put the League of Nations last.

The headquarters of Wilson and his delegation were in the beautiful Hotel Crillon facing the Place de la Concorde. Most of the discussions were held in the rooms of Colonel House, rather than in those of Secretary Lansing, who because of his official position should have been given a place only second to the President himself. Wilson appears never even to have thought of the feelings of his secretary of State, although House once suggested that the commissioners should occcasionally meet at Lansing's office. Perhaps

240

the arrangement may be explained by Lansing's unwillingness to conceal his convictions that the League of Nations and other items from the Fourteen Points were unimportant compared to the drafting of some sort of a definite peace treaty; but if Wilson had only treated the secretary with greater consideration and discussed his problems with him at greater length, Lansing might not have been so indifferent to the League.

Wilson hurt Lansing's feelings further when he remarked "he did not intend to have lawyers drafting the treaty of peace." General Bliss stood up for his principles and showed remarkable insight, while Henry White, the fourth of the Commissioners, became convinced that Wilson was far wiser than he had previously realized. Baruch, Hoover, Lamont, Norman Davis and Pershing were also on hand to give advice and helpful counsel.

Wilson wasted valuable time and exhausted precious energy not only by using his own system of shorthand and by typing memoranda himself but also by receiving all sorts of delegations who asked to see him. Some of these represented oppressed minorities whose problems already had been gone over by his specialists, while others were groups representing interests which were relatively insignificant or with which he had no concern, such as a union delegation of French railroad men. Perhaps he merely felt that each group was representing the people in general, so that he ought to keep in touch with them. But he worked so hard, he turned his intelligence and sympathy to so many problems, that it seemed doubtful if his frail physique could stand the strain.

The labor which he found most congenial was that devoted to the formation of the League. This task was turned over to a special commission organized to draft the League's covenant and its sessions frequently lasted until after midnight, because its members were occupied with all sorts of other issues during the day. Wilson and Orlando gave the League Commission their constant attention and the project was pushed through with success and considerable speed. But France wanted a somewhat different sort of League, wielding greater military powers, so that her acquiescence in the one adopted required subsequent concessions looking toward her defense against any new German aggression.

Wilson's method of establishing the kind of League he thought best has been investigated so closely that it has received criticism from almost every angle. Examination has shown that he did not delay the other work of the conference, and it seems that no equally propitious moment for setting up the League would ever have occurred again, at least not before the outbreak of World War II. In Wilson's eyes the covenant was a more pressing matter than drafting a quick preliminary treaty, especially since that might have resulted in the League being left out altogether.

Lloyd George was so sturdily built that he showed few signs of weariness during the discussions, nor did he often lose his friendly smile. He had risen from a simple Welsh attorney to prime minister largely through good fortune and hard work. He had designed a British budget which tapped the resources of the rich, brought in insurance against unemployment and sickness, became secretary of state for War and finally supplanted Asquith as head of the government. He wanted a League, but he also wanted to provide sufficient force to hold down the Germans if the League should fail; and these two purposes were difficult to reconcile with one another.

Clemenceau, "the Tiger of France," was seventy-eight, but even more menacing than in his youth. After practicing medicine and teaching in a female seminary, he had been mayor of Montmartre during the Franco-Prussian War. His small eyes shone in a yellow face, and he was also characterized by a skullcap and a thick white mustache. He wore gray gloves which some said were needed to conceal his claws. He wanted a League of Allies rather than a League of All Nations. Since he still feared Germany, he had announced to the Chamber of Deputies on December 29 that France depended for her safety upon a balance of power based on alliances, with economic, military and territorial guarantees. He felt that he "alone was representing continental interests," with England and America against him. When referring to his place between Lloyd George and Wilson he is said to have asked how you would like to

242

be placed between two men who thought of themselves as Napoleon and Jesus Christ.

Orlando of Italy disliked contention, but his foreign minister Sonnino kept demanding extravagant rewards to Italy for having joined the side of the Allies. The British Dominions were represented by the cold and philosophical Smuts of South Africa, Borden of Canada, Hughes of Australia and Massey of New Zealand. Venizelos obtained for Greece too much for his country to digest, Paderewski showed earnestness and love of country in picturing Poland as a bastion against the Bolsheviks. Benes was there for the Czechs, Makino and Chinda for Japan and Wellington Koo for China. Jews wanted protection in eastern Europe and Christians in Asia Minor. Representatives of the inhabitants of Montenegro, Arabia, Albania and Armenia were among those seeking to have their territories established as new nations. It must have seemed unlikely that so many different personalities with so many opposing national interests could ever come to an agreement. So a program was drawn up by Wilson "to establish peace for all time among the peoples of the Earth" as Clemenceau put it in his opening speech. The order of business which was agreed upon dealt with the League, reparations, new nations, other territorial arrangements, and colonies, in that order. It became nearly unavoidable that the representatives of the five most powerful Allies should settle these problems almost without consultation with the smaller countries.

Wilson was convinced that the secret treaties would have to be disregarded not only because they ignored his idea of the self-determination of nations but also because there were so many conflicting clauses hidden in them. For instance, Italy demanded the loot promised her in the Pact of Lonodon, but tried to ignore the Pact of Rome, when in her peril after Caporetto she had promised the Serbs to settle controversies upon the basis of the nationalities involved. When other statesmen maintained that their countries should be recompensed for the disasters they had suffered in the war, Wilson pointed out that they would be sure to expect the United States to help support and maintain any settlements which

243

were made. Meanwhile in America, although Theodore Roosevelt had died, Lodge and other Republican senators seemed to be preparing to tear to bits almost any League and treaty presented to them.

Wilson had expected a preliminary treaty to be drawn up imposing military and economic terms upon Germany and he had intended to connect his League with this so that both could be passed upon and authorized at once. When it became evident that the problems were too complicated to be settled quickly, so that no preliminary treaty was possible, he still believed that some organization for permanent international co-operation to carry out the decisions made by the conference should be set up as quickly as possible.

The five Great Powers soon took charge of drawing up the treaty. Their representatives, known as the Council of Ten, met in the large study of France's foreign minister, Stephan Pinchon, a room where Gobelin tapestries portrayed the various love affairs of King Henry IV. The ten statesmen sat in front of the fireplace to receive those who had some special plea to make. Clemenceau presided and kept the petitioners from taking up too much time. Most of the pleas were aimed at Wilson who heard them with apparent interest, while Lloyd George sat on the edge of his chair barking questions. This body established various general principles, but the detailed questions presented were passed on to various commissions established for the purpose. Fifty-eight of these commissions were required to deal with the work of the conference.

In this Council of Ten, Wilson often found it necessary to uphold the principles of his Fourteen Points against all sorts of other ideas. Indemnities as well as reparations for war losses were suggested, but Wilson was prompt to recommend that they be omitted. Agreement on proper reparations alone became very complicated.

Japan and the British Dominions both claimed rights to German colonies in the Pacific, but Smuts of South Africa suggested that such colonies become mandates, to be administered under the supervision of the League. Wilson approved of this and insisted that the colonies must not be parceled out as war loot. So it was agreed that they should simply be governed by various countries as agents of the League. In order to prevent the land-hungry countries from seizing them before these arrangements were completed, Wilson believed it was necessary to hasten the formation of the League, otherwise "the world would say that the Great Powers first portioned out the helpless parts of the world and then formed a League of Nations," which would cause the League to be "discredited from the beginning." Promises made to Italy, Japan and the Dominions were to be disregarded but this could only be done over their violent protests.

The most serious obstacle arose on February 11 when the French demanded the creation of an international police force under the control of the League. Both Wilson and Lord Robert Cecil of Great Britain said that their nations would not consent to such a delegation of sovereignty. Had such a force actually been created, not only would France have been far safer but future wars might have been prevented. But of course Wilson and Cecil were both perfectly accurate in their replies: neither of their countries would accept such a provision. There was also the objection that since Germany and Russia were being excluded from the League for the time being, any League army would be just like a force directed against them, so that they would be led to raise counter-forces of their own.

The League Committee required only eleven meetings because Wilson had worked the project over so thoroughly in advance. Authority in the League was divided between a Council of Great Powers and an Assembly where all nations were represented. A World Court was finally established after Colonel House won Wilson over to this idea. However, House was not entirely in sympathy with Wilson's views, for he felt that the League would never be able to prevent war altogether. Lansing had even less confidence in the effectiveness of the League and was inclined to believe that concentration upon the work of this committee was delaying all the other activities of the conference. Wilson did not have the unqualified support even of his own delegation, but he succeeded in pushing through a League which was very much in line with the one he had hoped to get.

The Covenant of the League began with seven articles dealing with organization and administration, including such matters as membership, voting and procedure. These articles also set up the machinery for the Assembly, Council, and Secretariat. All member nations were to be represented in the Assembly, while the executive Council was to include the five great Allied powers and at least four smaller nations, chosen by the Assembly for three years. Spain and Poland were frequently among those elected. Reduction of armaments and a permanent Military Commission were provided for in Articles VIII and IX. The plans for arms reduction were to be formulated by the Council, and the execution of its decisions was to be supervised by the Military Commission. Under Article X, source of later bitter contention, all members of the League undertook to preserve one another against external agression. Article XI declared that any war or threat of war was "a matter of concern to the whole League and the League shall take any action that may be deemed wise or effectual to safeguard the peace of nations." It was to be the "friendly right" of each member to point out any circumstance that threatened to disturb international peace. The next three articles dealt with various methods of settling disputes without war, among which was the creation by the Council of a World Court, actually established two years later at The Hague.

The "sanctions" or penalties to be used against any nation that broke the peace were included in Articles XVI and XVII. Financial and economic relations were to be severed, amounting almost to a boycott of the aggressor. Articles XVIII to XX concerned treaties and international obligations, while the next two dealt with the Monroe Doctrine and mandates. Article XXIII established various agencies for social betterment, which were to work for humane conditions of labor, and maintain international supervision of the traffic in drugs and women. All international bureaus were placed under the League and the members agreed to encourage national

Red Cross organizations. The last article provided for amendments which should become operative when approved by the members of the Council and a majority of the Assembly.

Then came the great day of Wilson's life. On February 14 he presented the Covenant before a plenary session of the Peace Conference. The setting was imposing. In the Room of the Clock, a part of the French Foreign Office, magnificent in proportions and adorned with beautiful sculpture and gilt trim created by the Ancient Regime in Europe when the king was in fact the state, he read in an even and clear voice the draft of the League Covenant of the democracies. Sixty or eighty diplomats were gathered around baize tables: gayly uniformed generals stood or sat round the wall. The very quietness and lack of histrionics in Wilson's delivery increased the impressiveness of the occasion.

After the reading Wilson made a quiet little speech, in which he announced "a living thing is born." Other speeches followed. The Belgians and some other delegates were prepared to protest and to suggest changes; but Clemenceau, who was presiding, pushed the draft over without giving anyone a chance to voice objections.

Driving back through the streets of Paris, Wilson said to his wife: "This is the first real step forward. The League can arbitrate and correct mistakes inevitable in the treaty." Then, contemplating a rest from the intricate arguments of Paris, he remarked contentedly: "It will be good to go home for a few days feeling I have kept faith with the people—and particularly with those boys, God bless them!"

CHAPTER XX

FIGHTING FOR
DEMOCRATIC PRINCIPLES

Wilson left for America the day after he presented the draft of the League of Nations Covenant to the Conference, but he was determined to go back to Paris to try to make sure that the peace treaty was based on the principles which he had proposed. Meanwhile, although Lansing was the official head of the delegation, it was House who was the genuine spokesman for the President during the few weeks that he was gone. Naval and military conditions had to be decided on during the interval, information had to be collected and recommendations had to be prepared by the experts.

The weather was pleasant on the voyage west. A cheerful group surrounded the President. Two thousand soldiers on board were pleased with his friendly ways. When the ship was entering the waters near Boston and a deep fog caused the captain to become confused, young Franklin D. Roosevelt was called upon to use his knowledge of those shoals and channels to discover just where the ship lay and set her on her proper course. Upon arrival Wilson drove to the Copley Plaza Hotel for lunch through streets thronged with people. An onlooker said his hair looked wispy in the breeze like that of an old man, and he seemed to be worn and tired, lacking the exuberance and power needed to carry the hopes of the world on his shoulders.

In a speech that evening at Mechanics Hall he said, "It warms my heart to see a great body of my fellow citizens again. . . .

America is the hope of the world. And if she does not justify that hope . . . men will be thrown back upon bitterness of disappointment, bitterness of despair." In conclusion he announced, "I have fighting blood in me and it is sometimes a delight to let it have scope." This belligerent climax was delivered in the home city of Henry Cabot Lodge, but it is not likely that it made that gentleman any more contentious than he already was.

After the peaceful voyage troubles were waiting for the President in Washington. He must have expected this, for although he had asked the senators not to discuss the Covenant until he had a chance to present it to them, many had resented this request, and those most opposed to the League had been busily attacking it even before it was officially presented to the Peace Conference. Poindexter said it would breed wars and be "a colossal burden of entangling alliances" and Reed of Missouri complained that it would be a renunciation of America's right to defend herself. Borah, Johnson and Knox were determined to postpone action on the League until the general treaty had been signed, while Borah agreed with Poindexter in opposing American membership in any such organization. A dinner at the White House for members of the Foreign Relations Committees of both houses of Congress apparently failed to win over any of the dissenters. Nor was Congress willing for the President to carry on without its being able to take action, for a filibuster of necessary appropriation bills was organized for the sole purpose of forcing him to call a special session.

On March 3 enough senators of the new Congress to block ratification of any treaty signed a "round robin" in which they asserted that the Covenant of the League "in the form now proposed to the Peace Conference should not be accepted by the United States." This should have been a warning to Wilson, but he regarded their suggested changes as inconsequential or even undesirable and felt that to adopt them would simply open up the question of other amendments at the demand of other governments. He was unable to decide immediately whether or not to place these suggestions before the Peace Conference.

In his frustration and anger Wilson lost control of himself in a final speech at the Metropolitan Opera House the next day. William Howard Taft preceded the President's address with an explanation of the Covenant, placing emphasis upon its importance to an enduring peace. Most of Wilson's talk was impressive and moving. He began with a picture of a group of wounded Italian soldiers presenting a petition for the League and referred to "the crusading spirit of these youngsters who went over there not to glorify America but to serve their fellow men." He felt that "an overwhelming majority of the American people is in favor of the League," as opposed to any "doctrine of careful selfishness." Then came the passage which aroused great indignation in certain quarters in Washington. "When that treaty comes back, gentlemen on this side will find the Covenant not only in it, but so many threads of the treaty tied to the Covenant that you cannot dissect the Covenant from the treaty without destroying the whole vital structure." Probably actually intended as a threat, its utterance seriously angered many senators who had not previously openly opposed the League.

Sailing back to Paris early in March, Wilson became convinced that he must make demands for amendments to the Covenant to win for it the approval of the Senate; but at the same time he was running into all sorts of renewed troubles and arguments with the European statesmen. When he reached Brest and Colonel House came on board to report on developments at the conference, Wilson emerged from the interview looking to his wife as if he had "aged ten years." She records that he remarked with a bitter smile, "House has given away everything I had won before we left Paris."

Mrs. Wilson sees in this interview the beginning of her husband's ultimate collapse, but there is little other evidence to support the opinion. Actually House had conceded little except for agreeing that the French might occupy the Rhineland for about five years, which did no harm since the idea was rejected by Lloyd George. The real damage from the interview came in its terminating the confidence which Wilson had placed in the Colonel. This was the more unfortunate because during the next six months he was going to need counsel urging conciliation of opponents more than he ever had needed it before. Yet it is very probable that House would have stayed in Europe when Wilson came home in any case. Nor was the breach due wholly to this interview. Ike Hoover felt that it might have been developing ever since enemies of House obtained the President's ear on the voyage to Europe in December. The estrangement was partly due to Wilson's feeling that House was always willing to concede too much in order to please the Allies; and perhaps also to the influence of Mrs. Wilson.

Almost immediately upon arrival Wilson consented to two new proposals. He followed Lloyd George in agreeing that if France would accept mere temporary occupation of the Rhineland, their countries would come to her assistance in case of German attack. The three other commissioners realized that the Senate would never consent to such terms, but Wilson felt that popular opinion would force the senators to approve any terms which he found satisfactory.

More serious was the decision to follow a French recommendation to have no preliminary treaty but only a final one. He wanted to get his work completed and had promised not to "come back till it was over over there." But Germany's delegates had expected to take part in drawing up the final treaty; now they would have no part in negotiating its terms so that Hitler was later given an opportunity to orate about the *"Diktat"* of Versailles. The quickening pace was also partly responsible for assessing reparations upon Germany with no regard for her ability to pay.

Wilson believed that any mistakes could later be changed through action of the League. The Council of Ten was quickly reduced for speedier operation to the Big Four, who were immediately confronted with problems concerning reparations, the Rhine Valley, and the frontiers of Italy and Poland. Affairs were becoming highly critical and Wilson was having great difficulty maintaining his aims among so many antagonistic purposes. The stress and strain exhausted him.

His difficulties were made more serious by the need for presenting four amendments to the League Covenant demanded by the senators. These would exclude any interference with the Monroe Doctrine or such domestic issues as tariffs and immigration laws, allow America to quit the League and refuse to accept mandates. The French protested that the Monroe Doctrine might turn Americans' thoughts away from Europe, but Wilson was angered when he heard later that Léon Bourgeois admitted he had brought this up only for trading purposes. France also felt that the freedom to withdraw would endanger the entire edifice of the League.

The French were busy presenting other demands of their own. These included an occupation of the Rhineland for thirty years with inspection by a sort of general staff of Allied officers. On March 29 Clemenceau called Wilson "pro-German" and stalked out of the President's study in the little palace where the Big Four meetings were held. Another time Clemenceau said to Wilson: "I do not wish you to go home, but I intend to do so myself." Finally about the middle of April, after the Saar question was determined, a compromise was arranged on the demilitarization and occupation of the Rhineland. Attacks on Wilson in the French press, which had been virulent, immediately stopped, and before long Danzig was made a free city to give Poland access to the sea.

On April 1, Wilson showed his exhaustion in an exclamation unlike his usual self: "Logic! Logic! I don't give a damn for logic!" and in his assent, over the objection of his experts, to the incorporation of pensions and separation allowances among the items for which Germany must make reimbursement. This turned out to be the worst of all his concessions, but at the time it seemed only to be giving more to England and less to France since both British and Americans appeared to agree that the total sum should not be fixed beyond Germany's capacity to pay. But France kept on demanding the entire cost of the war, with no time limit. Lloyd George was assailed at home for failing to fulfill his election promises to destroy Germany; and, when Wilson was sick in bed a few days later, Colonel House agreed to the French demands. Wilson failed to reverse House's compliance when he returned to the conference. He also unfortunately gave his approval to the "war guilt" clause which later furnished the Nazis with another basis for stirring up the German people against the treaty.

Wilson's illness, which began on April 3, started with a fit of coughing. His temperature shot up to 103°. Dr. Grayson thought at first perhaps he had been poisoned, but later publicly diagnosed the illness as influenza, of which a serious epidemic was in progress. Yet many of those nearest to the President believed it was a light stroke. The patient showed his strength of character by trying to work even while ill. But Hoover felt that during his convalescence Wilson's mind was no longer alert and flexible with the result that he avoided making decisions. Perhaps that is the reason he failed to denounce the unlimited reparations and the "war guilt" clause. When he reappeared his face twitched and he was said to look like a corpse. He soon regained his courage and tenacity and some of his ability to act boldly in an emergency, but his health and judgment seemed never to be quite the same again.

The new democracies of central Europe that sprang up after the war felt that they owed their existence to Wilson. If he had not insisted upon the self-determination of peoples they could never have been born. His views on nationality were expressed in his Fourteen Points, especially numbers VI to XIII. Since the Fourteen Points had been regarded by the Central Powers as setting the pattern for the peace, these new nations had relied upon Wilson's statements when they undertook to establish themselves even before the Peace Conference. For Wilson had said in his Fourteen Points that the frontiers of Italy should be adjusted upon the basis of nationality, that the peoples of Austria-Hungary should be given a real opportunity for autonomous development, and that Serbia was to be given free access to the Sea, while international guarantees would underpin the independence and territorial integrity of the various Balkan states. Point XII assured nationalities under Turkish rule against interference in their lives or autonomous development, and also opened the Dardanelles to ships of all nations. According to number XIII a new Polish state with access to the sea was to be guaranteed by international covenants.

253

The new leaders of Yugoslavia, Czechoslovakia, Hungary and Poland felt that by these promises Wilson had given them authority to set up their democracies. In Prague not only were the new railroad station and the principal avenue named after Wilson, but also his statue was erected in the main square. Similar evidence that his influence was almost universally recognized abounded throughout Europe. He was the acknowledged father of the new nations. The peace treaty itself had only to determine their boundaries, protect their minorities and help them work out friendly relations with their neighbors.

Yugoslavia had been enlarged from the old Serbia by the addition of substantial Austrian territory including the port of Fiume. Although the population of this city was predominantly Italian, its suburbs and all the back country were filled with Yugoslavs. It was the only good port on the east coast of the Adriatic, but the Italians wanted the whole sea to be under their control. With this in view they tried to influence Dr. Mezes and other American advisers by persuasion and even by hospitality to give Fiume to them. House in turn was influenced by Mezes, so their group became known as "upstairs," because of the location of House's rooms at the Hotel Crillon.

But the American technical experts felt that Fiume should go to Yugoslavia, saying that "It would be charged that we had betrayed the rights of small nations. . . . The Italian government may fall, but the Italian people cannot long withstand the opinion of the world." Wilson believed this was true and he even tried to appeal directly to the Italian people, with no effect except leading them to regard their former friend as nothing but a hypocrite. Italo-Americans also turned against Wilson because of his stand on Fiume. Worst of all, perhaps, Wilson lost still more confidence in House, since he and the other three commissioners all felt that House had tried to give the impression that the advice of qualified experts was the same as that presented by "upstairs." Perhaps this was the reason House stayed in Europe until fall, just when his tact and conciliatory counsel might have been most useful to the President. Orlando and

254

Sonnino immediately left Paris in indignation, which led the remaining Big Three to omit Italy from the final distribution of mandates, thus again wounding the pride of all patriotic Italians.

On that same day Japan asked what was going to be done about the Shantung Peninsula in northern China. Her treaty with England purported to transfer to her all the rights Germany had possessed. These rights were also ostensibly confirmed by treaties which Japan had extorted from China and the Japanese were in actual control of the peninsula. Although everything was in their favor, the Japanese quite reasonably agreed to keep only the economic holdings which Germany had possessed. The settlement seemed fair and could scarcely have been avoided, at least not without running the risk of a Japanese-Russian-Italian alliance against the League. But the concession was bitterly attacked in America and perhaps did more than any other clause, except Article X of the Covenant, to defeat the treaty in the Senate fight.

Of the other problems Wilson met at the Peace Conference, many might have been expected, some were utterly surprising. Irish-Americans demanded that De Valera and two other commissioners be admitted to plead for an independent Ireland before the Big Four. Although this was interfering in the internal affairs of the British Empire and although no other small nation had been permitted to plead its case, Lloyd George received a delegation headed by Frank P. Walsh, former co-chairman with Taft of the War Labor Board, and showed some signs of allowing De Valera and other Irishmen to appear at Paris. But the delegation then went to Ireland on a destroyer provided by Lloyd George, took nips of Irish whisky offered by the populace to settle their stomachs and rode down Sackville Street in Dublin in a jaunting car with all Dublin cheering. One of them took the driver's seat and announced that "We Irish Yankees have come to proclaim Ireland a nation" and called upon all within the sound of his voice to "join the boys from America and throw George the Fifth into the River Shannon."

This put an end to their prospect of a hearing; but the incidents in Dublin were not published in the American press and therefore were not known to the American public. So the pressure continued. Walsh and former Governor Dunne of Illinois asserted that the American Federation of Labor had voted unanimously in favor of the recognition of the Irish Republic. They then went unsuccessfully to Clemenceau as president of the conference with their plea. Walsh's letters are full of anger over their failure to win their point.

Another reaction that seemed trivial at the time but later had serious consequences was the indignation of William Bullitt. This had been aroused when he was sent to Moscow to inquire as to the terms on which the Bolshevik leaders would reach an understanding with the Allies. Until then he had merely been employed to collect news and documents for the American delegation, but he accomplished his mission quickly and returned with an answer that did not seem unreasonable. But both Lloyd George and Wilson distrusted the Bolsheviks and were so busy with other affairs that they neglected to take any action on his report. At this inattention Bullitt became so furious that on May 17 he tendered his resignation in a letter accusing Wilson of having "so little faith in the millions of men like myself in every nation who had faith in you." This anger was probably the reason he later offered damaging testimony before the Senate Committee, which had probably been distorted and was certainly confidential.

Wilson made other minor mistakes. He went against the advice of his experts to uphold the capture of Smyrna by Greece, giving that country temporary control of more territory than it was in her power to hold and digest. He scorned a recommendation of Lloyd George, tendered in early June, that several terms of the treaty be made less back-breaking for Germany, asserting that it made him "very tired" to see concessions offered to Germany merely for fear she would not sign, an attitude which he would scarcely have taken if his temper had not been rendered unstable by illness, since he well knew the general limitations of Germany's ability to pay and he had previously consistently stood for generous terms toward the enemy.

The Allied draft of the Treaty of Versailles was presented to the

German delegates on May 7 in a small room of the Trianon Palace. Everyone sat in silence while the Germans came into the room. Clemenceau then rose with fury in his voice, saying: "The time has come when we must settle our accounts. You have asked for peace. We are ready to give you peace." Brocdorff-Rantzau did not even stand while he read the German answer. Bitterness and arrogance thickened his speech. Wilson was furious and turning to Lloyd George said, "Isn't that just like them!" Later Germany was able to gain some small concessions, and might have gained more if her representative had used tact instead of gall. But with the armies of Foch ready to strike the moment that the Germans balked, few changes were tolerated. The final treaty was signed in the great Hall of Mirrors at Versailles on June 28. Germany had been left no alternative.

CHAPTER XXI

DISASTER AT THE SENATE'S HANDS

When Wilson came home to fight for the League and the treaty, he knew he must convince two thirds of the Senate to get the treaty ratified and to accomplish this he was willing to make any personal sacrifice. But the more important question was whether he would be willing to negotiate and meet the senators in a conciliatory spirit such as Colonel House urged upon him when he set sail from Brest. He does not seem to have been impressed with the necessity for this, for his rejoinder was: "House, I have found that one can never get anything in this life that is worth while without fighting for it." Although House then reminded him that "Anglo-Saxon civilization is built on compromise," he was not willing to heed this advice, even when House repeated it by letter some months later.

Wilson looked fresh after his sea voyage; but it was not to be long before he would become overtired again under the pressure of the numerous problems that came with the ending of the war, worry about the Senate's activities, and the heat of a Washington summer. His opponents were ready and waiting for him; they had already begun their open opposition to whatever proposals he might bring home. Hiram Johnson shouted that to join the League would subject America forever to "the sordid, cunning, secret and crafty designs of European and Asiatic governments." Senator Reed was accustomed to pulling a slip of paper from his pocket, referring to the treaty which was still not widely published and crying, "I have it here and I seem to see the bloody footprints of John Bull tracking all over the dastardly document," neglecting to state that the printed version actually covered several hundred pages. Lodge made fun of Wilson's scholarship on the grounds that the President expressed his thoughts directly in his own words without encumbering them with a host of classical allusions. Borah with his Websterian language and lack of stamina, Poindexter with his ignorance, Fall with utter nothingness, Knox with his selfishness, and Lodge with his vanity were some of his opponents, as characterized by their fellow Republican, Ex-President Taft. To these might be added Senators Smoot of Utah, Moses of New Hampshire, Brandegee and Harding. Lodge, perhaps, might have been less bitter if he had not suffered a personal tragedy a few months before in the loss of his sensible and charming wife.

The Democrats had seven members on the Senate Foreign Relations Committee against ten Republicans. Gilbert Hitchcock, a publisher from Nebraska, was the minority leader of the Senate and most of the other Democrats were of considerable ability, but Shields of Tennessee was opposed to the Administration. Of the Republicans only McCumber supported the League. But, since Lodge realized that the population in general favored a League, he told Borah that the attack should be "by way of amendment and reservation" rather than frontal assault.

Two lines of argument were still open to the opposition; namely, that the treaty ought to be rejected and that it could be substantially improved. Johnson, Reed, and Borah were ready to argue against it in any form; Knox and Lodge said they could make it better. Whichever proposition seemed most likely to be in line with the mood of the country could be emphasized. And time was on their side. People were beginning to worry about taxes, strikes, prohibition and the cost of living, instead of maintaining any lively interest in the affairs of Europe. As Taft remarked, the Committee on Foreign Relations seemed to have been packed with opponents of the League, so it is not surprising that, led by Lodge and his faction, it postponed reporting the treaty for two months after Wilson officially submitted it to the Senate. Nor were the members moved from the strategy of delay by the fact that unsettled conditions all over the world made speed of the utmost importance to the peoples of Europe and Asia.

Wilson did his best to win over to his side those who were wavering. All through his first months in Washington he kept inviting senators of both parties to confer with him. The *New York Times* helped his cause by pointing out that the power and prestige of the United States would enable it to secure any changes in the League which proved to be necessary. Herbert Hoover, President Eliot of Harvard and other prominent Republicans including George W. Wickersham, insisted upon the need for immediate ratification. But on August 12, Lodge suddenly made a two-hour speech attacking the treaty. He used Wilson's plea for service to the world as the basis for a violent attack on Article X and other provisions of the Covenant, asserting that they limited America's freedom of action. He also demanded that the four other great Allied powers would have to approve his proposed reservations. The galleries of the Senate burst into thunderous applause. Perhaps the mild reservationists, who wished to make minor changes in the treaty, were tempted to uphold more drastic alterations as a result of this ovation received by Lodge.

Wilson himself offered to appear before the Foreign Relations Committee. Secretary Lansing had already given extensive testimony in a correct fashion but with no enthusiasm for the League, combined with actual opposition to the Shantung article contained in the peace treaty. The committee members finally came to the White House at Wilson's invitation on August 19, when he answered their questions for three and one-half hours. First he emphasized that if amendments or reservations were made part of the resolution of ratification they would give other nations, including Germany, a basis for demanding changes of their own. But he admitted that some matters might need elucidation saying, "There can be no reasonable objection to such interpretations accompanying the act of ratification." He also pointed out that four changes had already been made to satisfy American demands after his first trip home. He described the making of the treaty and Covenant. He showed that Article X could not lead us into wars because the Council of the League could not even advise action to protect the boundaries of other member nations without the concurrence of the American representatives, who would be members of the League Council of Five. And he remarked that unless the United States was a party to the dispute the real difficulty with the article would probably be an unwillingness on the part of the Great Powers to take the steps necessary to enforce it, which proved to be the case.

Senator Harding seemed unable to understand the binding force of a moral obligation and argued over this for over an hour, wasting so much time and energy that Wilson later informed his Cabinet that Harding had a disturbingly dull mind. After forcing the President to admit that words may have numerous different meanings, Senator Brandegee contended that Article X was only "a rope of sand" and that no treaty was technically needed for peace. The committee members called for documents which it would have been improper for the President to provide, since they would have divulged confidential negotiations with other countries. The Republicans quoted Lansing's opinion that Japan would have accepted the treaty without receiving concessions on Shantung and they protested against the right of the British Dominions to vote in the League Assembly.

The interview apparently failed to win Wilson any converts and under constant questioning by Borah and Hiram Johnson he made the great mistake of saying that he had not been told about the secret treaties between the Allies until he arrived in Paris after the armistice. But the terms of some of these had been published in American newspapers the previous August and the Fourteen Points had partially been intended to nullify them. It is true that the Treaty on Shantung had been disclosed to Wilson only when he reached Paris and that, as he said, "Yes, the whole series of understandings were disclosed to me for the first time then." This was true of "the whole series," but he had learned about most of them beforehand from Balfour, so he was being very technical. Worse was his reply to a question by Johnson as to whether he had intended his Fourteen Points to countermand the secret treaties: "Since I knew nothing of them, necessarily not."

What was the reason for the lie? Some historians have argued that perhaps Wilson simply felt that it was sometimes unavoidable to lie in political discussions or that he did not want to spend time upon a non-essential issue. But the lie was too obvious to serve any good purpose.

The explanation for the falsehood seems to rest in the state of Wilson's health. He was undergoing a severe cross-examination under difficult conditions. He may have been caught off guard, but Lansing had been asked the same question only two weeks before so that he must have expected to be quizzed on this subject. It was logically impossible to expect the denial to be believed. He simply must have had a failure of memory upon this point. Even if he were believed, it would have done him no good to appear to have been fooled in such an important point, while the Allies would be made to appear dishonest and despicable. The misstatement could bring him no advantage at all.

It is necessary to remember that Wilson had always been frail, and that as a boy he was seldom seen in fights or games requiring physical contact. As a man he still tended to avoid open quarrels and dissensions. His digestion had always bothered him. It is probable that he had already had a stroke in April and possibly one the previous October. Within six weeks he was going to suffer a definite and severe stroke which paralyzed him. Such a stroke, according to some physicians, may be preceded by a complete failure of memory on one particular subject. This could easily occur in moments of tense mental concentration and anxiety. The strains and difficulties he had already undergone would have made him still more susceptible to an attack of this kind. But the slip was a serious blow to his cause.

Senators Borah, Knox, and Johnson immediately took up Wilson's statement, declaring that the treaty would obligate America to guarantee for an indefinite period agreements made by secret treaties which had been concealed from the President until the beginning of the Peace Conference, and that "Europe would be under the same impelling force to take part in the settlement of American affairs." Yet Brandegee had already called Article X merely "a rope of sand," by which America could scarcely be much obligated.

After going back again to the interpretations of Article X, Shantung and the system of mandates, Wilson invited them all to lunch which was reported to have been a "jovial" occasion with a number of good stories by the President. Nothing was said during the three-and-one-half-hour hearing about such real defects in the treaty as the hopeless economic conditions imposed upon Germany, the failure to deal with the problems of minorities in central Europe, or the thirst for retaliations which its provisions inspired in Germany. These were matters which seemed to have no direct bearing upon the problems and worries of Americans at the moment, however important they might prove to be later.

A group of Irish-Americans led by Frank Walsh were received by the committee. They assailed the League as an instrument of monarchy in general and the British government in particular. This shed no real light on the issues but was of assistance in what Wilson called "poisoning the wells of public sentiment." Then on September 12 the hearings closed with the appearance of William C. Bullitt, the State Department employee who had resigned with such an unpleasant letter to the President. He produced documents which although not of any special importance should still not have been made public. Then he told about a supposed conversation in which Lansing was quoted as saying, "I consider the League of Nations at present is entirely useless. . . . I believe that if the Senate could only understand what this treaty means, and if the American people could really understand, it would unquestionably be defeated." Lansing wired Wilson a somewhat different version of the interview which stated that he had told Bullitt that he recognized the faults of the treaty to be unavoidable and that he doubted ratification only of American membership on League commissions. But Lansing refused to make any public comment and his disavowals were not sufficiently strong to hide his general feeling against the treaty, so that the harm caused by Bullitt's breach of confidence was not repaired.

Another disappointment for Wilson arose from the failure of many prominent Republicans who had formerly supported the League to come forward to uphold it now. Root had demanded a limitation of national sovereignty a few months before, but now he kept quiet since to speak out would have been to oppose the position which his party had espoused. Taft still believed in the need for Article X or its equivalent, but he confined his opinion of anti-League senators to private remarks, and he was willing to accept almost any compromise in order to get a peaceful agreement. Colonel House might have given Wilson helpful advice on how to win over some of the wavering Republicans, but he was in Europe so that he only sent a letter deploring the rumors of a break between Wilson and himself. Anyway, it is doubtful if his habit of compromise would have appealed to his determined chief.

Meanwhile, politically-minded Republicans were freely attacking the League and the treaty. The boys were home from the war and nobody wanted them to go away again. Article X was the principal object of attack, since it was felt that its terms would require the sending of American soldiers to any part of the world. The orators failed to point out that soldiers could not be sent abroad without the consent of the American representatives on the League Council, unless their country was a party to the dispute. Wilson regarded this article as the heart of the Covenant so that he was unwilling to have it removed or substantially changed. He had left its wording purposely vague in the hope that his Republican opponents would be more willing to accept it that way; but this step toward conciliation did not prevent their condemnation.

By the last of August, prospects for ratification of the treaty and the League were becoming so poor that Wilson decided it was vital for him to take a trip around the country to help his cause. He believed himself to be the only one who could present the arguments strongly enough, and without doubt he was their most able champion. He was convinced of the League's supreme importance and he knew the problems which had led to the solutions which he now proposed.

He had not been robust enough to take the trip earlier for it would require addressing large audiences, meeting the prominent citizens of various cities and attending social affairs arranged in his honor. Actually he still was not strong enough to undertake such a task. Sir William Wiseman described him as he appeared at a luncheon shortly before he left on the journey: "His face was drawn and of a gray color, and frequently twitching in a pitiful effort to control nerves which had broken down under the burden of the world's distress." But the President was willing to give all he had, and told Wiseman that "I ask nothing better than to lay my case before the American people."

That was his decision, no matter what might be the cost to himself. Mrs. Wilson tried to dissuade him and Dr. Grayson warned him that the price of the trip might be his life. In spite of all this he ordered the Presidential train to be ready to leave on the evening of September 3 for the West Coast and points between. Nor would he allow the trip to be cut to proportions which would not be too exhausting; he insisted on planning to give an average of more than one major speech a day for almost four weeks. This schedule would not give him any adequate rest, especially since each day he must also write the next day's speeches because he had been too busy to prepare them beforehand.

The train was full of reporters, photographers and secretaries. Wilson began to have bursting headaches almost as soon as the trip started; but he showed such endurance and self-control that he won an affection from the newspapermen he had never before enjoyed. One of them recorded that no President he had known had been "so entirely free from presidential consciousness" and from "any petty vanity." Wilson was winning friends for the treaty and the League at every stop and his audiences increased steadily in size and enthusiasm. But Hiram Johnson and Borah were both in pursuit of him, trying at each place where he had gone to stir up hatred and distrust of the treaty by violent diatribes against it.

In twenty-two days he delivered thirty major speeches and ten minor ones in Columbus, St. Louis, the Dakotas, Montana, Oregon and California. His theme was the cost of war in money and in suffering. His principal plea was that the 7,500,000 men of all nations who had died in battle in the war should not be betrayed. He was sure their hopes of peace would best be carried out by the establishment of the League which he was presenting for his countrymen's approval. He believed that only by some such means could new wars be prevented and he said that rejection of the League by America would "break the heart of the world."

With such a cause to plead for he would not consent to stop. Before his speech at San Francisco he had a headache for two days but he kept his audience quiet and attentive even though the hall was dangerously overcrowded. Loud-speakers were then unknown, so that day after day he had the strain of throwing his voice to reach the fringes of enormous crowds. Finally, after a morning speech in Denver on September 25 he had such a bad headache that he told friends he intended to make an address at Pueblo that afternoon somewhat brief. He joked with the reporters as he went to the rostrum, "Aren't you fellows getting pretty sick of this?" and then made one of his longest and most appealing speeches. He replied to criticism of the League and told a story about two hot-tempered men swearing at each other who were persuaded to continue their brawl outside the town but by the time they arrived there had no inclination to swear at all. He concluded by describing his visit to an American Army cemetery as Suresnes, France, saying "I wish some men in public life who are now opposing the settlement for which these men died could visit such a spot as that. . . . I believe that men will see the truth . . . and it is going to lead us, and through us the world, out into pastures of quietness and peace such as the world never dreamed of before."

It was a great speech but it was his last. As the train sped toward

Kansas it stopped for half an hour while the President took a peaceful country walk. This revived him so that dinner that night was gayer than usual. But before midnight he tapped on the door of his wife's compartment. The agony inside his skull was so persistent that Dr. Grayson could not lessen it even a little. The President could not talk without an effort nor keep the tears of pain and frustration from his eyes. In spite of this he sent for Tumulty, hoping to prepare for a morning appearance at Wichita. He shaved and dressed himself with the greatest effort, but when the train began to slow down for the stop he had to surrender. It was decided that he must be taken immediately back to Washington, and he was able to walk to his automobile upon arrival. But one morning a week after this collapse Mrs. Wilson found him unconscious on the bathroom floor. His whole left side was paralyzed by a stroke.

CHAPTER XXII

ONLY THE UNBENDING
WILL REMAINS

The rest of the story is only of disaster, of a strong man broken, of a great cause lost. But even in its loss Wilson had made a lasting change in the direction of American foreign policy. Never since that time has America been so isolationist in feeling as she was before. Some such sentiment may still remain, but most Americans probably now believe that their destiny is inseparable from the rest of the world, that their country has become one of the great world leaders, and there is no turning back.

Wilson's will remained firm, unflinching and uncompromising. But his force, his power, was gone. He could only refuse to lose his spirit and his faith in God. Nor would he give up his hope for the League. But he could no longer lead the fight with anything like the same skill and eloquence as before, nor was anyone else properly qualified to take up the struggle.

The nature of the President's illness was concealed from the people. At first his wife, Dr. Grayson and some medical specialists were the only ones permitted to see him. Grayson's bulletins would refer to the trouble as some vague sort of sickness such as a "nervous breakdown" accentuated by "indigestion and a depleted system." The whole affair makes clear the need for some method of determining whether or not a President is incapacitated so that the vice president may take over his duties. No one has been given any Constitutional authority to make the decision.

In this case the evidence seems to indicate that the decision not to retire was made by the President and Mrs. Wilson. She has denied this, saying that it was made by the doctors. But George Sylvester Viereck, who subsequently interviewed many of those concerned, came to the conclusion that the doctors advised resignation, a view upheld by the investigations of Professor Thomas A. Bailey. It seems entirely logical that they should have so advised, for Wilson was never again much more than the shell of his former self. He undoubtedly needed quiet and a rest from the cares of office. He was the only President between Grant and Franklin Roosevelt to serve two full consecutive terms, and he collapsed before the end. Perhaps he was never told the true nature of his illness for fear the knowledge would hinder his recovery. Since he never wanted to be a "quitter," the necessity for resignation might have killed him; and this undoubtedly was a factor with Mrs. Wilson in making her decision to urge him to remain in office.

She really had to make the decision because no one else had the authority. Yet it should have been made by some disinterested person or body of persons. A similar problem presented itself in 1955 and is almost certain to arise again under conditions which may be even worse. Mrs. Wilson herself wrote that "Woodrow Wilson was first my beloved husband whose life I was trying to save, fighting with my back to the wall—after that he was the President of the United States." This was a proper wifely attitude, but it was not unprejudiced and it did not put the interests of the nation first. It was not fair that the ultimate decision should have been left up to Mrs. Wilson.

A movement arose demanding that Vice President Marshall be authorized to take over the Presidency. When Secretary Lansing called to suggest this a few days after Wilson's breakdown, Tumulty indignantly replied that he and Dr. Grayson would fight any such idea, even though it seemed probable that Wilson would be completely incapacitated for a long period. Actually, Marshall does not seem to have been a man of much force and it is probable that he could have done little to push the treaty through the Senate. He himself modestly remarked that it would be a tragedy both for him and for the country if he had to take over the duties of the Presidency.

For nearly three full months after Wilson's collapse of October 3, Secretary Lane was unable to see him, even about the important question of Lane's resignation from the Cabinet. The government seems to have been run during that time largely by Mrs. Wilson. Even later it was she who decided what documents should be presented to her husband and when. She also reduced the problems to tabloid form. The decisions may have been the President's, but it must have been almost impossible for her to avoid some interpretation and perhaps partiality. Her self-justification maintained that she had learned to know his views during their years of marriage, which was probably to some extent true. But if she was virtually the President during those first bad months, it was an office for which she was neither properly equipped nor properly trained. Meanwhile the government ran along mostly from its own momentum, with the various department heads in charge. The Cabinet met informally and irregularly. Twenty-eight bills became law without the President's signature.

The effect on the treaty's chances was disastrous. Wilson's illness apparently made him more than ever stubborn and unyielding. Nor were those around him willing to tell him that opinion both in the Senate and the country was turning more and more to approval of reservations. A letter urging compromise from H. H. Kohlsaat in October was returned unopened, while three similar appeals from Colonel House were never answered. Nor were the Cabinet members able to meet with him and impress on him the necessity for compromise. Even Senator Hitchcock, the minority leader, was not allowed to see him in October and only twice briefly in November, just before a vote was taken on the treaty, so that he could not help exclaiming, "What a hopeless situation!"

Some visitors were admitted during the first months, the Prince of Wales and the King and Queen of the Belgians. There was a veto of the Volstead Prohibition act and a request to the United Mine

Workers to call off a strike against terms which had been arranged with the sanction of the Fuel Administration. Since few people had access to Wilson, Senator Fall, later disgraced in the Teapot Dome scandal, told the Foreign Relations Committee that he believed Mrs. Wilson was acting as President. Early in December he wanted to make a visit to the sickroom to find out, but because he was a bitter opponent of Wilson, it was suggested that Senator Hitchcock go with him. The two received a strong handshake from the President who discussed Mexican affairs so intelligently that Fall admitted to reporters that he found the patient's mind "vigorous and active." But the affair embittered Wilson, who later referred to the visitors as a "smelling committee." When Fall said "We have been praying for you," Wilson snapped back, "Which way, Senator?" Later Wilson told Secretary Houston, "If I could have got out of bed, I would have hit the man. Why did he want to put me in bad with the Almighty?"

Not long afterward in December the President's message to Congress asked that the criminal courts of the federal government be empowered to deal with those who sought to destroy America's "time-tested institutions by violent methods" and reminded high-tariff men that "if we want to sell, we must be prepared to buy." By the middle of the month Wilson was very much better, so much better that he was capable of dressing himself and walking around with a cane. But the improvement did not temper his stubbornness or fighting spirit.

He had hoped to keep the debate on the League and treaty on a nonpartisan basis and some of the senators at first appeared willing to appraise the problem objectively. But Lodge and other Republican leaders were able to turn it into a party issue, perhaps partly because they did not want Wilson and the Democratic administration to get the credit for so great an achievement.

No compromise seemed possible in connection with Article X, which was regarded by the opposition as likely to draw the country into foreign wars. The proposed Republican reservations served notice that in joining the League Americans assumed no obligation under this article to join in defending the territorial integrity or political independence of any state, except as the result of an Act of Congress. The Democratic stand merely recommended that when the Council advised action under Article X, it should be recognized that Congress alone could declare war.

Another main source of contention was the provision of the Covenant which gave one vote each to Australia, Canada, India, New Zealand and South Africa, the self-governing dominions of the British Empire. The Lodge reservations turned down this arrangement altogether, stating that no nation should have more votes than the United States. Wilson felt that any such action would place the whole issue of the League before the nations of the world all over again; but he was willing to approve the Democratic or Hitchcock reservations denying any British colony the right to vote upon purely British problems.

Wilson's position that the Republican reservations would amend the Covenant so drastically as to remove its very heart was not realistic. It is scarcely true that the League's power to guarantee territorial integrity would be destroyed completely if the consent of Congress were needed for each specific action which might have to be taken, and some agreement could undoubtedly have been reached, even though an attempt to reduce the representation of the British self-governing dominions might have opened the way for new issues and claims. Discussion of the League and treaty problems was so intense that the attention of both people and Congress was distracted from the problems of returning the domestic economy to peacetime conditions. Even when the elections of 1920 rolled around, the League was still generally regarded as the primary issue before the country.

One of the best prospects of a compromise appeared on November 5, when Colonel Stephan Bonsal conferring with Lodge obtained a signed memorandum of the minimum changes the senator would accept. But when this was forwarded to the President through Colonel House, nothing more was heard of it. Wilson's attitude was made clear two weeks later when Senator Hitchcock called and asked Mrs. Wilson to plead with her husband to accept the Lodge reservations. She reported that Wilson replied it was "better a thousand times to go down fighting than to dip your colors to dishonorable compromise." Yet it is possible that Wilson never saw the memorandum obtained by Bonsal, for Mrs. Wilson liked neither Lodge nor House. This failure to receive an answer may well have increased the rancour of the senator.

When Lodge on November 19 offered a resolution that the treaty be ratified with his fourteen reservations, the Democrats voted against it upon Wilson's unsound advice that the resolution "does not provide for the ratification but rather the nullification of the Treaty." The motion did not come close to receiving a majority, nor did Hitchcock's substitute demanding ratification without change approach obtaining a two-thirds vote of approval.

Wilson did not give up the fight because of this vote, although the treaty had little chance of passage after such a deadlock. He only became the more determined to get well and lead the struggle. Colonel House and other friends of the President, as well as various organizations and individuals, urged him to accept the reservations; but in his message to the Jackson Day dinner, he said there must be no changes which would "alter the meaning" of the treaty. Polls were taken showing majorities for the treaty without reservations or only mild ones; but when Lodge seemed inclined to pay this sentiment some attention, Senator Borah and the "battalion of death" told him any such action would be either hypocrisy or betrayal, so that Lodge abandoned the idea of compromise.

Wilson gave his approval to the interpretive resolutions of Senator Hitchcock, one of which specified that the United States assumed no obligation under Article X to use its armed forces or an economic boycott, except after action of its own Congress. But this was not enough to satisfy Lodge and his partisans. On January 31, 1920, Sir Edward Grey revealed the attitude of the British government by the publication of a letter in the London *Times* which stated that he was writing as a private individual to explain the position of the Senate in American treaty-making, and he suggested that it was better to have the United States in the League as a willing partner with limited obligations than as an unwilling partner with unlimited obligations. He said that although the proposed reservations were important, they might never be invoked in actual practice. He implied a willingness to accept all the fourteen reservations, except the one denying the British dominions a vote in the Assembly.

The letter was a breach of diplomatic etiquette, since it seemed to be an attempt to appeal to the American people over the head of their President; but it was much the same sort of thing that Wilson had done with the Italian people during the Paris Conference. Lloyd George, as Prime Minister, denied any knowledge of the letter before it appeared; but he also said it was the business of the United States to decide what conditions it wished to impose, so long as the other powers were not expressly required to agree to the American conditions. The leading French newspapers, like the *Temps* and the *Journal des Debats,* which were recognized as expressing the views of the French government, had been writing for weeks that it was preferable to have the United States in with reservations than not to have her in at all.

These statements weakened Wilson's position, making his refusal to yield appear more like unjustifiable stubbornness. When the final vote in the Senate came on March 19, he insisted that the Democrats should remain united in their refusal to accept the Republican reservations. This action blocked any two-thirds majority for the treaty and League, since the followers of Borah and Lodge combined against acceptance by America with only the Democratic reservations. Wilson's fight for the treaty and the League had met its final defeat; a defeat which he could have prevented by bowing to the inevitable and accepting the Republican reservations.

One reason for Wilson's refusal to accept any substantial changes in the Covenant or treaty was his confidence that his cause would win the support of the country at the next election. But he did not have a clear view of the situation. It probably was both lack of information and failure of judgment due to his illness that made him certain that the people would rally in support of the League. Up to the very moment when the votes were counted, he continued to believe that the Democratic Party would win both Congress and the Presidency in the autumn elections of 1920.

Wilson called the Cabinet together for the first time since his illness on April 13, 1920, although he could neither see clearly nor talk without difficulty. Mrs. Wilson came in after an hour with the suggestion that they had better go; but Wilson appeared to have more strength at later meetings. He did not send a message to the Democratic Presidential convention in July; so that no one knew whether he favored his son-in law McAdoo for the nomination. But when the Republican convention adopted an indefinite platform and nominated Harding, he summoned the chief political reporter of the New York *World* and gave him a scorching interview, attacking the Republican Party as the "apotheosis of reaction." He appeared to the reporter mentally keen, with sound judgment and unwavering convictions.

The Republicans succeeded in straddling the treaty issue, with Johnson and Borah remaining on one side, while Taft, Hughes and Root were on the other. Wilson told his Cabinet before the election, "You need not worry. The American people will not turn down Cox and elect Harding. A great moral issue is involved." But the people were forgetting their wartime idealism when they voted for what what was called a return to "normalcy." After Harding won easily, it was suggested that Wilson could embarrass him by leaving the treaty on his desk, but the President replied, "I do not wish to put Mr. Harding in a hole."

The decision to have the first meeting of the Assembly of the League of Nations on November 15 gave Wilson great satisfaction. He was asked to issue the call for this meeting and he was also selected for the Nobel Peace Prize in December. But he did not recover his old strength. As he came to his last Cabinet meeting on March 1, 1921, Houston saw him weakly and painfully hobbling down the hall and felt it better to step aside into a doorway while the President passed. When the members started to make little speeches of farewell, Wilson's eyes filled with tears and he was forced to stop them, saying, "I cannot control myself as I have been accustomed to do. God bless you all." After they were gone, he still sat there gray-faced and broken, as he sought to recover control of his feelings.

On inauguration day, Wilson looked feeble and wan, almost shrunken, as he drove with the robust Harding from the White House to the Capitol. The retiring President was able to appear cheerful and content while riding before the people, but he was not so successful later in the President's Room where he signed the last bills passed by the expiring Congress. The committee which came to announce the end of the session and ask if he had any last message to deliver was headed by Henry Cabot Lodge, but Wilson maintained his composure as, with a somewhat grim countenance, he informed his old antagonist, "I have no further communications to make. Thank you. Good morning."

The Wilsons retired to a beautiful brick house on S Street in Washington. The former President believed that he would settle down to working on his old project of a "Philosophy of Politics," but he only succeeded in inscribing a most appreciative dedication to his wife. After forming a law partnership with Bainbridge Colby, his last secretary of State, he felt only one of the many cases offered to them was proper for a former President to undertake, so for the second time he quickly abandoned the practice of the law.

He really could do little more than go to the movies and Keith's theater, listen to books and magazines being read aloud, and sometimes have close friends to lunch. Ray Stannard Baker and Frank Cobb, Bliss Perry and Bernard Baruch, Lloyd George and Clemenceau were among those with whom he talked about old times and discussed the problems of the day. Bliss Perry reported his mind as clear as ever but not so alert. During this interview, Wilson sat in his library with bent head, slumped in a chair and holding a cane. The old warrior was unable to forgive Henry Cabot Lodge and still maintained his faith that "a revival of more idealism was bound to come to our American people."

With much effort and polishing late into the night, he wrote an article for the *Atlantic Monthly* inveighing against the Harding idea of a return to "normalcy" and protesting against the high-tariff policy of the Republicans, which he regarded as a method of granting unfair privileges to certain vested interests. He believed the war had "made the world safe for democracy," but that in the Harding-Coolidge kind of democracy there was always danger of national revolution. He pleaded for "a Christian conception of justice, where capitalists would no longer use other men as mere instruments of profit." Although brief and without any especially new ideas, it showed his continuing devotion to the principles for which he had fought so long.

In his first radio speech on Armistice Day, 1923, he deplored America's withdrawal into "a sullen and selfish isolation, which is deeply ignoble because cowardly and dishonorable," but he was confident that the country would "assume once more the role of courage, self-respect and helpfulness which every true American must regard as our natural part in the affairs of the world."

There were times when his optimism and faith drowned out his resentment at the cruel destiny which forced him to endure what he jokingly described as "the unique experience of attending my own obsequies." This cheerful humor showed in an unexpected statement to one of his daughters that he thought "it was best after all that the United States did not join the League of Nations." When she asked him why, he replied, "Because our entry into the League at the time I returned from Europe might have been only a personal victory. Now, it will be because they are convinced it is the right thing to do, and *then* will be the only right time for them to do it." He added with a little grin, "Perhaps God knew better than I did after all."

Death must have been a relief when it came to Woodrow Wilson on the morning of February 3, 1924, and terminated a life which had been sincerely devoted to the service of mankind. Buffeted by snow, only a small crowd knelt outside the house on S Street to honor him whom the whole world had once been eager to acclaim.

Along with greatness he possessed faults and made mistakes for which he suffered dearly. He was endued with excessive partisanship, obstinacy and self-assurance, which grew worse as he grew older, and he ended by arousing violent opposition in all the three great offices he occupied. His interference in Mexico was not appreciated by its inhabitants, he failed to prepare the United States adequately for participation in World War I, and by his extreme stubbornness he prevented America's entry into the League of Nations.

But to his credit are the reforms which he introduced, including the Federal Reserve Bank System, lowering of tariffs, better regulation of large corporations, and many other liberal measures. He was a capable war President and he turned the United States from isolationism to a leading role in world affairs. He suffered incurable illness and death in working for his League and lasting peace. He died as he had lived; a stubborn idealist with an unconquerable soul.

A BRIEF BIBLIOGRAPHY

The most extensive single source of knowledge about Wilson is the eight volumes of his *Life and Letters,* by Ray Stannard Baker. For his early years, in particular, there is no other comparable source of information, although a biography by William Allen White includes many items of interest collected shortly after Wilson's death. Baker also published three volumes on the Peace Conference. Wilson's speeches are compiled by Baker and William E. Dodd in six volumes of his *Public Papers. The Intimate Papers of Colonel House* edited by Charles Seymour, are important volumes of printed source material, and there are also the letters and memoirs of many others who were associated with him in public life, including *The Life and Letters of Walter Hines Page* and volumes by Secretaries Lane and Houston. A valuable insight into Wilson's thinking may also be gained from his own books and essays discussed in Chapter VIII.

Books by those who knew Wilson well include Bliss Perry's *And Gladly Teach,* Josephus Daniels' *The Wilson Era,* Mrs. Edith Bolling Wilson's *My Memoir* and Eleanor Wilson McAdoo's *The Woodrow Wilsons,* all of them friendly and sympathetic. To these may be added Mrs. E. G. Reid's *Woodrow Wilson* and Tumulty's *Woodrow Wilson As I Knew Him,* which may be supplemented by Blum's recent *Tumulty and the Wilson Era.* Harley Notter investigated the origins of Wilson's foreign policy, William Diamond examined the development of his *Economic Thought,* and Donald Day has published a collection of extracts from his writings and speeches.

279

Scholarly and thorough discussions of Wilson's activities in peace-making include Harry R. Rudin's excellent work on the *Armistice 1918;* Thomas A. Bailey's *Woodrow Wilson and the Lost Peace* and Paul Birdsall's *Versailles Twenty After.* Lloyd George and Lansing are among the participants who have written about the Peace Conference, and Stephen Bonsal's *Unfinished Business* is a readable personal account, while there are numerous studies of special aspects of the treaty-making. The *Senate Documents* and *Congressional Record* give details of the Senate fight over the treaty, which is also covered by Bailey in *Woodrow Wilson and the Great Betrayal.*

An exhaustive biography in several volumes has been begun by Arthur S. Link with *Wilson, The Road to the White House,* published in 1947, and *Woodrow Wilson and the Progressive Era, 1910—1917,* published in 1954. Indications of how Wilson appeared to contemporaries may be found in biographies of Theodore Roosevelt, Taft, Bryan, Lodge, Carter Glass, and others, as well as in numerous magazine articles, which can be traced through the *Readers' Guide.* The best one-volume biographies of Wilson himself are those by William Allen White, David Loth and Professor H. C. F. Bell.

Wilson is so large a figure and the printed source materials on his career are so extensive that the little which has remained unpublished is almost certainly of slight importance. An odd assortment of mail received subsequent to his return from Europe in 1919 has been deposited in the Library of Congress by his widow and may be examined with her permission. The Library staff will also point out other available collections which are in its charge, while some additional manuscripts can be found in the libraries of Princeton and Yale.

INDEX

Adams, Herbert B., 51
Armour, George, 65
Axson, Edward, 42
Axson, Ellen (*see also* Wilson, Ellen Axson), 38-42, 49, 50
Axson, Rev. I. S. K., 42
Axson, Stockton, 42, 61, 64, 66, 73

Bagehot, Walter, 26, 28, 38, 55, 101
Bailey, Thomas A., 228, 269, 280
Baker, George F., 180
Baker, Newton D., 197, 209
Baker, Ray Stannard, 276
Balfour, Arthur James, 213, 216
Baruch, Bernard, 200, 208, 241, 276
Beck, James M., 204
Beecher, Henry Ward, 54
Bellamy, Dr. William, 21-22
Bellamy, Ellen, 20
Bellamy, John, 19, 20-21, 23, 38, 171
Bergson, Henri, 227
Big Four, The, 251
Bliss, Gen. Tasker H., 234, 241
Bones, Helen, 207, 208
Bones, James, 38
Bones, Jessie, 6, 15, 38, 45, 140
Bonsal, Col. Stephan, 272, 280
Borah, William E., 249, 259, 262, 265, 273, 275
Bourgeois, Léon, 231, 252
Bradford, Gamaliel, 56, 96
Brandeis, Louis D., 136, 179, 228
Bridges, Robert, 25, 28, 29, 58, 67
Bright, John, 32
Brooke, Francis J., 16
Brougham, Henry B., 89

Bryan, William Jennings, 125, 126, 128, 130, 132, 133-134, 136, 141-142, 148, 149-150, 155, 159, 160-161, 162, 166, 169, 170, 175, 194, 196, 197, 199, 200
Bryant, Dave, 115, 140
Bryce, James, 54, 56, 92, 231
Bullitt, William C., 256, 263
Burke, Edmund, 26, 28, 38
Burleson, Albert S., 142, 144, 145, 175, 229

Carnegie, Andrew, 75, 174
Carranza, Venustiano, 167, 169, 171, 172, 173
Cecil, Lord Robert, 245
Choate, Joseph A., 174
Clark, Champ, 131, 133, 134, 175
Clemenceau, Georges, 226, 227, 232, 234, 240, 242, 243, 244, 247, 252, 257, 276
Cleveland, Grover, 72, 80, 83, 85, 86, 102, 118
Cobb, Frank, 203, 276
Colby, Bainbridge, 276
Congressional Government, 55-57, 58, 95
Constitutional Government, 80, 94, 108, 145
Council of Ten, 244, 251
Crandall, John J., 114
Creel, George, 208, 236

Daniels, Josephus, 129, 130, 142, 171, 200, 208
Davies, Joseph E., 145, 196
Davis, Jefferson, 5
Davis, Mrs. John W., 220-221

Davis, Norman, 241
Davis, Robert, 113, 118
Devlin, Martin P., 114
Dewey, Davis R., 51
Division and Reunion, 105-106, 107
Dodge, Cleveland H., 84, 144

Edison, Thomas A., 200
Eisenhower, Dwight D., 178
Eliot, Charles William, 143, 191, 199, 260

Fall, Albert B., 259, 271
Fine, H. B., 31
Fleming, Will, 5, 6
Foch, Marshal, 211, 213, 222
Ford, Henry, 200, 230
Ford, Henry Jones, 176
Forgan, James B., 160
Fourteen Points, 215, 217, 223, 233, 241, 244, 253, 261-262
Francis, David R., 131

Galt, Mrs. Edith Bolling (*see also* Wilson, Edith Bolling Galt), 47, 195
Ganfield, Harry, 208
Garrison, Lindley M., 143, 197
Gerard, James W., 144, 196
Glass, Carter, 142, 156, 157-158, 159-160, 161, 163
Gompers, Samuel, 136, 181
Grayson, Dr. Cary T, 140-141, 143, 161, 208, 221, 253, 265, 267, 268
Grey, Sir Edward, 169, 196, 231, 273

Hale, William Bayard, 103, 157, 167
Harding, Warren G., 259, 261, 275, 276
Harvey, George 70, 111-112, 113, 115, 116, 129-130
History of the American People, 72, 107
Hitchcock, Gilbert, 259, 270, 271, 272
Hoover, Herbert, 208, 241, 260
House, Col. Edward M., 126-127, 132, 139, 142, 144, 159, 162, 173, 189, 191, 194, 195, 199, 207, 216, 225, 226, 232, 233, 234, 245, 248, 250-251, 252, 254, 258, 264, 270, 272, 273

Houston, David F., 142, 154, 163, 166, 276
Huerta, Victoriano, 147, 166-168, 170, 171, 172, 173, 178
Hughes, Charles Evans, 198, 199, 200, 235, 275
Hulbert, Mrs. Mary (Mrs. Mary Hulbert Peck), 159
Hull, Cordell, 154
Hurley, Edward M., 208

James, Ollie, 133, 198
Johnson, Hiram, 149, 200, 249, 258, 261, 262, 265, 275
Joline, Adrian H., 90, 91, 128
Jones, David B., 84
Jones, Thomas D., 144
J. P. Morgan and Co., 135, 148
Katzenbach, Frank S., 114
Kenny, Edward, 121
Kerney, James, 115, 123
Keynes, J. M., 233
Kohlsaat, H. H., 270
Knox, Philander, 235, 249, 259, 262

Lane, Franklin K., 143, 166, 169, 195, 270
Lansing, Robert, 194, 212, 233, 234, 240-241, 245, 248, 260, 261, 263-264, 269, 280
Lawrence, David, 91
League of Nations, 223, 228, 231, 234, 238, 242
   Covenant of, 246-247, 261
Lenin, Nikolai, 212, 214
Life of George Washington, 106-107
Lind, John, 167
Lindabury, Richard V., 113
Link, Arthur S., 56, 69, 280
Lloyd George, David, 216, 226, 231, 239, 240, 242, 244, 250, 251, 252, 255, 256, 274, 276, 280
Lodge, Henry Cabot, 163, 175, 196, 198, 218, 224, 230, 231, 244, 249, 259, 260, 271, 273, 276

McAdoo, William Gibbs, 126, 133, 134, 135, 142, 159, 162, 163, 166, 175, 192, 194, 196, 275

McCombs, William F., 125, 127, 128, 130, 133, 134, 135, 141, 142, 200
McCormick, Cyrus, 84
McCormick, Vance, 200
McCosh, James, 25, 26, 79
McLemore, Jeff, 197
MacMasters, Ellen, 16, 140
McReynolds, James Clark, 142-143, 153
Madero, Francisco, 147, 166
Martine, James E., 117, 118, 125
Mayraw, Katie, 36
Mexican crisis, 47, 166-174
Mezes, Sidney, 216, 254
Mitchell, Edward P., 127
Morgan, J. Pierpont, 180
Murphy, Charles Francis, 133

New Freedom, The, 156
Newberry, Truman, 230
Nugent, James, 113, 116, 120-121, 122-123
Orlando, Vittorio, 73, 226, 240, 241, 243, 254-255

Page, Walter Hines, 36, 50, 70, 124, 144, 174, 194, 196
Palmer, A. Mitchell, 143
Parker, Alton B., 132, 133
Patton, Francis Landez, 62, 64, 69
Peck, Mrs. Mary Hulbert (*see also* Hulbert, Mrs. Mary), 45-47, 85, 135, 139
Perry, Bliss, 64, 103-104, 220, 276
Pershing, Gen. John J., 173, 208, 210, 211, 222, 241
Phelan, James, 149
Prohibition, 183-184
Pyne, Moses Taylor, 82, 84, 85, 86, 88, 89

Reading, Lord, 196, 220
Record, George L., 112, 116, 120
Redfield, William F., 143, 153
Reed, James A., 131, 162, 249, 258-259
Reid, Mrs. Edith, 53
Renick, Edward Ireland, 36, 49, 58
Roosevelt, Franklin D., 145, 197, 204, 248

Roosevelt, Theodore, 47, 74, 86, 124, 132, 133, 135, 136, 153, 175, 177, 183, 187-188, 192, 196, 198, 209-210, 218, 229
Root, Elihu, 17, 212, 213, 231, 235, 264, 275
Royce, Josiah, 54
Ryan, Thomas Fortune, 165-166

St. John, William W., 114, 117
Sayre, Francis B., 161
Smith, Adam, 101
Smith, Goldwin, 101
Smith, Hope, 125
Smith, James, Jr., 113, 114, 115, 116, 117, 118, 123
Smuts, Gen. Jan, 231, 243, 244
State, The, 58-59, 96, 109
Stephens, Alexander, 3, 5
Story of a Style, The, 103
Straus, Oscar, 174

Taft, William Howard, 132, 133, 135, 140, 147, 165, 176, 224, 231, 234, 235, 250, 259, 264, 275
Talcott, Charles, 30, 31, 32
Tansill, Charles, 204
Tedcastle, Agnes, 38
Thilly, Frank, 76
Thomas, Miss M. Carey, 57
Thompson, Mrs. H. D., 77
Treaty of Versailles, 256-257
Trotsky, Leon, 214, 216
Truman, Harry S., 178
Tumulty, Joseph P., 114, 117, 119, 123, 143, 161, 194, 202, 205, 209, 224, 229, 233, 269
Turner, Frederick Jackson, 98, 105, 107

Underwood, Oscar, 153, 154

Van Dyke, Henry, 82
Van Dyke, Paul, 90
Vanderlip, Frank A., 163
Viereck, George Sylvester, 269
Villa, Francisco, 169, 173

Wade, Festus J., 160, 163

283

Walsh, Frank P., 255, 256, 263
Walsh, Thomas J., 235
Warburg, Paul M., 158-159
Watson, Tom, 127
Watterson, Col. Henry, 113, 129-130
West, Andrew F., 74, 80, 83-85, 86, 87, 88, 89, 91
Westcott, John W., 114
White, Henry, 234, 241
Wickersham, George W., 260
Willis, H. Parker, 157
Wilson, Anne Adams, 9
Wilson, Edith Bolling Golt, 195, 198, 207-208, 221, 229, 250-251, 265, 267, 269, 270, 271-272, 275
Wilson, Eleanor Randolph, 61, 77
Wilson, Ellen Axson, 42-44, 45, 46, 47, 48, 64, 66, 125, 126, 130, 140, 153, 166, 187, 190
Wilson Henry Lane, 147, 167
Wilson, James, 8-9
Wilson, James Ruggles, Jr., 35
Wilson, Jessie Woodrow (daughter), 59, 161
Wilson, Jessie Woodrow (mother), 1, 10, 11, 12, 20
Wilson, Joseph Ruggles, 1, 2, 3-4, 9-10, 11-12, 14-15, 19, 26, 36-37
Wilson, Margaret, 58, 186, 208

Wilson, Thomas Woodrow:
    at Princeton University, 24-31
    political studies, 26-28
    at University of Virginia, 31-34
    first marriage, 41
    friendship with Mary Hulbert Peck, 45-47
    at Johns Hopkins University, 50-54
    at Bryn Mawr, 57-58
    at Wesleyan University 59-62
    as professor at Princeton University, 63-69
    as President of Princeton, 69-91
    writings of, 93-110
    as Governor of New Jersey, 116-123
    as President of U.S., first term, 138-199
    second marriage, 195
    as President, second term, 200-276
    in retirement, 276-277
Wilson, William B., 143
Wiseman, Sir William, 265
Wodrow, James, 10
Woman Suffrage Amendment, 184
Wood, Gen. Leonard, 196, 210
Woodrow, Harriet, 33
Woodrow, James, 15
Woodrow, Thomas, 10
Woods, Charles A., 144